THE NEW CAMBRIDGE SHAKESPEARE

GENERAL EDITOR
Brian Gibbons, *University of Münster*

ASSOCIATE GENERAL EDITOR
A. R. Braunmuller, *University of California, Los Angeles*

From the publication of the first volumes in 1984 the General Editor of the New Cambridge Shakespeare was Philip Brockbank and the Associate General Editors were Brian Gibbons and Robin Hood. From 1990 to 1994 the General Editor was Brian Gibbons and the Associate General Editors were A. R. Braunmuller and Robin Hood.

JULIUS CAESAR

This revised edition preserves the play text as it was edited by Marvin Spevack for the 1988 first edition. Jeremy Lopez's new introduction provides a detailed discussion of *Julius Caesar*'s strange and innovative form by focusing on the interpretive challenges the play has presented to audiences, scholars and theatre companies from Shakespeare's time to our own. The textual commentary has been revised and updated with an eye, and an ear, to the contemporary student reader, and the list of further reading has been updated to reflect the latest developments in Shakespearean criticism. Like the first edition, this edition concludes with an appendix containing relevant excerpts from Shakespeare's main source, Plutarch's histories of the lives of Caesar and Brutus as translated by Sir Thomas North in 1579.

THE NEW CAMBRIDGE SHAKESPEARE

All's Well That Ends Well, edited by Russell Fraser
Antony and Cleopatra, edited by David Bevington
As You Like It, edited by Michael Hattaway
The Comedy of Errors, edited by T. S. Dorsch
Coriolanus, edited by Lee Bliss
Hamlet, edited by Philip Edwards
Julius Caesar, edited by Marvin Spevack
King Edward III, edited by Giorgio Melchiori
The First Part of King Henry IV, edited by Herbert Weil and Judith Weil
The Second Part of King Henry IV, edited by Giorgio Melchiori
King Henry V, edited by Andrew Gurr
The First Part of King Henry VI, edited by Michael Hattaway
The Second Part of King Henry VI, edited by Michael Hattaway
The Third Part of King Henry VI, edited by Michael Hattaway
King Henry VIII, edited by John Margeson
King John, edited by L. A. Beaurline
The Tragedy of King Lear, edited by Jay L. Halio
King Richard II, edited by Andrew Gurr
King Richard III, edited by Janis Lull
Love's Labour's Lost, edited by William C. Carroll
Macbeth, edited by A. R. Braunmuller
Measure for Measure, edited by Brian Gibbons
The Merchant of Venice, edited by M. M. Mahood
The Merry Wives of Windsor, edited by David Crane
A Midsummer Night's Dream, edited by R. A. Foakes
Much Ado About Nothing, edited by F. H. Mares
Othello, edited by Norman Sanders
Pericles, edited by Doreen DelVecchio and Antony Hammond
The Poems, edited by John Roe
Romeo and Juliet, edited by G. Blakemore Evans
The Sonnets, edited by G. Blakemore Evans
The Taming of the Shrew, edited by Ann Thompson
The Tempest, edited by David Lindley
Timon of Athens, edited by Karl Klein
Titus Andronicus, edited by Alan Hughes
Troilus and Cressida, edited by Anthony B. Dawson
Twelfth Night, edited by Elizabeth Story Donno
The Two Gentlemen of Verona, edited by Kurt Schlueter
The Two Noble Kinsmen, edited by Robert Kean Turner
The Winter's Tale, edited by Susan Snyder and Deborah T. Curren-Aquino

THE EARLY QUARTOS
The First Quarto of Hamlet, edited by Kathleen O. Irace
The First Quarto of King Henry V, edited by Andrew Gurr
The First Quarto of King Lear, edited by Jay L. Halio
The First Quarto of King Richard III, edited by Peter Davison
The First Quarto of Othello, edited by Scott McMillin
The First Quarto of Romeo and Juliet, edited by Lukas Erne
The Taming of a Shrew: The 1594 Quarto, edited by Stephen Roy Miller

JULIUS CAESAR

Third Edition

Edited by
MARVIN SPEVACK

Revised and with a new introduction by

JEREMY LOPEZ
University of Toronto

CAMBRIDGE
UNIVERSITY PRESS

University Printing House, Cambridge CB2 8BS, United Kingdom

One Liberty Plaza, 20th Floor, New York, NY 10006, USA

477 Williamstown Road, Port Melbourne, VIC 3207, Australia

4843/24, 2nd Floor, Ansari Road, Daryaganj, Delhi – 110002, India

79 Anson Road, #06–#04/06, Singapore 079906

Cambridge University Press is part of the University of Cambridge.

It furthers the University's mission by disseminating knowledge in the pursuit of education, learning, and research at the highest international levels of excellence.

www.cambridge.org
Information on this title: www.cambridge.org/9781107459748

© Cambridge University Press 1988, 2003, 2017

First published 1988

Reprinted 1989, 1996, 1999, 2000 (twice), 2001 (twice), 2002 (twice)

Updated edition 2004

12th printing 2012

Third edition published 2017

Printed in the United Kingdom by TJ International Ltd. Padstow Cornwall

A catalogue record for this book is available from the British Library

Library of Congress Cataloguing in Publication data
NAMES: Shakespeare, William, 1564–1616, author. | Spevack, Marvin, editor. | Lopez, Jeremy, writer of introduction.
TITLE: Julius Caesar / William Shakespeare ; edited by Marvin Spevack ; revised and with a new introduction by Jeremy Lopez.
DESCRIPTION: Third edition. | New York : Cambridge University Press, 2017. | Series: The New Cambridge Shakespeare | Includes bibliographical references.
IDENTIFIERS: LCCN 2017009173 | ISBN 9781107088665 (hardback)
SUBJECTS: LCSH: Caesar, Julius – Assassination – Drama. | Conspiracies – Drama. | Assassins – Drama. | Rome – Drama. | Tragedies. | Shakespeare, William, 1564–1616. Julius Caesar. | BISAC: LITERARY COLLECTIONS / General.
CLASSIFICATION: LCC PR2808.A2 S64 2017 | DDC 822.3/3–dc23
LC record available at https://lccn.loc.gov/2017009173

ISBN 0 978-1-107-08866-5 Hardback
ISBN 0 978-1-107-45974-8 Paperback

For DIANNE AND BILLY

CONTENTS

List of Illustrations   *page* viii

Acknowledgements   ix

Abbreviations and Conventions   xi

Introduction   1

by Jeremy Lopez

     Date   1

     Source   2

     Caesar in the English Renaissance Theatre   6

     The Play   12

         Personal and Political Caesar   14

         Rituals of Power   20

         Witnessing History   23

     The Text   26

     Julius Caesar on the Stage   28

     Note on this Edition   41

Note on the Text   42

List of Characters   44

THE PLAY   46

Appendix: Excerpts from Plutarch   138

Reading List   169

ILLUSTRATIONS

1 *The Emperor Julius Caesar on Horseback* by Antonio Tempesta (The Metropolitan Museum of Art, The Elisha Whittelsey Collection, The Elisha Whittelsey Fund, 1951 (51.501.3475))   *page* 13

2 Julius Caesar by Marcantonio Raimondi (reproduced by permission of the Trustees of the British Museum)   14

3 Julius Caesar by Martino Rota (Graphische Sammlung Albertina, Vienna)   15

4 Julius Caesar by Egidius Sadeler, after Titian (reproduced by permission of the Staatliche Graphische Sammlung, Munich)   16

5 *The Triumphator Julius Caesar on his Chariot* by Andrea Mantegna (copyright reserved to Her Majesty Queen Elizabeth II; Royal Collection at Hampton Court)   17

6 The assassination of Julius Caesar: Her Majesty's Theatre, 1898 (reproduced by courtesy of the Board of Trustees of the Victoria and Albert Museum)   31

7 Paul Richard as Julius Caesar: Meiningen production, 1881 (reproduced by permission of the Staatliche Museen, Meiningen)   32

8 Antony's funeral oration. Mercury Theatre, 1937 (reproduced by permission of the Billy Rose Theatre Collection, The New York Public Library at Lincoln Center, Astor, Lenox and Tilden Foundations)   34

9 The death of Brutus, Act 5, Scene 5: Shakespeare Memorial Theatre, 1957 (Angus McBean)   38

10 Mark Antony, Octavius, and the dead Brutus before a backdrop with Caesar's head in the 1995/6 production at the RST Stratford/Barbican London, directed by Sir Peter Hall (Donald Cooper)   39

11 Soothsayer and ensemble. RSC production, 2012 (photo by Kwame Lestrade © RSC)   40

12 Production of Julius Caesar, 1999. Photographer: John Tramper. © The Globe.   41

ACKNOWLEDGEMENTS

I am privileged to acknowledge the help I have received from students and colleagues, friends and strangers, who contributed their expertise and goodwill to this enterprise. I take pleasure in the fact that my debt is great and to many on both sides of the Atlantic.

In seminars in Münster and New Mexico (where I spent the academic year 1985–6), I was able to profit from the remarks of the prospective users of a work of this kind: the reactions of students to the necessity and nature of the commentary. In Münster, my thanks go to Sabine Ulrike Bückmann-de Villegas, Peter Hellfeuer, Michael Hiltscher, Thomas Pago, Ulrich Paul, Elisabeth Pirke, Clemens Sorgenfrey, Elke Stracke, Krishnan Venkatesh, Martin Wolny, and Angela Zatsch. In Albuquerque, to Mohamed Ali, Mary Lou Fisk, David Kreuter, Catherine Mecklenburg, Linda Oldham, and Jon Tuttle.

For help in the preparation of the manuscript in Albuquerque, I am indebted to Marta Field and K. T. Martin, for administrative encouragement to Hamlin C. Hill, and for computer support to Harry C. Broussard; in Münster, to Lydia Remke for typing, and Carsten Ehmke and Bernhard Friederici for computing. Marga Munkelt, as always, provided ready solutions to many and varied scholarly problems. Special credit is due to Elisabeth Pirke, who worked on all aspects in Münster and Albuquerque, and to Sabine Ulrike Bückmann-de Villegas, who saw to all the final details as well as writing the section of the Introduction dealing with the stage history.

For the selection of illustrations, I was able to draw on the experience of J. W. Binns, Hildegard Hammerschmidt-Hummel, Fortunato Israël, Julian-Matthias Kliemann, Vera Liebert, Giorgio Melchiori, Sylvia Morris, Karl Noehles, Robert Rockman, and Robert Smallwood.

For their unfailing assistance on individual questions, I thank G. Blakemore Evans, C. Walter Hodges, Helga Spevack-Husmann, Michael Steppat, and Hans-Jürgen Weckermann. Brian Gibbons read the manuscript with professional crispness and courtesy. Paul Chipchase supplied the necessary editorial consistency and concern. I am particularly grateful to John W. Velz, who went to great trouble checking the collation and making available, in countless ways, his profound knowledge of this play, and to Krishnan Venkatesh, who was a source of sensitivity, insight, and common sense all along the way.

M. S.
Münster 1988

I am grateful to Sarah Stanton at Cambridge University Press for asking me to undertake this revision, and to Brian Gibbons and A. R. Braunmuller for their careful reading of the revised commentary and Introduction. I was greatly assisted in the early stages of this project by Lauren Paré, a student research-assistant at the University of Toronto.

J. L.
Toronto 2015

ABBREVIATIONS AND CONVENTIONS

Shakespeare's plays, when cited in this edition, are abbreviated in a style modified slightly from that used in the *Harvard Concordance to Shakespeare*. Other editions of Shakespeare are abbreviated under the editor's surname (Ridley, Sanders) unless they are the work of more than one editor. In such cases, an abbreviated series name is used (Cam.). When more than one edition by the same editor is cited, later editions are discriminated with a raised figure (Collier). References to Abbott's *Shakespearian Grammar* are to paragraph numbers. All quotations from Shakespeare, except those from *Julius Caesar*, use the text and lineation of *The Riverside Shakespeare*, under the general editorship of G. Blakemore Evans.

1. Shakespeare's Plays

Ado	*Much Ado about Nothing*
Ant.	*Antony and Cleopatra*
AWW	*All's Well That Ends Well*
AYLI	*As You Like It*
Cor.	*Coriolanus*
Cym.	*Cymbeline*
Err.	*The Comedy of Errors*
Ham.	*Hamlet*
1H4	*The First Part of King Henry the Fourth*
2H4	*The Second Part of King Henry the Fourth*
H5	*King Henry the Fifth*
1H6	*The First Part of King Henry the Sixth*
2H6	*The Second Part of King Henry the Sixth*
3H6	*The Third Part of King Henry the Sixth*
H8	*King Henry the Eighth*
JC	*Julius Caesar*
John	*King John*
Lear	*King Lear*
LLL	*Love's Labour's Lost*
MM	*Measure for Measure*
MND	*A Midsummer Night's Dream*
MV	*The Merchant of Venice*
Oth.	*Othello*
Per.	*Pericles*
R2	*King Richard the Second*
R3	*King Richard the Third*
Rom.	*Romeo and Juliet*
Shr.	*The Taming of the Shrew*
STM	*Sir Thomas More*
Temp.	*The Tempest*

TGV	*The Two Gentlemen of Verona*
Tim.	*Timon of Athens*
Tit.	*Titus Andronicus*
TN	*Twelfth Night*
TNK	*The Two Noble Kinsmen*
Tro.	*Troilus and Cressida*
Wiv.	*The Merry Wives of Windsor*
WT	*The Winter's Tale*

2. Other Works Cited and General References

Abbott	E. A. Abbott, *A Shakespearian Grammar*, 3rd edn, 1870
Anon.	Anonymous
apud	in
Badham	Charles Badham, 'The text of Shakespeare', *Cambridge Essays*, vol. II, 1856, pp. 261–91
Becket	Andrew Becket, *Shakespeare's Himself Again*, 2 vols., 1815
Bevington	*Works*, ed. David Bevington, 1980
Blair	*Works*, ed. Hugh Blair, 1753
Blake	N. F. Blake, *Shakespeare's Language: An Introduction*, 1983
Boswell	*Plays & Poems*, ed. James Boswell, 1821
Bulloch	John Bulloch, *Studies on the Text of Shakespeare*, 1878
Bullough	Geoffrey Bullough (ed.), *Narrative and Dramatic Sources of Shakespeare*, vol. V, 1964
CahiersE	*Cahiers Elisabéthains*
Cam.	*Works*, ed. William George Clark and William Aldis Wright, 1863–6 (Cambridge Shakespeare)
Capell	*Comedies, Histories, and Tragedies*, ed. Edward Capell, [1768]
Capell MS.	MS. holograph of Capell's edition, before 1751 (Trinity College Library, Cambridge)
Cartwright	Robert Cartwright, *New Readings in Shakspere*, 1866
Charney	*Julius Caesar*, ed. Maurice Charney, 1969 (Bobbs-Merrill Shakespeare Series)
Collier	*Works*, ed. John Payne Collier, 1842–4
Collier[2]	*Plays*, ed. John Payne Collier, 1853
Collier[3]	*Comedies, Histories, Tragedies, and Poems*, ed. John Payne Collier, 1858
Collier[4]	*Plays and Poems*, ed. John Payne Collier, 1875–8
Collier MS.	MS. notes by J. P. Collier in a copy of F2 (Perkins Folio in the Huntington Library), before 1852
conj.	conjecture
Craig	*Works*, ed. W.J. Craig, [1891] (Oxford Shakespeare)
Craik	*The English of Shakespeare*, ed. George L. Craik, 1857
Daniel	Peter A. Daniel, *Notes and Conjectural Emendations of Certain Doubtful Passages in Shakespeare's Plays*, 1870
Daniell	*Julius Caesar*, ed. David Daniell, 1998 (Arden Shakespeare)

Deighton	*Julius Caesar*, ed. Kenneth Deighton, 1890 (Grey Cover Shakespeare)
Delius	*Werke*, ed. Nicolaus Delius, 1854–[61]
Dent	R. W. Dent, *Shakespeare's Proverbial Language: An Index*, 1981 (references are to numbered proverbs)
Dessen and Thomson	Alan C. Dessen and Leslie Thomson, *A Dictionary of Stage Directions in English Drama 1580–1642*, 1999
Dorsch	*Julius Caesar*, ed. T. S. Dorsch, 1955 (Arden Shakespeare)
Douai MS.	Douai MS. 7.87, *c.* 1694 (Douai Public Library)
Dyce	*Works*, ed. Alexander Dyce, 1857
Evans	*The Riverside Shakespeare*, ed. G. Blakemore Evans et al., 1974
F	*Mr. William Shakespeares Comedies, Histories, and Tragedies*, 1623 (First Folio)
F2	*Mr. William Shakespeares Comedies, Histories, and Tragedies*, 1632 (Second Folio)
F3	*Mr. William Shakespear's Comedies, Histories, and Tragedies*, 1663–4 (Third Folio)
F4	*Mr. William Shakespear's Comedies, Histories, and Tragedies*, 1685 (Fourth Folio)
Farmer	Richard Farmer, contributor to Steevens (1773 edn) and Steevens[2] (1778 edn)
Folger MS.	Folger Shakespeare Library MS. V.a.85, *c.* 1665
Furness	*Julius Caesar*, ed. Horace Howard Furness, Jr, 1913 (New Variorum Shakespeare)
Globe	*Works*, ed. William George Clark and William Aldis Wright, 1864 (Globe Edition)
Hall	'Mr. Hall' mentioned in Thirlby
Hanmer	*Works*, ed. Thomas Hanmer, 1743–4
Heraud	John A. Heraud, contributor to Cam. (1863–6 edn)
Herr	J. G. Herr, *Scattered Notes on the Text of Shakespeare*, 1879
Hudson	*Works*, ed. Henry N. Hudson, 1851–6
Hudson[2]	*Works*, ed. Henry N. Hudson, 1880–1 (Harvard Edition)
Humphreys	*Julius Caesar*, ed. Arthur Humphreys, 1984 (Oxford Shakespeare)
JEGP	*Journal of English and Germanic Philology*
John Hunter	*Julius Caesar*, ed. John Hunter, [1869] (Hunter's Annotated Shakespeare)
Mark Hunter	*Julius Caesar*, ed. Mark Hunter, 1900 (College Classics Series)
Irving	*Works*, ed. Henry Irving and Frank A. Marshall, 1888–90 (Henry Irving Shakespeare)
J.D.	J.D., 5 *N&Q* 8 (1877), 262–3
Jennens	*Julius Caesar*, ed. Charles Jennens, 1774
Jervis	Swynfen Jervis, *Proposed Emendations of the Text of Shakspeare's Plays*, 1860
Johnson	*Plays*, ed. Samuel Johnson, 1765
S. F. Johnson	*Julius Caesar*, ed. S. F. Johnson, 1960 (Pelican Shakespeare)
Thomas Johnson	*Plays*, ed. Thomas Johnson, 1711
Thomas Johnson[2]	*Plays*, ed. Thomas Johnson, *c.* 1720
Keightley	*Plays*, ed. Thomas Keightley, 1864

Kittredge	*Works*, ed. George Lyman Kittredge, 1936; *Julius Caesar*, 1939
Knight	*Comedies, Histories, Tragedies, & Poems*, ed. Charles Knight, [1838–43] (Pictorial Edition)
Lettsom	William Nanson Lettsom, 'New readings in Shakespeare', *Blackwood's Edinburgh Magazine* 74 (Aug. 1853), 181–202
Macmillan	*Julius Caesar*, ed. Michael Macmillan, 1902 (Arden Shakespeare)
Malone	*Plays & Poems*, ed. Edmond Malone, 1790
Mason	John Monck Mason, *Comments on the Last Edition of Shakespeare's Plays*, 1785
Mason 1919	*Julius Caesar*, ed. Lawrence Mason, 1919 (Yale Shakespeare)
Mitford	John Mitford, 'Conjectural emendations on the text of Shakspere', *Gentleman's Magazine* n.s. 22 (1844), 451–72
Morley	Henry Morley, contributor to Mark Hunter (1900 edn)
Nicholson	Brinsley M. Nicholson, contributor to William Aldis Wright, MS. Notes (Add. MS. b.58) in Trinity College Library, Cambridge
OCD	*The Oxford Classical Dictionary*, ed. N. G. L. Hammond and H. H. Scullard, 2nd edn, 1970
OED	*The Oxford English Dictionary*, online edn, June 2015
Onions	C. T. Onions, *A Shakespeare Glossary*, revised by Robert D. Eagleson, 1986
PBSA	*Publications of the Bibliographical Society of America*
Plutarch	*The Lives of the Noble Grecians and Romanes*, translated by Sir Thomas North, 1579 (page references are to the extracts given in the Appendix, pp. 160–90 below)
Pope	*Works*, ed. Alexander Pope, 1723–5
Pope²	*Works*, ed. Alexander Pope, 1728
PQ	*Philological Quarterly*
Q (1684)	*Julius Caesar* quarto
Q (1691)	*Julius Caesar* quarto
QU1, QU2, QU3, QU4	Undated quartos of *Julius Caesar* issued between the late seventeenth and early eighteenth centuries
Rann	*Dramatic Works*, ed. Joseph Rann, 1786–[94]
Reed	*Plays*, ed. Isaac Reed, 1803
Ritson	Joseph Ritson, contributor to Steevens³ (1793 edn)
Rowe	*Works*, ed. Nicholas Rowe, 1709
Sanders	*Julius Caesar*, ed. Norman Sanders, 1967 (New Penguin Shakespeare)
SD	stage direction
SH	speech heading
S.St.	*Shakespeare Studies*
S.Sur.	*Shakespeare Survey*
Singer	Samuel W. Singer, contributor to Cam. (1863–6 edn) and Hudson² (1880–1 edn)
Singer	*Dramatic Works*, ed. Samuel W. Singer, 1826
Singer²	*Dramatic Works*, ed. Samuel W. Singer, 1856
Singer 1858	Samuel W. Singer, 2 *N&Q* 5 (1858), 289–90
Sisson	*Works*, ed. Charles Jasper Sisson, [1954]
SQ	*Shakespeare Quarterly*

Staunton	*Plays*, ed. Howard Staunton, 1858–60
Steevens	*Plays*, ed. Samuel Johnson and George Steevens, 1773
Steevens²	*Plays*, ed. Samuel Johnson and George Steevens, 1778
Steevens³	*Plays*, ed. Samuel Johnson and George Steevens, 1793
subst.	substantively
Theobald 1730	Lewis Theobald, letter to William Warburton (14 Feb. 1729/30)
Theobald	*Works*, ed. Lewis Theobald, 1733
Theobald²	*Works*, ed. Lewis Theobald, 1740
Theobald³	*Works*, ed. Lewis Theobald, 1752
Theobald⁴	*Works*, ed. Lewis Theobald, 1757
Thirlby	Styan Thirlby, MS. notes in eighteenth-century editions of Shakespeare, 1723–51
Tyrwhitt	Thomas Tyrwhitt, contributor to Steevens² (1778 edn)
Walker	William Sidney Walker, *A Critical Examination of the Text of Shakespeare*, ed. W. Nanson Lettsom, 3 vols., 1860
W. S. Walker	William Sidney Walker, *Shakespeare's Versification*, 1854
Warburton 1734	William Warburton, letter to Lewis Theobald (2 June 1734)
Warburton	*Works*, ed. William Warburton, 1747
Wells and Taylor	*Works*, ed. Stanley Wells and Gary Taylor, 1986 (Oxford Shakespeare)
White	*Works*, ed. Richard Grant White, 1857–66
White²	*Comedies, Histories, Tragedies, and Poems*, ed. Richard Grant White, 1883 (Riverside Shakespeare)
Wilson	*Julius Caesar*, ed. John Dover Wilson, 1949 (New Shakespeare)
Wordsworth	*Historical Plays*, ed. Charles Wordsworth, 1883

INTRODUCTION

Date

> On the 21st of September, after dinner, at about two o' clock, I went with my party across the water; in the straw-thatched house we saw the tragedy of the Emperor Julius Caesar, very pleasingly performed, with approximately fifteen characters; at the end of the play they danced together admirably and exceedingly gracefully, according to their custom, two in each group dressed in men's and two in women's apparel.[1]

Thus begins one of the most famous diary entries ever written: it records a day in the life of Thomas Platter, a Swiss tourist visiting London in 1599. A physician and the son of a minor humanist scholar, Platter would probably be unknown to history if literary scholars did not believe, on the basis of this diary entry, that he was a lucky spectator at one of the earliest productions of Shakespeare's *Julius Caesar*. The circumstantial evidence in support of this belief is strong: in 1599, Shakespeare was writing plays for a company called the Lord Chamberlain's Servants, and that company had recently moved into a theatre called the Globe. The Globe did have a thatched roof, and was located in the suburb of Southwark; in order to get to it from the city of London you had to cross the river Thames. But this evidence is *only* circumstantial. Platter does not give the title or the author of the play. He does not name the theatre, nor refer to it as a *new* theatre; the older Rose Theatre, just steps away from the Globe, also had a thatched roof.

There is, moreover, no certain evidence that Shakespeare wrote *Julius Caesar* in or around 1599. It is true that some lines in Ben Jonson's *Every Man Out of his Humour* – which can be certainly dated to 1599 – seem to allude parodically to *Julius Caesar*; and it is true that a conversation between Polonius and Hamlet in *Hamlet* (*c.* 1600) seems to depend for its ironic humour upon a spectator's awareness that the actors playing these characters also played Shakespeare's Caesar and Brutus. But such internal, inferential evidence is hard to rely on. When *Every Man Out*'s Carlo Buffone says 'Et tu, Brute?' to his antagonist Macilente (who is about to seal up the loquacious Buffone's lips with molten wax), he *might* be quoting *Julius Caesar*, but he also might be quoting *The True Tragedy of Richard, Duke of York* (printed in 1595), where Edward IV says it to his traitorous son Clarence. And *True Tragedy*'s Edward was himself translating and adapting the Greek 'You too, child?', given by the Roman historian Suetonius as the last words Caesar spoke. Various versions of this phrase were in circulation during Shakespeare's time, and it is quite possible that playwrights made use of it without thinking of

---

[1] Translated by Ernest Schanzer, in 'Thomas Platter's observations on the Elizabethan stage', *N&Q* 201 (1956), 466.

themselves as alluding to one another. The case for a connection between *Julius Caesar* and *Every Man Out* does not rest solely upon 'Et tu, Brute': there is also a moment in Jonson's play where a foolish character, trying to sound sophisticated, says 'Reason long since is fled to the animals, you know.' Some critics believe this to be a parody of Antony's plaintive apostrophe at 3.2.96: 'O judgement, thou art fled to brutish beasts.' But this evidence, such as it is, is only as convincing as you allow yourself to find it.

The most precise evidence we have for determining the date of *Julius Caesar* provides us with a range of a little over ten years. The play was probably not written before 1598, because it is not mentioned in Frances Meres's *Palladis Tamia*, where he lists the tragedies for which Shakespeare was known. And it was definitely written before 1612, when it is known to have been performed as part of the festivities in honour of the wedding of James I's daughter Elizabeth.

On balance, I think it is likely that Shakespeare's *Julius Caesar* was written and first performed in or around 1599, and also that Shakespeare's *Julius Caesar* is the play Thomas Platter saw on 21 September of that year. I will be assuming the truth of both things throughout the remainder of this Introduction. But it is essential to emphasise that these assumptions can only be made inferentially and, indeed, imaginatively. If we make them by way of Platter's diary, we must push past, and to some extent disregard, the details in the foreground of Platter's account in order to discover – and indeed to supply – the important details that remain hidden in the background: not only the playwright's or the theatre's name, but also the entire plot of the play. To do this is, however, to misread Platter's account of his outing to the theatre – an account that is, to some extent, *all* background. For Platter, 'the Emperor Julius Caesar' is just one small, almost incidental detail in a glittering recollection of late-summer leisure in one of the world's great cities. His lunch, his boat ride, the 'party' of friends going to the theatre, the conventional after-play dance – all of these details could have coalesced around any play; there is no sense at all that Platter sought this one out. We might think of *Julius Caesar*, and the actor playing the title character, as the lucky ones, randomly but thankfully memorialised as a representative detail of sixteenth-century cosmopolitan life. To seek the date of Shakespeare's *Julius Caesar* by reading Thomas Platter's diary, and then to contextualise the play within its historical moment of composition and performance, requires that we shift our perspective – fluidly, critically, and constantly – between background and foreground; this is a skill we must cultivate in reading the play as well.

Source

In writing *Julius Caesar*, Shakespeare drew primarily upon Plutarch's *Lives of the Noble Grecians and Romans*, which was written in the first century AD and translated into English by Thomas North in 1579. The sections of Plutarch which Shakespeare relies upon most heavily are his life of Julius Caesar and his life of Brutus. Excerpts from both have been provided in the Appendix to this edition so that you can see for yourself where and how Shakespeare followed, and where and how he departed from, his source material.[1] It is very likely that Shakespeare had read and was familiar with other accounts of the life of Caesar. Caesar's own account of his Gallic wars was required reading for Elizabethan schoolboys, and Shakespeare certainly could have read, or read about representations of Caesar in, other first- and second-century histories, such as Suetonius's *History of the Twelve Caesars*, Tacitus's *Annals*, Appian's *Civil Wars* – or in more contemporaneous works such as Sir Thomas Elyot's *Book called the Governour* (1531) or the collaboratively authored *Mirror for Magistrates* (the 1587 edition of which contained a poem about Caesar). Precise echoes of or divergences from these other works cannot, however, be definitively or reliably identified; the discussion of Shakespeare's use of his sources which follows will, therefore, focus entirely on Plutarch. Of course, this should not be understood to imply that Shakespeare had not read more broadly in Roman history.[2]

When we discuss the relation between a Shakespeare play and its sources, we tend first of all to look for differences between the two. Those places where we can see Shakespeare most deliberately altering the historical material upon which his play is based seem to provide us with clear insight into his intentions and priorities as a dramatic artist. The most obvious difference between Plutarch's history of Caesar and Shakespeare's is their treatment of the common people. In the first scene of his play, Shakespeare suggests that Caesar rises to power on a wave of popular support: the common people, in the words of the tribune Murellus, 'strew flowers in his way, / That comes in triumph over Pompey's blood' (1.1.49–50). Plutarch's life of Caesar provides an emphatically different representation of the common people: 'the triumph he made into Rome', Plutarch writes, 'did as much offend the Romans, and more, than anything that ever he had done before; because he had not overcome captains that were strangers, nor barbarous kings, but had destroyed the sons of the noblest man in Rome, whom fortune had overthrown'.[3] Moreover, while Shakespeare's first scene implies that the common people have 'decked with ceremonies' the statues of Caesar throughout the city, and that the tribunes remove the decorations in response (1.1.63–4), Plutarch writes that when Flavius and Murellus pulled down the images that had been adorned by Caesar's followers, the people 'followed them rejoicing at it, and called them "Brutes", because of Brutus, who had in old time driven the kings out of Rome . . . ' (p. 141). It is true that Plutarch says (as Shakespeare implies) that the Romans, weary of civil war and grateful for the relative peace and prosperity Caesar's victory brought to the land, willingly 'chose him perpetual Dictator' (p. 139). And, like Shakespeare, Plutarch vividly represents mob rule taking hold of the city through the episode where the poet

---

[1] You can also read North's translations of Plutarch's lives of Caesar and Brutus in their entirety in Geoffrey Bullough (ed.), *Narrative and Dramatic Sources of Shakespeare*, vol. v, 1964. Some passages from Bullough are cited in the commentary.

[2] Vivian Thomas's essay, 'Shakespeare's sources: translations, transformations, and intertextuality in *Julius Caesar*', in *Julius Caesar: New Critical Essays*, ed. Horst Zander, 2005, pp. 91–110, is a useful complement and supplement to my discussion here.

[3] This quotation can be found in Plutarch's *Life of Julius Caesar* as excerpted in this edition's Appendix, p. 138. The page numbers for further quotations of Plutarch from the Appendix will be given parenthetically.

Cinna is murdered simply for having the same name as one of the conspirators. But Plutarch also says that it was Caesar's desire to be called king 'which first gave the people just cause, and next his secret enemies honest colour, to bear him ill will' (p. 140). And, at the same time, Plutarch makes clear that the brutality of Caesar's assassination turned the people against Brutus and the conspirators from the start – and that the conspirators had, even before the funeral, made preparations for their own escape, in case the Roman citizens did not welcome their act of liberation. Plutarch presents a somewhat more nuanced picture of the common people than Shakespeare does; he refuses to represent their shifting responses to political violence as wholly unreasonable.

This is not to say that Shakespeare's unsympathetic representation of the common people is entirely unhistorical, nor that it must be understood as Shakespeare's own point of view. The divergence between play and source on this point provides an invitation to interpretation, and a careful reader of both the play-text and the historical excerpts given in the Appendix might discover any number of other interpretive avenues – in, for example, the difference between Shakespeare's and Plutarch's representation of the murder of the poet Cinna; or the different portrayal of Cassius in each; and so on. But interpretive rewards await, as well, the careful reader who compares Shakespeare and Plutarch in order to find moments of close correspondence or surprising historical fidelity. Such moments might shed some light upon Shakespeare's method of dramatic composition. I will try to explain what I mean by looking at how Shakespeare builds the scene of Brutus's death out of materials he finds in Plutarch.

In Plutarch's *Life of Caesar* and his *Life of Brutus*, there are about four accounts of Brutus's death. At the end of the *Life of Caesar*, Brutus, on the battlefield near Philippi, sees the ghost that had earlier visited him in his tent and understands this to be a sign that he will die. He plunges himself headlong into the battle, 'but yet fighting could not be slain. So, seeing his men put to flight and overthrown, he ran unto a little rock not far off; and there setting his sword's point to his breast fell upon it and slew himself . . . ' (p. 146). Having described this dramatic death scene, Plutarch immediately and conditionally revises it: 'but yet, as it is reported, with the help of his friend that dispatched him' – that is, an unnamed friend might have finished the job Brutus could not complete himself. A rather different pair of stories is presented at the end of the *Life of Brutus*. There, Brutus and his army have been beaten into a retreat. Over the course of a long night, they realise that their situation is hopeless and Brutus asks first Volumnius ('a grave and wise philosopher, that had been with Brutus from the beginning of this war', p. 165) and then Dardanus (Brutus's servant) to help him kill himself. Both refuse, and so Brutus makes a speech of thanks and farewell to all, and then moves aside, getting himself as close as possible to his friend Strato ('with whom he came first acquainted by the study of rhetoric', p. 167). At this point, Brutus takes 'his sword by the hilts with both his hands and falling down upon the point of it, ran himself through' (p. 167). Once again, and immediately, Plutarch partially revises this dramatic moment: 'Others say that not he [i.e. Brutus], but Strato, at his request, held the sword in his hand, and turned his head aside, and that Brutus fell down upon it.'

The histories of Plutarch, then, shift between a Brutus who dies nearly in the midst of battle and a Brutus who dies to avoid a battle; and they shift between a Brutus who kills himself by himself and a Brutus who dies among, and is helped to die by, his friends.

Plutarch's method of writing history, in particular his narrating of crucial events by giving different accounts of them and refusing to choose between them, was quite ordinary in his own time and in Shakespeare's. Shakespeare would have been accustomed, when developing plays out of both classical histories and more recently written English histories (such as *Holinshed's Chronicles*, 1587), to choosing among multiple possible narratives of or perspectives on the same event. In writing the scene of Brutus's death in *Julius Caesar*, he chooses those pieces from Plutarch which show Brutus among his friends and assisted in his suicide. Here, as throughout a play in which Brutus is almost always surrounded by people (he has only one soliloquy), Shakespeare seems interested to show that the extraordinary man can never be separated from – and in fact longs *not* to be separated from – the society he seeks to change. And Shakespeare commits to dramatising this version of Brutus in spite of its considerable theatrical inefficiency. The last scene of the play begins with the stage direction '*Enter* BRUTUS, DARDANIUS, CLITUS, STRATO, *and* VOLUMNIUS.' With the sole exception of Brutus, none of these characters has appeared anywhere in the play before. Now that they are on the stage, these characters are called very particularly by their names – all names that an audience or a reader will not have encountered previously. The actual suicide must be a complicated, potentially awkward, very-necessary-to-rehearse four-handed affair: 'Hold then my sword and turn away thy face, / While I do run upon it', Brutus orders (5.5.47–8) – surely easier said than done! It would be an easier staging, it would require less rehearsal, and it would leave us with a more obviously heroic view of Brutus to follow the first version of Brutus's death which Plutarch recounts in the *Life of Caesar*: the soldier, weary from the fierce fighting into which he has thrown himself, retires to a quiet corner – which becomes the centre of the stage – and resolutely stabs himself. But what Shakespeare gets from Plutarch, and what he wants to put on the stage, however briefly, is the vivid sense of a whole world inhabited by all of the characters. It is a world with personal histories and long-standing relationships: 'Good Volumnius, / Thou know'st that we two went to school together', Brutus says (5.5.25–6 – and here perhaps Shakespeare is confusing or conflating Volumnius and Strato). And it is a world of precise, meaningful, emotional gestures – ordinary movements that are so expressive that they are commemorated by historians, and so passed down into history: Brutus goes among his friends and servants, whispering to them in hopes of finding someone to help him die; Strato, in a phrase very clearly inspired by Plutarch, must 'turn away' his face as he holds the sword.

Both examples I have given of Shakespeare's interaction with his source material are centred on the representation of crowds. 'The people' in Plutarch are never given a very particular identity: more often than not, Plutarch seems to use the term to lump together the common people, Roman citizenry irrespective of class, and the politicians who represent them. In this lack of particularisation, Plutarch is able to maintain an apparently objective view of crowd behaviour in political crisis. Shakespeare, on the other hand, particularises the crowd, and represents it as a mob: idle, fickle, always searching for an outlet for its inherent violent tendencies. Against the foil of this crowd, Shakespeare is able to represent the dangerous but exciting charisma of powerful men: the stoic Brutus, the eloquent and calculating Antony, the godlike Caesar, even the feverishly tenacious Cassius. But if Shakespeare discards Plutarch's objective view of the crowd in order to focus a spectator's attention, desire, and sympathy on a would-be heroic figure like Brutus, he also, and perhaps paradoxically, goes out of his way to follow Plutarch in representing Brutus, in the final moments of his life, as inseparable from and sustained by a community of nearly anonymous friends and supporters. At the moment we might most expect to see a solitary Brutus, we find him surrounded by people. The dynamic shift – so crucial to the structure and to an audience's experience of *Julius Caesar* – between foreground and background, extraordinary historical figures and the ordinary lives they touch, is everywhere apparent in Shakespeare's interpretation and selection of events recorded by Plutarch.

Caesar in the English Renaissance Theatre

In 1598, the Lord Chamberlain's Servants lost their lease on the playhouse called the Theatre. Built in 1576 in Shoreditch, a suburb just north of the city of London, the Theatre had been one of the first permanent, purpose-built playing spaces in England. Audiences there had probably seen the first productions of many of Shakespeare's plays: *Romeo and Juliet*, for example, and *A Midsummer Night's Dream*, *Richard II*, *1 Henry IV*, and *The Merchant of Venice*. The company did not own the land on which the Theatre stood, but it did own the timber out of which it had been constructed: in 1598–9 they dismantled the building and transported the wood through the city and across the river, where it was reused in the construction of their new home, the Globe. Some scholars have suggested that this new theatre was opened with a production of *Julius Caesar*, though there is no certain evidence of that: *Henry V*, whose Chorus self-consciously refers to the 'wooden O' in which epic history will be represented, or *As You Like It*, with its 'All the world's a stage' speech, are equally plausible candidates. It is also entirely possible that the Globe opened with a performance of a play by another playwright. In any case, audiences at the Globe would see the first productions of many of the plays Shakespeare wrote in the remainder of his career, including those we now think of as his most famous: *Hamlet*, *Othello*, *King Lear*, and *Macbeth*. In 1613, audiences would flee the Globe as it burned to the ground, its thatched roof having been ignited by a firework set off during a production of Shakespeare and John Fletcher's *Henry VIII*. We do not know whether Shakespeare was in the house on this catastrophic occasion: he seems to have taken a break from playwriting and moved to Stratford-upon-Avon around 1611, though his collaboration with Fletcher on *Henry VIII* suggests that he did not consider himself completely retired. We do know that, by 1613, his plays had helped bring his company – known, since 1603, as the King's Majesty's Servants – to sufficient financial success for them to be able to rebuild the Globe almost immediately, and bigger and better than before. And his plays, even those written a decade or more earlier, remained an important part of the company's repertoire: the King's Majesty's Servants performed numerous plays at the court of King James in 1612–13, in celebration of his daughter Elizabeth's wedding. Among these were *The Tempest* (probably composed *c.* 1610–11), *The Winter's Tale* (1610–11), *Othello* (1603–4), *Much Ado About Nothing* (1598–9), and *Julius Caesar*.

We can, then, catch fleeting glimpses of *Julius Caesar* at some of the most significant moments in Shakespeare's career: the founding of the Globe and the onset of an extraordinary phase in the playwright's artistic production; the destruction of the Globe and the playwright's gradual withdrawal from the world of the commercial theatre. But we must not be led by these historical coincidences into thinking that the name 'Julius Caesar', as a theatrical commodity, orbits only around the name 'William Shakespeare'. Rather, Shakespeare was one of numerous playwrights (most of the others remain anonymous even to this day) drawn into the orbit of the story of the great leader.[1] One of the earliest sixteenth-century English Caesar-plays that we know anything about is the now-lost *Caesar Interfectus* (*Caesar Murdered*), probably performed at Christ Church, Oxford around 1582, and probably written (in Latin) by Richard Edes, master of that college. What little evidence there is of this play's existence – a fragment of a sixteenth-century manuscript containing what might have been the play's epilogue – suggests that it probably told a similar story to the one told by Shakespeare's play. 'Caesar triumphed forcibly over the Republic', it reads, 'Brutus over Caesar':

> It was evil that Caesar seized the Republic; good that he seized it without slaughter or bloodshed. Brutus acted rightly when he restored its liberty; but wickedly when he thought to restore it by killing Caesar … The former behaved admirably in the worst, the latter reprehensibly in the best, of causes … Cassius was as much the better General as Brutus was the better Man; in one Force was greater, in the other Virtue. You would prefer to have Brutus as a friend, but you would fear more to have Cassius as an enemy. The former hated tyranny, the latter the tyrant. Caesar's fate seems just if we consider his tyranny, but unjust if we consider the man he was …[2]

There is no evidence that Shakespeare knew *Caesar Interfectus* (indeed, it is most likely that he did not), and for that reason it is all the more significant that the subtle and ambivalent treatment of personal and political relationships in the Oxford manuscript fragment is similar to what we see in Shakespeare's play. Both plays participate in a tradition of sixteenth-century thinking about Caesar which locates the essential drama

---

[1] For an excellent, fuller accounting of other Caesar-plays – and Caesar in other plays – see Clifford Ronan, 'Caesar on and off the Renaissance English stage', in *'Julius Caesar': New Critical Essays*, ed. Horst Zander, 2005, pp. 71–90. In the same volume, Barbara L. Parker provides a discussion of *Julius Caesar* in the context of Shakespeare's other Roman plays: 'From monarchy to tyranny: *Julius Caesar* among Shakespeare's Roman works', pp. 111–26.

[2] The fragment from *Caesar Interfectus* is translated in Bullough, *Narrative and Dramatic Sources of Shakespeare*, 195.

of the story in the difficulty of separating the motives and passions of individuals from the political circumstances that frame and often seem to govern their actions.

Another thing the *Caesar Interfectus* manuscript fragment has in common with Shakespeare's *Julius Caesar* – and the thing that seems most to distinguish these plays from other Caesar-plays in the period – is an apparent lack of interest in the figure of Pompey the Great. Gnaeus Pompeius Magnus was, with Caesar and Marcus Licinius Crassus, a member of the First Triumvirate, which ruled the Roman empire starting in 61 BC; he was also the husband of Caesar's daughter Julia. The death of Crassus in 53 BC dissolved the triumvirate, and was closely followed by the death of Julia in childbirth. Caesar tried to re-seal the alliance by giving his grand-niece Octavia to Pompey in marriage, but Pompey refused. Instead, he married Cornelia, the widow of Crassus's son. By 51 BC, due to a range of complex political disagreements, Caesar and Pompey had become antagonists in a civil war. Pompey was defeated by Caesar at the battle of Pharsalus in 48 BC. He fled to Egypt and sought refuge with its young king, Ptolemy. The Egyptians were reluctant to open themselves to the possibility of Roman aggression by welcoming Ptolemy into their midst, and keen to take an opportunity to stay on the right side of Caesar. In an act of betrayal described in high dramatic style by Plutarch, Ptolemy's men met Pompey's fleet and lured him ashore with the promise of aid. Pompey's wife Cornelia

stood on the trireme watching with great anxiety for the outcome, and began to take heart when she saw many of the king's people assembling at the landing as if to give him an honourable welcome. But at this point, while Pompey was clasping the hand of Philip that he might rise to his feet more easily, Septimius, from behind, ran him through the body with his sword, then Salvius next, and then Achillas, drew their daggers and stabbed him. And Pompey, drawing his toga down over his face with both hands, without an act or a word that was unworthy of himself, but with a groan merely, submitted to their blows, being sixty years of age less one, and ending his life only one day after his birth-day.[1]

While the triumph for Caesar that followed upon the battle of Pharsalus is the first thing that happens in *Julius Caesar* – and while, at 1.1.31–54, the tribunes upbraid the citizens for transferring their allegiance so easily from Pompey to Caesar – Shakespeare's play contains almost no other reference to the remarkable events comprised by the long association of Caesar and Pompey.[2] In this surprising omission, we might see Shakespeare deliberately setting himself in opposition to a dramatic tradition in which the relationship between the two triumvirs, where political and familial bonds were inextricable, was seen as the heart of Caesar's history.

On Twelfth Night (January 6) 1581, a play called *The Story of Pompey* was performed before Queen Elizabeth at Whitehall. This was one of many plays to be acted at court during Christmas festivities, and the performing company was the Children of St Paul's – actors drawn from among the choirboys at the cathedral and directed by their choir-master Sebastian Westcott. There is no extant copy of *The*

---

[1] This passage is from Plutarch's *Life of Pompey*, as translated by Bernadotte Perrin in the Loeb Classical Library edition of Plutarch's *Lives*, 1917, vol. v, pp. 321 and 323.
[2] At 5.1.71–5, Cassius, about to face Antony at Philippi, compares himself to Pompey at Pharsalus.

Story of Pompey, so we can only speculate that the play dramatised events involving Caesar as well as Pompey – but this is probably a safe speculation. If we are reading the admittedly scarce evidence correctly, 1581 seems to have been a good year for Pompey plays. An antitheatrical pamphlet called *Plays Confuted in Five Actions* (1582) seems to indicate that a 'history of Caesar and Pompey' was staged that year at Shakespeare's future theatrical home, the Theatre. This play, whatever it was, has also been lost, as have the two plays performed a little more than a decade later: *1 Caesar and Pompey* and *2 Caesar and Pompey*, staged by the Lord Admiral's Servants at their house with the thatched roof, the Rose Theatre, in 1594 and 1595. We can be almost certain that Shakespeare would have known – had very likely seen – the plays staged at the Rose in 1594 and 1595. Given what we know about the Rose repertory, these were probably sprawling and spectacular plays, and probably drew extensively upon Plutarch's histories in order to represent the rise and fall of the First Triumvirate in great historical detail and with great theatrical vigour. When Shakespeare decided, perhaps in 1598, to write a Caesar-play of his own, his first thought must have been to try something different – to replace Caesar and Pompey with Caesar and Brutus, and thus to represent not the beginning but the end of Caesar's extraordinary career.[1]

To contextualise *Julius Caesar* by means of lost plays is an enjoyable and productive enterprise, but also a dangerously speculative one. Fortunately, not all Caesar-plays from the period are lost, and in those that survive (most written after Shakespeare's), we see that Pompey remains a focal point of interest. In 1594, the dramatist Thomas Kyd published a 'closet' drama (that is, a verse-play not intended for stage performance) called *Cornelia*, which covers the life of Cornelia both before and after her marriage to Pompey. Sometime (most likely) between 1599 and 1607, the playwright George Chapman composed a play called *Caesar and Pompey*, which makes Brutus a central figure in the civil wars between Caesar and Pompey – he switches sides twice – and which ends (unhistorically) with Pompey being killed by Ptolemy's men in his own home after bidding his wife and children good-night. Chapman's play was also probably never performed. It was printed in 1631, about ten years after the early modern period's final extant Caesar-play, John Fletcher and Philip Massinger's *The False One* (1619–20). A sort of prequel to Shakespeare's *Antony and Cleopatra*, *The False One* is about Cleopatra's ascent to the throne of Egypt through her political–romantic alliance with Caesar. This play begins in Egypt, with Ptolemy and his councillors discussing the Roman civil war and Pompey's request for aid. Pompey himself never appears in the play, but his severed head is brought on in the second act and presented to Caesar who, as happy as he might be to have his rival out of the way, promises to punish the murderers of his fellow Roman.

All of these other Caesar-plays make clear how much of the pre-history of Caesar's assassination Shakespeare *left out* of his play – even as a memory – and so give us some idea of what a strange and unconventional history he set out to write. Shakespeare never refers to the fact that Pompey was married to Caesar's daughter, nor to his flight to and

---

[1] Perhaps significantly, there is no extant or known-but-lost early modern play titled *Marcus Brutus* – nor any that contains the name Marcus Brutus in its title.

betrayal in Egypt, nor to Brutus's alliance with Pompey during the civil war, nor even to the alliance that was the First Triumvirate. 'Crassus' is not a name any character speaks. A reader unfamiliar with Roman history might assume from the first act of *Julius Caesar* that Pompey and Caesar were merely rivals for control of Rome, not rivals who had once been co-rulers. Of course, Shakespeare himself *was* familiar with Roman history and, moreover, he probably assumed that the spectators who would get the most out of his play would also be familiar with Roman history. Nevertheless, I suggest that, much more than assuming that his audience would fill in the historical blanks he left en route to telling the story he was most interested in, Shakespeare hoped that his audience would be surprised by the *theatrical* blanks left in his dramatisation of a history that had probably, by 1599, taken on a conventional shape. He wanted his audience gradually to realise that the story of Caesar and Pompey had been transmuted into the story of Caesar and Brutus. We can see this perhaps most clearly by looking at the relationship between Shakespeare's play and one final Caesar-play of the period: *The Tragedy of Caesar and Pompey, or Caesar's Revenge*, a play written in English and performed by students at Trinity College, Oxford, probably in the mid-1590s.

Scholars are generally in agreement that Shakespeare was familiar with *Caesar's Revenge*, most likely from seeing it in performance (it was not printed until 1606 or 1607), and that he borrowed many details from it. In both *Caesar's Revenge* and *Julius Caesar*, for example, when Titinius finds Cassius's body and commits suicide (5.3.90 in Shakespeare's play), he kills himself with Cassius's weapon rather than his own – a detail that is not in Plutarch. There are many other such examples of rather minute overlap between the two plays, but there is also one quite major difference, and it is the one I have been talking about throughout this section: Pompey is an important character in the Trinity College play. *Caesar's Revenge* begins with the battle of Pharsalus, and its first two acts follow Pompey's flight from the battlefield, his attempt to take refuge in Egypt, and his betrayal and death at the hands of Ptolemy upon arriving there. Cornelia makes an appearance in the fifth scene, where she bids farewell to Pompey as he sets out for Egypt, and after he is gone she seems to have a vision of his betrayal. She appears once more in 2.2, where she bewails her husband's murder and (unhistorically) kills herself. After this series of scenes, Pompey's name is on every character's lips throughout the play, and the effect of his broken alliance with Caesar upon Caesar's fate is inescapable. Trebonius, for example, says this to the bleeding corpse of Caesar just after the assassination:

> How heavens have justly on the author's head
> Returned the guiltless blood which he hath shed, . . .
> And, Pompey, he who caused thy tragedy, . . .
> Here breathless lies before thy noble statue.[1]

Later, the Ghost of Caesar will offer a lengthy catalogue of the 'wrongs' he has committed – among them 'both the Pompeys by me done to death' (1996).

---

[1] These are lines 1736–9 of the play as it was edited and transcribed by F. S. Boas in his 1911 Malone Society edition. I have modernised the spelling and punctuation.

Shakespeare borrows or retains many elements from this play, but in each case removes Pompey from the equation: the visionary spouse who foresees her husband's murder is now Calpurnia dreaming of Caesar spouting blood; the suicidal spouse is now the distracted Portia; and the Ghost is raised as a reminder of Brutus's, not Caesar's own, wrongs. The irony of Caesar being murdered at the very foot of Pompey's statue is under-emphasised in Shakespeare: Brutus at 3.1.115 and Antony, 3.2.179, simply mention the fact, but no one refers to Caesar's death, even hypothetically, as a just quittance for Pompey's murder. In a strange way, Shakespeare seems to want to remove Caesar from history, transforming the man of action who in many ways earned his own betrayal into an idea that haunts the minds of men so powerfully that it must be either worshipped or destroyed. As ordinary as this might seem to us now, it was, in the early modern theatre, a novel conception of Caesar.

In *Julius Caesar*, Shakespeare offered something new in terms of Elizabethan dramatic representations of Caesar, and he did so by writing the kind of play we have come to understand as typically 'Shakespearean': the kind of play in which the protagonist is his own antagonist, and where the significance of the action lies not so much in how it plays out on stage as how it is played out, before and as it unfolds, in the protagonist's mind. If the Lord Chamberlain's Servants did in fact choose *Julius Caesar* as the first play for their new stage, it may have been because they recognised its startlingly innovative approach to a familiar story, and because they thought that London theatre-goers were ready for something new and challenging. In such a narrative, the Globe, Shakespeare, and *Julius Caesar* become the site of a real turning point in western theatre, where the most serious dramatic writing does not seek (as Aristotle advised) to express character through action, but rather seeks to demonstrate how action is determined by character. It may seem intuitive to us, now, to claim that the true meaning, and the truth, of a play's action can be found in the protagonist's head, but this was a radical, if rapidly adopted, idea for dramatists at the end of the sixteenth century. It took hold in the course of the seventeenth century in no small part through the work of Shakespeare, as he progressed from *Julius Caesar* to *Hamlet* to *Lear* to *Macbeth* to *The Tempest*.

As compelling as this view of Shakespeare's plays, career, and influence is, it is worth reminding ourselves (as Brutus must be reminded) that real historical change comes only very slowly, and the process by which it is achieved is often obvious only in retrospect. The genuinely new is as often as not rejected by, or perceived as alien to, the historical moment into which it bursts. There is absolutely no evidence that *Julius Caesar* was a particularly popular play, and if it *was* the play that the Lord Chamberlain's Servants chose to open their new theatre, it was – if we take into account the other drama happening at the time – definitely a risk, and not necessarily one that we need to assume was immediately rewarded. The years 1598–1600 also saw the production of a number of plays that shared with *Julius Caesar* a pastiche-like, or mosaic, approach to action, but differed from it in an externalised approach to character: Jonson's *Every Man Out*, the anonymous disguise-comedy-history-play *Look About You*, Thomas Dekker's urban romance *The Shoemaker's Holiday*, Anthony Munday and Henry Chettle's sprawling Robin Hood plays (*The Downfall* and *The Death of Robert, Earl of Huntington*), John Marston's self-consciously erratic *Antonio and Mellida*, and so on. We have no idea whether these plays – all more like one another than they are like *Julius Caesar* – were more popular or well-liked than Shakespeare's, but we can get some sense of the kind of thing that really captured a sixteenth-century spectator's imagination from the diary of Thomas Platter. For a play about Julius Caesar was not the only play that Platter saw on his trip to London. Another passage in his diary – much less well known, in spite of the fact that it follows immediately upon his brief description of the Caesar-play – describes, in considerably more detail, a very different play he saw.

On another occasion not far from our inn, in the suburb at Bishopsgate, if I remember, also after lunch, I beheld a play in which they presented diverse nations and an Englishman struggling together for a maiden; he overcame them all except the German who won the girl in a tussle, and then sat down by her side, when he and his servant drank themselves tipsy, so that they were both fuddled and the servant proceeded to hurl his shoe at his master's head, whereupon they both fell asleep; meanwhile the Englishman stole into the tent and absconded with the German's prize, thus in his turn outwitting the German; in conclusion they danced very charmingly in English and Irish fashion.

The theatre to which Platter refers was almost certainly the Curtain, which was not far from the now-abandoned site of the Theatre. As with the Caesar-play, Platter does not give the title of this play, and while its plot and comic devices resemble many plays that have come down to us (most particularly William Haughton's *Englishmen for My Money*, *c.* 1598), it cannot be precisely identified with any extant work. For our purposes, the most important thing about this part of Platter's diary is how much time, and obvious pleasure, he takes in recounting the plot of this ridiculous play – what a particular impression this play registers in his diary when compared to what he says of the 'excellent performance' of the presumably much more serious Caesar-play. Years later, if Platter or his heirs returned to this diary, the unknown comedy is what would leap into focus, and the Caesar-play, even if it was Shakespeare's, would simply be a part of the background – just another play in the busy and exciting landscape of London theatre. To say this is not to denigrate or diminish *Julius Caesar* but rather to gain a new perspective on the astonishing fact of its longevity and enduring theatrical power. We might draw an analogy between what Platter's diary does, incidentally, to the Caesar-play and what Shakespeare does, deliberately, to the familiar and ubiquitous figure of Caesar himself: he brings Caesar to the fore only to relegate him to the background, and in this way he shows that the work of history never belongs solely to one man.

The Play

I have attempted to demonstrate two things in the previous two sections. First, Shakespeare knew his Plutarch (in particular, North's translation of Plutarch) very well – probably well enough not to have to look at it very closely as he wrote his plays. He had events and phrases from different parts of different *Lives* knocking around in his head, and he was sufficiently confident in his understanding and interpretation of the history of Caesar to redeploy and recombine pieces from Plutarch freely and creatively. Second, Shakespeare was familiar with the English tradition of Caesar-plays, and had a strong sense of what kinds of things dramatists and audiences would be most likely to find interesting about Caesar's life and death. He therefore, with a deliberate perversity that characterises most of his career as a dramatist, set out to write exactly the kind of Caesar-play that people would not expect to see.

1 *The Emperor Julius Caesar on Horseback.* An engraving by Antonio Tempesta from *The First Twelve Roman Caesars* (Rome, 1596)

2 Julius Caesar. An engraving by Marcantonio Raimondi from the series *The Twelve Caesars* (*c.* 1520)

PERSONAL AND POLITICAL CAESAR

In her introduction to the recent Norton edition of *Julius Caesar*, S. P. Cerasano argues that Shakespeare selected Caesar as the subject for one of his earliest plays at his new theatre because Caesar was

a character whose mythic life was well known, a larger-than-life presence who could easily take over the Globe stage. Generations of English schoolboys had translated Caesar's *Gallic Wars*, as well as Cicero's orations addressing ... contemporary politics during the period when Caesar ruled the Roman Republic. There were, as well, references to Caesar and his time in the writings of many classical authors whose works were standard reading for sixteenth-century students.[1]

Cerasano accurately represents the ubiquity of Caesar in literate culture of the late sixteenth century, but she somewhat inaccurately represents the kind of character

[1] *Julius Caesar*, ed. S. P. Cerasano, 2012, p. xii.

3 Julius Caesar. An engraving by Martino Rota from *Twenty-four Portraits of Roman Emperors* (Venice, 1570)

Julius Caesar actually is. Shakespeare's Caesar is *not* really a 'larger than life presence' who takes over the stage. That is the kind of Caesar we see in *Caesar's Revenge*, and that audiences probably saw in the two *Caesar and Pompey* plays staged by the Lord Admiral's Servants at the Rose Theatre in the mid-1590s. The Caesar Shakespeare gives us has very little stage time and is dogged, at every moment he occupies the stage, by prophecies (or, to the audience, reminders) that his triumph will cost him his life. An audience coming to the Globe in 1599 might very well have expected to see a play that began by representing Caesar's military prowess; that proceeded to a dramatisation of his increasing political power, his rift with Pompey, and his triumph in Rome; and that concluded, appropriately and tragically, with his assassination. What they got instead was a play that might as easily have been called *Marcus Brutus* – a play that begins with Cassius planting the seed of rebellion in Brutus's head; that proceeds to dramatise the establishment of the conspiracy, the assassination of Caesar, and Brutus's generalship in the civil war; and that concludes, tragically, with Brutus's suicide. It seems very likely that Shakespeare wrote the kind of play he wrote as a tonic to the cultural ubiquity – which, perhaps, he felt was rather numbing and over-determined – that Cerasano discusses. The hold Caesar had, and continues to have, upon the western imagination derives in large part not from what he did but from what, by his assassination, he was stopped from doing. He represents a crucial ambiguity that always attends upon the leaders of free societies in times of crisis:

4 Julius Caesar. An engraving by Egidius Sadeler (*c.* 1593) after Titian's series *Roman Emperors*

whether great power must be resisted lest it inevitably lead to tyranny, or charges of tyranny amount to a misunderstanding, or mere envy, of great power. But Caesar only comes to represent this ambiguity by way of the actions of Brutus. It was, perhaps, just this paradox that Shakespeare sought to dramatise by building the action, and the tragic structure, of his play so explicitly around Brutus, even as he decided to title it *Julius Caesar.*

5 *The Triumphator Julius Caesar on his Chariot*. From *The Triumphs of Caesar* by Andrea Mantegna at Hampton Court (late fifteenth century)

Shakespeare's paradoxical handling of Caesar's larger-than-life identity is a function of the political context in which he wrote his play. Most simply, it is a play whose hero strives to overthrow an aspiring monarch; and it was written at a time when a society *not* governed by a monarch would have been difficult, if not impossible, for most people to imagine. For the characters of *Julius Caesar*, the Republic – a society based on representative government, where the individual citizen (or, at least, the individual male, property-owning citizen) is the fundamental unit of power – is a lost ideal. The Republic was traditionally said to have been founded in the sixth century BC by Lucius Junius Brutus, who led a rebellion against the corrupt king Lucius Tarquinius Superbus. The name and reputation of this famous revolutionary haunts the Brutus of the play. Alluding to the founding of the Republic in order to goad Brutus into action, Cassius says:

> There was a Brutus once that would have brooked
> Th'eternal devil to keep his state in Rome
> As easily as a king.   (1.2.159–61)

In passages like this, the play asks its audience to measure the actual, halting, self-destructive actions of the play's Brutus against the imagined, world-changing decisiveness of his legendary predecessor and namesake; the Republic thus becomes a lost ideal for the audience as well. The modern reader or spectator, living in a modern democracy, might take the dramatisation of this lost ideal as a matter of course: for us, what is most tragic about the play is probably Brutus's inability to bring into being a society, based on individual self-determination, that obviously *should* exist – and maybe did once. But the response of a reader or spectator in Shakespeare's time might have been somewhat more vexed. The sovereignty to which Caesar aspires was in some sense the power enjoyed by sixteenth- and seventeenth-century English monarchs, and regicide was not only a terrible crime but a near-certain recipe for social chaos; for an Elizabethan audience, what was most tragic about the play was probably Brutus's inability, or unwillingness, to fill the vacuum left by Caesar's death with a comparable and stabilising power. Returning to the paradoxical relation between the play's title and its structure, discussed in the previous paragraph, we might say that one of the largest and most forceful statements Shakespeare's play makes is that Marcus Brutus is no Julius Caesar.

While it would be true to say that Republicanism was in no sense a widely understood or accepted possible alternative to monarchy in Shakespeare's England, it would not be true to say that monarchs and monarchy were beyond question or sceptical analysis. The ideal of the Roman Republic, already so prevalent in early modern English literate culture, provided Shakespeare and his audience with a relatively safe lens through which to undertake such an analysis. For a spectator at the Globe in 1599, it is quite possible that *Julius Caesar* might have contained clear and subversive resonances with the contemporary political situation, which was characterised by widespread dissatisfaction with and anxiety about the reign of Elizabeth I. In 1599, Elizabeth was sixty-six years old and had been on the throne for forty-one years. She was childless, there was no clear plan for succession after her death, and her court was riven by factions. One faction, led by the Queen's chief minister Robert Cecil, was closely aligned with the history, and the institutional memory, of the Queen's reign; the other, led by the Earl of Essex, embodied a restless present and an unpredictable future. Perhaps something like Caesar upon his first appearance in Shakespeare's play, Elizabeth, even as she remained tenaciously, watchfully, at the centre of power, was a surprisingly diminished figure. To put this another way, it may be that Shakespeare had Queen Elizabeth partly in mind as he began deciding how to construct his dramatic portrait of Caesar – and that the surprisingly diminished Caesar his play gives us is the result of his meditations upon present-day problems of a royal power that is wilfully unaware of its own mortality. Indeed, for all Caesar's constant insistence upon his readiness to face death, he seems no more capable than Elizabeth I was of actually imagining a world without himself in it.

Although *Julius Caesar* is ostensibly about its title character's swift but thwarted rise to absolute power, the Caesar it gives us is not an upstart, but rather a thoroughly known quantity – so predictable in his rhetorical habits, and so transparent in his ambitions, that at times he is almost ridiculous. Casca tells the story of Caesar's refusal of the crown (1.2.233–65) with undisguised contempt, characterising Caesar's humility as an embarrassing charade. Decius Brutus also speaks contemptuously of Caesar, noting at 2.1.202–11 that Caesar is easily flattered. While we are never given the opportunity to judge the accuracy of Casca's story about the crown, we do see, when Caesar is persuaded to go to the senate against his wife's wishes (2.2), that Decius Brutus was speaking the truth. *Julius Caesar* represents a close-knit social world, a group of ambitious men who have known one another, and fought against and alongside one another, for many years, and who are thus able to speak about (and often to) one another in a frank and demystified way. In 4.3, when Brutus, quarrelling with Cassius, exhorts him to 'Remember March, the ides of March', it is not to relive the grandeur of their revolutionary act, but rather to suggest that Caesar's crimes were all too human, and that his assassination was in some sense disproportionate:

> What, shall one of us,
> That struck the foremost man of all this world,
> But for supporting robbers, shall we now
> Contaminate our fingers with base bribes . . .? (4.3.21–4)

This is the first time that we, the spectators or readers, have heard about Caesar supporting robbers, and while Plutarch does report that Brutus said this, he does not provide much in his *Life of Caesar* to corroborate it. When Brutus blurts out this accusation, I think we are meant to feel that this is one of the many complaints against Caesar that Brutus and his friends had always stored up. Justly and unjustly, with a mixture of petty envy and moral superiority, the conspirators are consumed with the feeling that there is something unfair about Caesar's elevation so far above them all.

To say, as Brutus does here, that Caesar was the 'foremost man of all this world', is not to preclude the possibility that he was also an opportunist, taking whatever he could in order to gather power to himself. Indeed, such opportunism is elsewhere in the play shown to be entirely characteristic of the 'foremost' men: Antony, Octavius, and Lepidus are no sooner behind closed doors after Caesar's funeral than they are already making plans to kill their enemies and renege on the promises they made about Caesar's will (4.1.1–9); and the instant Lepidus exits in order to fetch the will, Antony and Octavius begin to plot to deprive him of his one-third share of the Roman world. What *Julius Caesar* represents, then, might not be one political ideal (absolute, tyrannical power) colliding with another (revolutionary democracy), but rather a series of small and careful manipulations and calculations made by men who, in a state of perpetual and desperate competition with one another, grasp at any advantage. The powerful commentary that such a dramatic world might have made upon the political world of Shakespeare's own time is not necessarily Republican, but it would certainly have been anti-monarchical: it is that power is always a performance, must always dignify itself by disguising its rapaciousness, and must be ferociously defended because it does not inhere in any one person. This is the point of view Cassius relies upon as he tries to stir up revolution in Brutus's heart by recalling a swimming contest in which he got the better of Caesar (1.2.100–15). Cassius's fable is transparently manipulative, and to some extent myopic – obviously there is more to leading men, and a nation, than mere physical strength; Cassius's very reliance upon Brutus to lead the revolution is a telling indication of his own limitations. But the narrowly focussed, and very evocative, character of Cassius's fable is expressive of a resonant question – Why him and not me? – that pervades *Julius Caesar*'s demystified political world.

Shakespeare was, throughout his career, interested in dramatising situations where apparently inherent power, the 'greatness' such as a monarch might possess, is transferred – by chance of war or twist of fate, circumstance, or luck – from one person to another. This is the overarching concern of *Julius Caesar*, *Richard II*, the *Henry VI* plays, *King John*, *King Lear*, and *Measure for Measure*; and it is an under-lying concern in *Macbeth*, *Hamlet*, *Troilus and Cressida*, and even *The Tempest*. This concern is frequently expressed by means of a theatrical metaphor – the idea that to embody or take on the authority of greatness is merely to play a role. Thus, in the moments immediately following the assassination, Cassius exults:

> How many ages hence
> Shall this our lofty scene be acted over
> In states unborn and accents yet unknown!

And Brutus responds:

> How many times shall Caesar bleed in sport,
> That now on Pompey's basis lies along
> No worthier than the dust! (3.1.111–16)

The conspirators already see themselves – clearly have been seeing themselves – as actors in a great historical drama, and they anticipate an entire tradition of actual drama in which Caesar is endlessly overthrown, both in the re-enacting of his assassination and by the as-yet-unimagined political leaders for whom his body stands in. And it is not only the conspirators who think of themselves as actors in a historical drama, and seem, even in the midst of their actions, to behold themselves in retrospect from a distant future; Caesar does this as well. Persistently referring to himself in the third person, and frequently characterising himself in unembarrassedly self-aggrandising terms (see, for example, the speech he makes just before he is killed, 3.1.58–73), Caesar seems more aware than anyone else of the nearly mythical identity that subsequent history will confer upon him. He talks about himself as though he were already a character in a play. Theatrical performance is the idiom in which the greatest power on earth expresses itself, even as it is the medium that reveals that power's impermanence.

RITUALS OF POWER

There is another kind of performance in *Julius Caesar*, not precisely theatrical performance, which is closely associated with the expression and the impermanence of power: this is the performance of political and religious ritual. On one level,

Shakespeare seems interested in ritual simply as a way of locating the play's action realistically in its own historical moment. Somewhat notoriously, the first characters we see in the play include a rout of Elizabethan-sounding tradesmen who, with their punning spokesman the Cobbler, would be entirely at home in a London play like Dekker's *Shoemaker's Holiday*. As though to balance out the anachronism, Shakespeare at the end of the scene makes Murellus careful to point out that the tradesmen's celebration of Caesar's triumph happens to coincide with an official Roman holiday, the feast of Lupercal. One of that holiday's rituals is then staged at the beginning of the following scene: Antony, ordered by the stage direction to appear attired 'for the course', enters with almost no clothes on, holding a strip of goat-skin with which he will attempt to strike Roman women as he runs around the city. The look and sound of this scene could not be more different from the look and sound of the opening scene. The Roman world has unfolded before us, and it is a place where even the most powerful figures are deeply committed to the forms and imagined efficacy of pagan religious ritual: Caesar's first words are addressed to his wife, telling her to be sure to stand in Antony's way as he runs so that she might receive the gift of fertility supposed to be conferred by the runners and their strips of goat-skin. No wonder Murellus balks when, at the end of the first scene, Flavius orders him to remove all 'ceremonies' (that is, ceremonial decorations) adorning the statues of Caesar. 'You know it is the feast of Lupercal', he reminds his colleague (1.1.66). To diverge from or interfere with the proper order of ritual cannot be imagined to be inconsequential.

Of course, Shakespeare's representation of ritual in *Julius Caesar* is not only for the sake of historical accuracy. Ritual also becomes a crucial site for representing how characters strive for control over historical events whose significance is obvious but whose outcome is always uncertain. We learn in Act 3 that Caesar's concern with ritual form – 'leave no ceremony out', he tells Antony at 1.2.11 – might actually be a recent development: Cassius, worrying that Caesar might decide not to go to the Capitol because of the terrible and portentous storm, says that the general 'is superstitious grown of late, / Quite from the main opinion he held once / Of fantasy, of dreams, and ceremonies' (2.1.195–7). The implication may be that, as Caesar has gained more power, he has become increasingly preoccupied with the possibility of losing it, to the point that he now seeks supernatural confirmation of his confidence or his fears. When we see him at his house at the beginning of the next scene, he is indeed focussed on ceremony, ordering a servant to 'bid the priests do present sacrifice / And bring me their opinions of success' (2.2.5–6). The central contest of the scene then takes shape around the interpretation of the sacrifice – the priests 'could not find a heart within the beast' – and of Calpurnia's dream that preceded it. In the end, Caesar is able to go complacently to his death by seeming to dismiss supernatural portents, and their interpretation, as merely idle: 'How foolish do your fears seem now', he tells Calpurnia (105) after Decius suggests that the senators might think the 'mighty Caesar' (94) stayed home because his wife told him to. But Caesar does in fact have ceremony on his side in dismissing Calpurnia. He has been persuaded by Decius's reinterpretation of her terrifying dream (83–90) and has himself reinterpreted the ritual sacrifice in his own favour: 'Caesar should be a beast without a heart / If he should stay at home today for fear' (42–3). Whether or not dreams and ritual sacrifices have any real meaning in themselves, their interpretation is of great consequence.

Not all ritual in this play is religious or supernatural in character. Caesar turns out to be as vulnerable in his observance of political ritual as he is in his interpretation of ritual sacrifice. In Casca's story of Antony's offering Caesar a crown (1.2.233–44), Caesar seems compelled, both by a desire to please the people and by a hope that he will change their minds, repeatedly to refuse what is offered. From Casca's point of view, this refusal is a charade more than anything else, but there is certainly something ritualistic to it as well – as though Caesar, who offers the people 'his throat to cut' (1.2.258), understands that the power to which he aspires, whether it is freely given or forcibly taken, will inevitably make him a scapegoat. It is at this point in Casca's story that Caesar faints – overwhelmed, perhaps, by the conflicting demands of his own performance. This moment looks ahead to the final moments of Caesar's life, when he refuses to read the written warning Artemidorus hands him – because 'What touches us ourself shall be last served' (3.1.8) – and then allows the conspirators to crowd around him in aggressive supplication for the repeal of Publius Cimber. As a public figure who would have everyone believe that he is invulnerable, Caesar is paradoxically bound to rituals that insist upon his vulnerability. He must repeatedly put himself at the mercy of those below him in order to dramatise his own authority. Such ritual performances are of course conventional in statecraft, and are typically understood by everyone involved as a metaphorical representation of the relationship between leader and people: the people believe in the strength of the leader who seems ready to sacrifice himself to them. Julius Caesar is surprised when he finds that the men closest to him have decided to take the metaphor of sacrifice literally.

'Let's be sacrificers, but not butchers', says Brutus (2.1.166) as he overrides Cassius's suggestion that Antony should be assassinated along with Caesar. It is the same kind of mistake Caesar makes in refusing to look at the revelatory letter handed him by Artemidorus: at a moment when a pragmatic view is most required, each man seeks out the comforting significance of symbolic relationships and ritual actions. Just as Caesar seems unable to imagine the existence of something unseen and deadly to himself, so Brutus seems unable to imagine a moment after the assassination of Caesar; he is so completely caught up in the symbolic aptness of slaughtering the scapegoat dictator as an offering for the greater good of Rome that he feels no need to imagine a future beyond the act – a future in which, for example, he might have to reckon with the retributive anger of Caesar's friends. It is hard to say exactly how much the other conspirators share in Brutus's myopic idealism in 2.1. Cassius does not seem convinced, and Trebonius's claim that Antony 'will live and laugh at this hereafter' is both surprisingly casual and ominously equivocal; but the philosophical discussion is cut short at this point by the striking of a clock and the necessity to formulate a plan for ensuring that Caesar goes to the Capitol. When the assassination finally happens, the rest of the conspirators seem to embrace the symbolic language in which Brutus imagined the event – even if only because it is a way of simplifying and comprehending an almost unimaginable act. 'Stoop, Romans, stoop, / And let us bathe our hands in

Caesar's blood', Brutus says (3.1.105–6), and Cassius echoes him: 'Stoop then and wash' (111). What a terrible sight these men must be as they work to insist upon the ritual significance of their brutal act! Antony, when he arrives, cannot stop talking about what he sees. In this way, he acts as a kind of mirror for the conspirators, telling them that he is entirely prepared for them to kill him 'whilst your purpled hands do reek and smoke' (158). This is also the language of sacrifice – 'reek and smoke' is a phrase conventionally used of animal entrails – but Antony uses it to achieve an alienating effect: Caesar was a man, not an animal, and yet his assassins look like butchers. Hearing Antony's words, Brutus, suddenly, is less certain of the ritual meaning he had conferred upon the act in advance. It is as though he is seeing it for the first time.

> O Antony, beg not your death of us.
> Though now we must appear bloody and cruel,
> As by our hands and this our present act
> You see we do, yet see you but our hands
> And this the bleeding business they have done.
> Our hearts you see not, they are pitiful;
> And pity to the general wrong of Rome –
> As fire drives out fire, so pity pity –
> Hath done this deed on Caesar.   (164–72)

Brutus is caught in the trap of the visible ritual he insisted upon: he cannot fully control how others interpret the symbolic blood on the conspirators' hands and swords. Antony, at once perceptive and opportunistic, shakes hands with the conspirators – a rather hideous social ritual – in order to take the blood of Caesar onto his own body. It is the clearest possible way to show that the consequences of the act can no longer be confined to its symbolic significance for the conspirators.

Brutus's only recourse, once Antony has involved himself in Caesar's blood, is to adopt a new ritual posture that puts him, ironically, in a similar position to Caesar before the assassination. Brutus, that is, must now dramatise his invulnerability by performing vulnerability. With disastrous results that, once again, his faith in the structuring power of ritual does not allow him to anticipate, he decides – once again over the objections of Cassius – to allow Antony to speak at Caesar's funeral. 'I will protest / He speaks by leave and by permission', Brutus says optimistically, 'And that we are contented Caesar shall / Have all true rites and lawful ceremonies' (3.1.238–41). Much like Caesar himself, Brutus cannot imagine Caesar's body as anything other than the eternally powerful body that gives political rituals meaning. He cannot imagine Antony will be able to turn the people against the conspirators, turn a funeral into a riot, simply by showing the people the body of Caesar, and what has been done to it.

WITNESSING HISTORY

I have structured most of my analysis in this section around a central thematic concern of the play, namely *the way things are seen*. The play's language is replete with references to sight, eyes, image, and reflection. 'Tell me, good Brutus, can you see your face?' asks Cassius in a representative instance; and Brutus replies, 'No, Cassius, for the eye sees not itself / But by reflection, by some other things' (1.2.52–3). The two men are trying to arrive at a means of understanding how the qualities of a truly virtuous leader might be discerned. Later, when Brutus argues that the conspirators should not kill Antony, his reason is that Caesar's assassination should appear 'necessary, and not envious ... to the common eyes' (2.1.178–9). Still later, Cassius kills himself because he believes that he has seen his friend Titinius taken prisoner 'before my face' (5.3.35). He turns out to be wrong – just as Brutus turns out to be wrong about the consequences of keeping up appearances by sparing Antony. Almost everything that happens in this play is framed within some discussion of how things look, or what it means to say that something *is* the way it *seems*.

And yet, as the example of Cassius's suicide demonstrates, as much as the play is concerned with what is seen, and how what is seen is interpreted, it is also concerned with what is *not seen*. Not only does Cassius misinterpret the far-off meeting of Titinius and some soldiers, he does not even see it: the meeting is actually witnessed and reported by his servant Pindarus, who has been sent up a hill to look out because Cassius's own 'sight was ever thick' (5.3.21). During this episode, a spectator or reader is reliant upon Cassius's interpretation of events, and is thus deceived for as long as Cassius is alive: only after Cassius has killed himself do messengers arrive with news that the day is not lost – that 'Octavius / Is overthrown by noble Brutus' power, / As Cassius' legions are by Antony' (5.3.51–3). The terrible irony here is not only that Cassius might have lived to fight another day had he actually seen the truth of what he believed to be true, but also that his refusal to do so was in some sense inevitable: he was always possessed of '[m]istrust of good success' (66). The tragic feeling a reader or spectator experiences at Cassius's death indicates that much of the truth of the play really does reside in what is not seen – for, while we might agree that Cassius is the victim of what Messala calls 'hateful error, melancholy's child' (67), we probably do not feel that Brutus would have been victorious if Cassius could only have seen what was really happening with Titinius. Throughout *Julius Caesar*, we are presented with unseen events of the greatest significance: Caesar's refusal of the crown in 1.2, for example, and Portia's death in 4.3, and the non-appearance of Caesar's ghost (in spite of his promise in 4.3) at the battle of Philippi. These are moments that invite interpretation – moments where the reader's or spectator's understanding not only of what happened, but of what could have happened, becomes the ground of history.

I will conclude my analytical overview of the play with a brief discussion of how Shakespeare's very idea of history is best understood through his interest in the unseen. As with all of his historical plays, Shakespeare telescopes historical time so that it can fit into stage time. The events spanning from 3.1, where Caesar is assassinated, through 4.1, where Antony, Octavius, and Lepidus meet to consolidate their power, are all represented as one continuous action even though the meeting staged in 4.1 actually took place about eighteen months after the assassination. The events of 4.2–4.3, where the quarrelling Brutus and Cassius manage to arrive at an uneasy reconciliation, occurred a few months later than that. Modern productions often put an intermission between 4.1 and 4.2 in order to indicate the passage of time, but there were no such intermissions in Shakespeare's theatre. In just the time it takes for one group of actors to leave the stage and another to enter, Shakespeare jumps from Antony and Octavius's imminent military preparations ('we must straight make head. / Therefore let our alliance be combined', 4.1.42–3) to the dissension within the revolutionary army. What is elided in the gap is the entire first phase of the actual civil war – with Antony and Octavius on one side, Brutus and Cassius on the other. A reader or spectator encountering 4.2 for the first time might, understandably, assume that the scene that is about to unfold will represent Brutus and Cassius preparing their joint forces to encounter Antony and Octavius. Instead, Brutus and Cassius meet cautiously and suspiciously, like enemies, at the head of opposing armies. This is a surprise, and it will only be over the course of the scene that we learn the cause of their quarrel. In his telescoping of historical time, Shakespeare also makes clear his thematic priorities: history for him is not simply a succession of highly visible military and political conflicts, but rather, and more importantly, the interpersonal conflicts that remain hidden from public view. 'Before the eyes of both our armies here', says Brutus, 'Let us not wrangle' (43–5). These leaders of men then retire – and we follow them – into Brutus's tent, which is the location of 4.3.

The root cause of the quarrel between Brutus and Cassius is revealed as soon as they are out of sight of their soldiers: that is, the spectator or reader gets to see what remains unseen and unknown to all the other characters whose lives depend upon Brutus and Cassius. And what we see is surprising in its obscurity. Cassius speaks first:

> That you have wronged me doth appear in this:
> You have condemned and noted Lucius Pella
> For taking bribes here of the Sardians,
> Wherein my letters, praying on his side,
> Because I knew the man, were slighted off.   (1–5)

The story of Lucius Pella can be found in Plutarch, more or less as it appears in these five lines: Pella was a Roman official in Sardia, accused by the Sardians – and publicly disgraced by Brutus – for misappropriating public funds. In Plutarch, Cassius was angry not because he had written a letter on Pella's behalf but rather because he, Cassius, had privately acquitted some friends of his for a similar offence, and felt that Brutus had meted out too harsh a punishment at a time when he ought to be cultivating goodwill among the local officials. What is strange about Shakespeare's interjection of the story here, and his use of it as the basis of the quarrel between Brutus and Cassius, is that it has literally nothing to do with the story the play tells. 'Lucius Pella' is a name unattached to any event before or after this moment in the play – and even the most careful reader of Plutarch in Shakespeare's audience could have been forgiven for not recalling this very brief episode in the Roman history. You can arrive at a meaningful interpretation of the quarrel between Brutus and Cassius, and all its unseen, unspoken causes, without knowing, or troubling to find out, who Lucius Pella is. But, of course, Shakespeare's very inclusion of the name suggests that it is important, and, of course, he is: he displaces the person, Julius Caesar, the men are actually fighting over and in this way embodies the play's overarching project of the diminishment or diffusion of Caesar's iconic image. As the crimes of the slain tyrant disappear into the crimes of a minor official, we once again find ourselves looking at or looking for someone other than the play's title character.

The Text

Not everything about *Julius Caesar* has a mosaic quality, or demands a divided focus. There is only a single authoritative text of the play, and that is the text in the 1623 Folio. This text is clean and well printed. It presents the modern editor with only a few real puzzles. One of these puzzles, as we shall see, does ultimately return us to the problem of divided focus – movement between background and foreground – that characterises all interpetive engagement with the play.

Some of *Julius Caesar*'s textual puzzles are typical of what an editor will face with almost any Shakespearean text. Take, for example, 1.3.126–30, where Cassius talks to Casca about the storm. In the Folio, the text appears as follows (I have modernised the spelling):

> for now this fearful night,
> There is no stir, or walking in the streets;
> And the complexion of the element
> Is favours, like the work we have in hand,
> Most bloody, fiery, and most terrible.

The puzzle here is in the beginning of line 129: 'Is favours' does not make sense. The New Cambridge Shakespeare edition solves the puzzle in the following way:

> For now, this fearful night,
> There is no stir or walking in the streets,
> And the complexion of the element
> **In favour's** like the work we have in hand,
> Most bloody, fiery, and most terrible.

The editor assumes that the printer either misread the manuscript from which he was setting up type, or simply set the wrong piece of type, an *s* instead of an *n*. Early modern writers did not consistently use an apostrophe to mark a contraction, so the editor's change of 'favours' to 'favour's' is an acceptable modernisation. The edited text makes clear sense – 'the complexion of the element is, in appearance, like the work we have in hand' – in a way the Folio text does not.

While this is the most common emendation of the Folio text, it is not the only one possible. A late-seventeenth-century manuscript copy of the play changes 'Is favours' to 'Is favorous', which expresses the same idea as the modern text, only a bit more specifically: to Cassius, the thought of the violent but glorious act the conspirators are planning is exciting enough to make the terrible storm look like a good omen. Nicholas Rowe, who produced the first modern edition of Shakespeare in 1709, made a different change, with different consequences: 'Is favours' became

'Is feav'rous' – that is, feverous. The suggestion of sickness in this word (which Shakespeare also used in a similar context in *Macbeth* 2.3.59) gives a different idea of the kind of 'work' Cassius imagines the conspirators 'have in hand': it is as though the heavens, and perhaps Cassius himself, are sick – perhaps in a state of delirium – at the thought of the violence to come. Somewhat more prosaically than either of these, Edward Capell, in his 1768 edition of Shakespeare, changed 'Is favours' to 'Is favour'd'. This conveys essentially the same meaning as the modern text – that the sky's complexion and the planned assassination 'look' the same – with a different grammatical construction.

Any one of these readings can be justified, both interpretively and as a correction of a likely misreading of the copy-text or mis-setting of type. And any one of these readings is equally plausible because there is no extant Shakespearean manuscript against which we can compare the Folio text. All of these readings demonstrate the surprising significance just one or two letters can have not only for a reader's comprehension, but also his or her interpretation, of the play-text. Other, similar examples in *Julius Caesar* include 2.2.46, 3.1.39, and 3.2.211. In each case, the editor has emended the Folio text, and the textual notes record both the Folio reading and some other possible emendations; in this way a reader can see, and choose between, a range of different interpretations.

The most interesting textual puzzles in *Julius Caesar* have a direct bearing not only on the reading of a single line or passage, but also on the thematic content and structure of the play. One such is the apparently erroneous substitution of 'first of March' for 'Ides of March' at 2.1.40; this is discussed briefly in the footnote to the line in question. Another, which is perhaps the most famous puzzle in all of the play, is the double-report of Portia's death in 4.3. The first report is from Brutus himself, at the end of his quarrel with Cassius (147). Cassius is stunned both that Brutus said nothing about this before, and that he did not allow his sorrow to erupt in violence during the quarrel. The second report of Portia's death is given to Brutus by Messala, who comes to Brutus's tent to talk about recent intelligence from Rome. Here, Messala tries to see whether Brutus already knows of Portia's death, and only breaks the news when it seems clear that Brutus does not know what he is talking about (180–9). Like Cassius, Messala is surprised by how little outward show of grief Brutus makes upon hearing the news, and Cassius echoes his sentiments (194–5).

Some textual scholars have suggested that this weird repetition in 4.3 is a result of Shakespeare's revisions to the text. Perhaps the playwright could not decide which method of revealing Brutus's stoicism was more effective, and so he wrote both with the idea of choosing between them when the play came to be performed. Or perhaps he wrote one version in 1599 and then another version for a later revival (in 1612–13, for example). Perhaps he, or whoever was responsible for such things in the playhouse, ultimately forgot to mark one passage for deletion so that the copy-text used by the Folio printers gave no indication that the repetition was unintentional. Or perhaps any marks for deletion that were made at some stage in the process of textual transmission (e.g. on Shakespeare's manuscript, or on a prompt-book used by the playing company during performance) did make their way into the Folio copy-text but were overlooked by the compositors. In any one of these scenarios, the cleanly printed 1623 text ends up preserving, by accident, the somewhat messy creative process – Shakespeare's intentions, provisional attempts, second thoughts.

Exciting as this possibility is, it is by no means certain that the double-report of Portia's death is actually a textual puzzle. Many critics and editors – as well as many modern theatrical productions – have argued convincingly that the repetition is entirely characteristic of the tone and technique of 4.3, and that it deepens a reader's or spectator's sense of Brutus's character by showing him in two different relations to the news of Portia's death, first the reporter and then the receiver. Each individual critic must ultimately decide for him or herself how important narratives of textual transmission are for adjudicating formal and interpretive questions. The Reading List at the end of this edition provides some useful reading material on both sides of the question.

Julius Caesar on the Stage

In this section, I provide a broad overview of *Julius Caesar*'s performance history. In a general sense, even accounting for local and occasionally significant variations, this performance history is quite similar to the performance history of all of Shakespeare's plays, and it can be outlined briefly as follows. The earliest revivals of the play were in many ways expedient and, from what we can tell, relatively conservative: they were mounted largely due to the simple need for dramatic material after the long hiatus of 1642–60. In the later eighteenth century and throughout the nineteenth century, revivals became more frequent, and the play was adapted, with increasing ingenuity, to meet the demands or tastes of celebrity actor-managers and spectacle-hungry audiences. In the first part of the twentieth century, after the study of Shakespeare had become established in universities, actors and directors began to feel the influence of theatre-historical scholarship and, reacting against the spectacular tradition of the previous century, tried to return the play to its authentic Elizabethan roots. Revivals in the post-war period, riding a wave of popular interest in Shakespeare that was partly a product of increased access to higher education, reacted against the movement towards authenticity and sought, with great ingenuity and intensity, to achieve contemporary relevance, often by means of radical and unabashed adaptation. Finally, the end of the twentieth century saw a resurgent theatrical interest in theatre-historical scholarship, so that the theatrical tradition of the twenty-first century has been defined by a constant oscillation between radical adaptation and radical authenticity.

As is the case with any individual play, there are a few particular elements of the *Julius Caesar* performance tradition that have to do with the structure and content of the play itself, and that provide useful touchstones for both theatrical and textual interpretation. I will note these elements here so that you can understand them as focal points around which the rather lengthy chronological narrative that follows has been structured. As I have discussed in the preceding sections, and as you will probably know from your own experience of reading the play, a structural peculiarity of *Julius*

Caesar is its shifting centre: the title suggests that the play is about Caesar, much of the action suggests that it is about Brutus, but the latter half also pulls one's focus strongly in the direction of Antony. The interpretive consequences of this shifting centre are everywhere evident throughout the performance tradition, where the dominant figure has sometimes been Brutus, sometimes Antony, but almost never Caesar. The problem of performing the role of Caesar is one that implicitly underlies the entirety of the following performance history, and I address it explicitly at the end.

Another, related peculiarity of *Julius Caesar* is its episodic structure. Perhaps its most important scene, and for much of its performance history its most famous scene, is 4.3, the quarrel between Cassius and Brutus. Not only is the scene causally unconnected to anything that happens before or after it (that is, we do not see the events leading up to the quarrel, and the resolution of the quarrel does not materially affect what happens in the war with Antony and Octavius), but it also contains within itself many small episodes that are disjointed from one another: the lengthy and obscure discussion of Cassius allegedly making excuses for one who took bribes (1–28); the strange entrance of the camp poet (124–38); the two reports of Portia's death (147–9 and 188–9); the exchange between Brutus and Lucius about a book Brutus has been reading (252–5); the cryptic appearance of the Ghost of Caesar (275–86). The scene encourages a director to approach the text with what theatre historians refer to as the 'blue pencil' – the instrument with which the text is marked for deletion and reorganisation in order to tighten its structure, 'fix' or evade the problems it raises for a reader or audience, and emphasise certain relationships between a given scene and the rest of the play while downplaying others. Since the eighteenth century, the entrance of the camp poet, the second reference to Portia's death, and the conversation between Brutus and Lucius after the appearance of the Ghost have regularly been cut from the scene. Even to the modern reader or spectator who hopes to see a 'full text' performed on the stage, cuts such as these might seem to be merely practical – a way of streamlining the action and keeping the focus squarely on Brutus. But in such an episodic play as *Julius Caesar*, cutting for 'continuity' almost inevitably has a profound effect upon a spectator's interpretation of the play. Self-contained episodes such as the murder of Cinna the Poet (3.3), the 'proscription scene' in which Antony, Octavius, and Lepidus consolidate their power (4.1), and the scene where Lucilius pretends to be Brutus (5.4) are all episodes that most contemporary scholars and teachers would single out as among the most important in the play; but all have a long history of being deleted in the theatre. Just as we can learn a lot about Shakespeare's particular biases, and what he hoped to achieve in writing this play, by comparing his text to the histories of Plutarch, so we can learn a lot about the historically particular priorities of any theatrical production by comparing its text to the one Shakespeare wrote. The performance history that follows will give you some material with which you might begin to make such comparisons.[1]

---

[1] In this section, I have relied quite heavily on two magisterial surveys of the play's performance history: John Ripley's *'Julius Caesar' on Stage in England and America, 1599–1973*, 1980, and Andrew James Hartley's *Shakespeare in Performance: 'Julius Caesar'*, 2014. I cite these works parenthetically as necessary below.

We have evidence of only a few performances between *Julius Caesar*'s probable date of composition and the closing of the theatres in 1642: the (likely) performance at the Globe in September 1599, discussed above; the performance during the marriage festivities of Princess Elizabeth in 1612–13; and two performances in the 1630s, one at court (31 January 1637) and one at the Cockpit Theatre (13 November 1638). The fact that this Elizabethan play was revived as late as the mid-1630s is possibly a testament to its popularity with audiences during and after Shakespeare's lifetime. It is likely that the play was revived soon, and regularly, after the Restoration and the re-opening of the theatres in 1660: the plays of Shakespeare and his contemporaries provided much-needed material for the suddenly resurrected entertainment industry. But the first record we have of the play's performance is from a court payment in December 1676. Real evidence of a performance tradition begins to accumulate only in 1682, when *Julius Caesar* became a staple in the repertory of one of the period's most famous actor-managers, Thomas Betterton. He performed the role of Brutus until 1707. The play was very popular in the vigorous and competitive world of the eighteenth-century theatre: as Ripley notes, only five of the first fifty years of the eighteenth century were without a *Julius Caesar* revival in London, and productions featuring the leading actors of the day were mounted at all of the leading playhouses. This popularity fell off somewhat in England in the latter half of the eighteenth century, though the play began to establish its place in the American repertory around this time: a production was mounted by the American Company at the Southwark Theatre in Philadelphia on 1 June 1770, and subsequently in touring productions in Charleston (1774) and New York (1788, 1791, 1802).

We don't have much evidence about what the texts looked like which theatre companies in the seventeenth and eighteenth centuries used for their productions – that is, we don't know how much of Shakespeare's text they cut, or in what ways they altered it. Two 'acting editions' of *Julius Caesar*, one published in 1684 and the other in 1719, both purporting to represent the play as it had recently been acted, suggest that the text was not very heavily cut, and that some minor redistributions were made in order to eliminate some characters and bulk up others. In both editions, for example, the role of Casca in particular benefits from the redistribution of lines – he is given those of the tribune Murellus in 1684, and of both Murellus and Titinius in 1719 – while the role of Cicero is cut and his lines reassigned to Trebonius. The conservative approach to the text of *Julius Caesar* revealed by these editions is characteristic of theatrical treatments of Shakespeare's texts in general in the first half of the eighteenth century. It was over-thrown in the latter part of the century as charismatic, influential actor-managers began capitalising upon Shakespeare's ever more firmly established 'classic' status in order to adapt his plays such that they became vehicles for star performers and display-platforms for spectacular theatrical technology.

The nineteenth-century *Julius Caesar* tradition begins with John Philip Kemble, whose 1812 production at Covent Garden established the influential precedents of deep textual cuts (450 out of about 2,500 lines, or just under 20 per cent), lavish and historically accurate costumes and sets (togas and sandals, arches and columns), and the shaping or streamlining of the play's dramatic structure so that it was more clearly

6 The assassination of Julius Caesar, Act 3, Scene 1. Herbert Beerbohm Tree's production at Her Majesty's Theatre in 1898. Set designed by Lawrence Alma-Tadema

focussed around the main characters – and in particular around Brutus, the character played by Kemble. Kemble, who was fifty-five when he mounted this production, continued to play Brutus regularly until he retired in 1817. The precedents set by his five-year run were followed and elaborated by all the major English and American productions of the next eight decades: William Charles Macready's at Covent Garden and at Drury Lane in the 1830s and 1840s; Samuel Phelps's at Sadler's Wells in the 1850s and 1860s; Edwin Booth's at Booth's Theatre, New York, in 1871; and Herbert Beerbohm Tree's at Her Majesty's Theatre, London, in 1898. Perhaps the best, if somewhat simplified, descriptive term one can apply to all of these productions is *pictorial*. All of them sought opulence and historical accuracy in set-design and costuming, and made extravagant use of supernumeraries to create 'living scenery' for the play's street scenes and the scenes requiring crowds. In this way, they were part of a creative tradition of theatrical interpretation which continues to this day – one that encourages deep immersion in the 'world' imagined or evoked by the play-text. At the same time, all of them cut the text in order to create an outsized, idealised portrait of the play's central figure. Character was subordinated to, or an effect of, the sceno-graphic impulse.

While Tree's *fin-de-siècle* production of *Julius Caesar* was fully a part of – indeed, the apotheosis of – the nineteenth-century pictorial tradition, it did feature a

7 Paul Richard as Julius Caesar in the German production of the Company of the Duke of Saxe-Meiningen, brought to London in 1881

significant innovation: it was the first English or American production in 200 years to cut the text so that Antony rather than Brutus was the central focus of the play. Tree's Antony was no less outsized and idealised, no less a distortion, than the Brutuses of earlier productions, but the exact nature of the distortion was somewhat ambiguous. On one hand, Tree seemed to conceive the play as a tragedy of friendship: in the words of one reviewer, he emphasised from the outset 'Antony's affectionate and almost sentimental devotion to Caesar' (quoted in Ripley, p. 173) On the other hand, Tree was not as skilled an actor in the heroic tradition as Booth and Kemble before him, and critics found him to be 'incomparably better in passages where he was acting emotion than in those in which he was supposed to feel it' (Ripley, p. 173). For this reason, the real energetic centre of Tree's performance was Antony's manipulation of the crowd in Act 3. A focus on Antony does not necessarily preclude heroism but it does have the potential to bring to the surface the play's interest in the darker forces of revolutionary or anti-revolutionary idealism: political expediency, popular ignorance, and self-serving ambition. Productions of the twentieth and twenty-first centuries would actively harness this potential.

Tree's innovation was not only a function of his comparatively limited acting abilities, nor was it a mere stroke of inspiration. In an example of cross-cultural influence that would become fully characteristic of Shakespeare production in the modern era, he got the idea from a German-language production mounted by the Company of the Duke of Saxe-Meiningen at Drury Lane in 1881. Like other nineteenth-century productions, the Meiningen Company *Julius Caesar* was characterised by lavish, historically accurate scenery and scores of supernumeraries. The significant difference in this production was the indecorousness of the crowd: no longer the 'inert, living scenery of Kemble's revival' (Ripley, p. 148) the Romans of this play were fully a part of, and visibly and audibly responded to, the actions going on around them. As a consequence, the crowd became a force to be reckoned with during the funeral orations of Act 3. Fortunately, the role of Antony was played by an actor – Ludwig Barnay – who was fully capable of reckoning with this force. In Kipling's summary of the enthusiastic critical responses to Barnay's portrayal, Antony was something far more complex than the 'straight-line athlete and grief-stricken young noble' that had been conventional since Kemble; now he was 'the rising opportunist, the master diplomatist as well ... Suppressed grief characterised his reading in the early moments of [his meeting with the conspirators after the assassination], but rising excitement overshadowed it as his plan took shape' (p. 149). In his address over Caesar's body, he gradually took control of a hostile and inattentive mob, seeming with both improvisation and calculation to harness its energy to his purpose.

It is only a slight exaggeration to say that, in the twentieth century, *Julius Caesar* became Antony's play. In a century whose national and global upheavals were defined by the manipulation of citizens at the hands of charismatic tyrants, the proliferation and influence of mass media, and the politics of image, it is no surprise that theatre companies and audiences alike have been captivated by the character who can tame a hostile crowd by making promises about Caesar's will and then, behind closed doors, coolly set about to 'cut off some charge in legacies' (4.1.9). In perhaps the most

8 Antony's funeral oration, Act 3, Scene 2, from Orson Welles's modern-dress production at the Mercury Theatre, New York, in 1937. Antony was played by George Coulouris

influential modern production, Orson Welles's at the Mercury Theatre, New York, in 1937, the celebrity actor-manager, Welles, played, as had been traditional, the role of Brutus; but his was a deliberately weak and ineffectual Brutus – meant, as Welles famously said, to represent the 'eternal, impotent, ineffectual, fumbling liberal' (quoted in Hartley, p. 48). Welles conceived his production as a critique of the rise of fascism in Europe, and he emphasised above all the overwhelming power of first Caesar and then Antony, their terrifying self-confidence and brutal authority under-girded by the mobs whose violence they could unleash at will. George Coulouris played Antony as an 'arch opportunist, a schemer, and a hypocrite', whose funeral oration was 'a marvel of contemporary hucksterism' (Ripley, p. 232); the blatant untruth of his position gave rise to and licensed the indiscriminate violence of the citizens as, in 3.3, they knowingly killed the wrong Cinna. Although slightly more exaggerated in tone and more specifically political in focus, Welles's staging was a direct descendant of the Meiningen Company and Tree productions. And while few major productions since 1937 have been quite as uncompromising as Welles's in their representation of Antony's 'hucksterism', it is now thoroughly conventional to make a connection between Antony's deliberately manipulative oration and the unjust murder of the innocent Cinna the Poet – or, at the very least, to emphasise Antony's dangerous charisma. In another of the modern era's most influential productions, Joseph Mankiewicz's 1953 film, 3.3 was cut, but the role of Antony was played by the young Marlon Brando, who had just starred in *A Streetcar Named Desire*, was simultaneously working on *The Wild One*, and would appear a year later in *On the Waterfront*.

On the face of it, the 1937 Mercury Theatre production and the 1953 Mankiewicz film seem like very different artifacts. One was a live theatrical production and the other a film. Welles's actors were dressed in modern clothes and performed on a bare platform stage backed with a stark brick wall; the actors in the film wore togas and sandals, and the action took place in settings that were meant to represent real historical and geographical locations – the streets of Rome, the Capitol and Forum, the battlefield of Philippi, etc. Finally, Welles, a very young upstart director (he was only twenty-two), sought to make an explicit, self-aggrandising political statement in his production, while Mankiewicz, an experienced director and Hollywood insider, seemed content to disappear into the filmic conventions of the 'period piece', allowing history, Shakespeare's text, and an extraordinary cast of actors (including, besides Brando, John Gielgud, James Mason, and Deborah Kerr) to speak for themselves. Both productions are, however, recognisably part of a tradition that dates to the beginning of the twentieth century and that grew up as a response and challenge to the pictorial tradition of the nineteenth century. The most influential early exponent of this tradition was F. R. Benson, who sought to bring the 'simple strength' of Shakespeare's plays out from under all the layers of costume, scenery, and operatic grandeur piled on by nineteenth-century actor-managers. Benson's company toured extensively through the British Isles from the 1890s to the early 1930s, and his productions (including nearly a dozen *Julius Caesar*s between 1892 and 1915) at the annual Shakespeare Festival at the Memorial Theatre in Stratford-upon-Avon were an important step on the road towards the establishment of the Royal Shakespeare Company. While Benson preferred a heroic idiom for the acting of Shakespeare which would not have seemed out of place to Kemble or Tree, and while he cut the text freely and expediently in order to give prominence to the role he played (Antony), he was also genuinely interested in ensemble performance and in foregrounding Shakespeare's language. He sought always to maintain a vigorous pace, cutting the text, encouraging rapid and clear verse-speaking, and managing scene changes so that there was as little as possible to interfere with an audience's sense of thematic content and dramatic structure. His success in achieving this goal was not always appreciated; indeed, he was often criticised both for distorting the plays as Shakespeare wrote them and for performing them with an almost monotonous, manic energy. But he was also widely perceived to be providing an antidote to a now ponderous and overwrought tradition of staging. Imperfectly but unmistakably, Benson's productions represented a ground-clearing: his contradictory impulses demonstrated that a new theatrical language must be found if Shakespeare's plays were to communicate directly and intelligibly with contemporary audiences. It is the drive towards a new, ever more contemporary theatrical language that links Benson with Welles and Mankiewicz, and with all that came between and has come after.

Paradoxically, the 'new' language theatre professionals in the post-Benson era initially settled upon as most capable of communicating to contemporary audiences was the language that Shakespeare wrote. In 1919, William Bridges-Adams took over as director of the Festival at Stratford-upon-Avon, and his inaugural production was a staging of the uncut Folio text of *Julius Caesar*. Bridges-Adams was heavily influenced by the work of William Poel and Harley Granville-Barker, who had been, since the 1890s, at the forefront of an 'Elizabethan revival': Poel's productions (in which the young Granville-Barker acted before branching out on his own) sought to recover and deploy Elizabethan stage practices (a bare stage, fluid scene changes, rapid and metrical verse-speaking, etc.) on the theory that the plays would communicate most effectively through the performance-conventions Shakespeare had in mind when he wrote them. Bridges-Adams was not hidebound to Elizabethan staging conventions as such, but he did feel, like Poel, that 'it was a good thing to pass the whole of Shakespeare under review and see what he amounted to' (quoted in Ripley, p. 197) – a statement that is perhaps most remarkable for being an almost completely new idea in the long tradition of staging Shakespeare's plays. With the complete, or nearly complete, text and historically evocative (but not pedantically accurate) costumes and set, Bridges-Adams was able to arrive at revolutionary, nuanced characterisations: a Brutus who was not an idealised, impassive Stoic, but an actively self-conflicted politician, at once too certain of his own virtue and haunted by doubt; a Cassius who was not purely driven by envy, but struggled through envy to express a real sense of the injustice of Caesar's tyranny; an Antony who was neither a blandly noble company-man nor a consummate manipulative orator, but instead subtle, watchful, and improvisatory in pursuing his self-interest. Whether or not he set out to do it, Bridges-Adams refashioned the nearly archetypal, or mythical, qualities of the play, making them more life-sized, making the characters seem complexly flawed and uncertainly virtuous – in a word, 'realistic'. And he did this by worrying less than his predecessors had about the contradictions and inconsistencies of the play's text as it has been preserved in the first Folio. The anti-heroical *Julius Caesar* that emerged from Bridges-Adams's fuller treatment of the text, the *Julius Caesar* that is surprisingly sceptical of all the idealisations it stages, is, with few exceptions, the *Julius Caesar* that critics, students, and audiences have encountered for the past century.

In Mankiewicz's 1953 film, Caesar was played by Louis Calhern, a well-known character-actor generally more at home in comic parts – *Duck Soup* and *Heaven Can Wait* were among his most successful films. His main qualification for the part of Caesar seems to have been his natural patrician bearing: tall, imposing but not intimidating, and possessed of a Roman profile and a fine speaking voice, he seems like someone whom other people would be happy to have in charge – if not of a sprawling political and military empire then certainly of a large corporation. Far outshone by the star-power and charismatic acting of John Gielgud (Cassius – a role he had played in Stratford-upon-Avon three years earlier), James Mason (Brutus), and Marlon Brando (Antony), Calhern is the perfect representative of Caesar in this anti-heroic period of the play's performance history. In the assassination scene, he is obviously overmatched by the conspirators; the scene's drama lies in his surprise that Brutus was involved and in Brutus's reluctant involvement even at this late stage. Brutus initially stands aloof from the murder, clearly uncertain whether this was the heroic act he had been planning for, and possibly on the verge of fleeing the scene altogether. When Caesar has been thoroughly stabbed, he emerges from the crowd of assailants and moves towards Brutus, his arm extended as though to ask for help. Brutus looks sick, half shakes his head as if to beg Caesar not to step any further, and then, with a look of infinite regret, steels himself and thrusts his dagger into his friend's chest. The 'most unkindest cut of all' takes the form of an embrace. It is perhaps the most powerful moment in the film, and its power derives, paradoxically, from the inability of either character to be what we think he ought to be or what he wants to be.

It has been conventional, since the middle of the twentieth century, to represent Caesar not only as Calhern did, as a bland and ineffectual figurehead, but also as past his prime – either myopically basking in past triumphs that mean nothing to a new generation of politicians, or visibly aging and physically weak. Peter Hall's 1995 production for the Royal Shakespeare Company took the idea of the *figurehead* quite literally: during the battle scenes of Act 5, a huge statue-head of Caesar rose out of the stage floor, occasionally dripping with blood – and the dominance of this prop was in marked contrast to Christopher Benjamin's nervous and ineffectual Caesar. But, of course, antiheroism need not take shape only around incapacity. The Caesar of Welles's 1937 production was, as I have noted above, a terrifying Hitler- or Mussolini-like dictator, and it has been equally conventional, since Welles, for productions to draw analogues between Caesar and contemporary political figures who might be seen as dangerously powerful: Castro, Ceausescu, Margaret Thatcher, George W. Bush, etc. Brewster Mason's Caesar for the Royal Shakespeare Company production of 1968 (directed by John Barton) was a courageous, magnetic figure of integrity and paternal authority; his response to the assassination was indignant anger, and he himself guided

9 The death of Brutus, Act 5, Scene 5: Shakespeare Memorial Theatre, 1957 (Angus McBean)

Brutus's dagger into his own body – Brutus was almost unable to do it himself. In Stephen Pimlott's 1991 production for the Royal Shakespeare Company, the Caesar portrayed by Robert Stephens was a forceful, authoritative figure who fought back viciously against the conspirators as they began to stab him. More recent productions – Edward Hall's for the Royal Shakespeare Company in 2001 and Deborah Warner's at the Barbican in 2005 are perhaps the most obvious examples – tend to see Caesar as

10 Mark Antony, Octavius, and the dead Brutus before a backdrop with Caesar's head in the 1995/6 production at the RST Stratford/Barbican London, directed by Sir Peter Hall (Donald Cooper)

a complicit member of a self-indulgently glamorous political elite, a charismatic master of 'spin', who has every reason to believe himself invulnerable until the moment he is brought down either by a discontent he never allowed himself to imagine (as in Hall's production) or (as in Warner's production) by a cynical and opportunistic violence of which he himself has been the best model. Whether blandly ineffectual or charismatically dangerous, Caesar, who must according to the text and the facts of history be assassinated, ends up serving, in the theatre, a primarily symbolic function. Like all symbols, he ends up being important not so much in himself as for what he reveals about everything and everyone around him.

In the spring of 1999, just under 400 years after its supposed inaugural production, *Julius Caesar* was revived in an all-male production at Shakespeare's Globe Theatre in Southwark, not far from the original site of the theatre where the play may have been first performed. In 2007, *Julius Caesar* was one of three plays (the other two were *Coriolanus* and *Antony and Cleopatra*) performed together by Toneelgroep Amsterdam in a highly experimental, six-hour, electronic-media-saturated production called *Shakespeare's Roman Tragedies*. In 2012, Gregory Doran staged the play for the Royal Shakespeare Company with an all-black British cast, and set the action in modern-day Africa. This is only the smallest, crudest sampling of the diversity of approaches to the play in the past two decades; like all Shakespeare plays, *Julius Caesar* has become (if it was ever anything else) a lens through which, or a mirror in which, successive historical generations try to understand themselves. '[T]he eye sees not itself / But by reflection, by some other things', as Brutus says (1.2.52–3). Ironically, but predictably, the least successful part of the Globe production was, by all accounts, its attempt to recreate an authentic Elizabethan atmosphere by encouraging audience participation: for example, actors planted in the pit encouraged spectators to respond loudly and contrarily to Antony's and Brutus's funeral orations. Besides being historically inaccurate (audiences in Shakespeare's time would have been very unlikely to

11 Soothsayer and ensemble. RSC production, 2012 (Kwame Lestrade)

12 Production of Julius Caesar, 1999. Photographer: John Tramper. © The Globe

shout down actors in a play they had paid to see), the Globe's 'interactive' staging was oddly myopic. Trying to force late-twentieth-century spectators to inhabit and adopt a late-sixteenth-century idiom, the Globe seems to have forgotten that Shakespeare already anticipated his play's translation – indeed, had already perceived himself as part of a tradition of translation that began in the first moments after Caesar was assassinated: 'How many ages hence', says Cassius as he looks upon Caesar's dead body, 'Shall this our lofty scene be acted over / In states unborn and accents yet unknown!' (3.1.111–13). The significance of the action lies in the fact that it will be repeated and reinterpreted in ways that the original actors themselves could neither imagine nor understand.

Note on this Edition

The edited text that follows is the one prepared by Marvin Spevack for the first New Cambridge Shakespeare edition and I reproduce his Note on the Text below. I have thoroughly revised the commentary with an eye, and ear, to the contemporary student reader, but I have also retained, to the letter or in substance, many of Professor Spevack's notes.

NOTE ON THE TEXT

The copy-text for this edition is the First Folio of 1623 (F), the sole authority. All substantive departures, together with their origin, are recorded in the collation, as are substantive emendations and conjectures which have been adopted in well-known editions or are of textual interest or are plausible orthographic alternatives. Changes involving accidentals, modernisation or normalisation of spelling, metre, or the like have not as a rule been recorded. Obsolete forms have been silently modernised when there is little phonetic or euphonic variation – 'strook', for example, is rendered as 'struck'. Variations in morphology, including inflections, are retained – 'strucken', for example, is not replaced by 'struck'. As for lineation, departures from F are recorded, and other significant alternatives given; in some important instances, alternatives are given even when F is retained. Obvious or inevitable combinations of short lines to produce single verse lines, generally following Steevens[3], are not recorded. The placing of stage directions involving a change of one or two lines only is also normally not recorded. Italicised names in entrance directions indicate mutes. Readings from the Folger and Douai MSS., as well as the six quartos, have been supplied by John W. Velz. Also consulted was G. Blakemore Evans, 'Shakespeare's *Julius Caesar* – a seventeenth-century manuscript', *JEGP* 41 (1942), 401–17, and 'The Douai manuscript – six Shakespearean transcripts (1694–95)', *PQ* 41 (1962), 158–72. The dating and description of the quartos – QU1–4, Q (1684), Q (1691) – are based on John W. Velz, '"Pirate Hills" and the quartos of *Julius Caesar*', *PBSA* 63 (1969), 177–93. The uncorrected F readings in the collation are from Charlton Hinman, *The Printing and Proof-reading of the First Folio of Shakespeare*, 2 vols., 1963, I, 300. In the format of the collations, the authority for this edition's reading follows immediately after the square bracket enclosing the quotation from the text. Other readings, if any, follow in chronological order. A conjecture not made in an edition is placed in round brackets and is preceded by the first edition to adopt it. The origins of a very select group of unadopted conjectures are also to be found in the List of Abbreviations and Conventions. Additional information may at times be found in the commentary, where also asterisks in the lemmas indicate words emended in the text. The punctuation of the text in this edition is considerably lighter than that employed by the compositors of F.

JULIUS CAESAR

LIST OF CHARACTERS

CAESAR	(Caius Julius Caesar)	
OCTAVIUS	(Caius Octavius Caesar)	*Triumvirs after*
MARK ANTONY	(Marcus Antonius)	*the death of*
LEPIDUS	(Marcus Aemilius Lepidus)	*Julius Caesar*
CICERO	(Marcus Tullius Cicero)	
PUBLIUS	(possibly Publius Silicius Corona, who spoke up against the persecution of Brutus by Octavius and was proscribed. See 4.1.4–5 n.)	*Senators*
POPILLIUS LENA	(Caius Popillius Laenas)	
BRUTUS	(Marcus Junius Brutus)	
CASSIUS	(Caius Cassius Longinus)	
CASCA	(Publius Servilius Casca Longus)	
TREBONIUS	(Caius Trebonius)	
CAIUS LIGARIUS	(Quintus Ligarius)	*Conspirators*
DECIUS BRUTUS	(Decimus Junius Brutus)	*against Julius*
METELLUS CIMBER	(Lucius Tillius Cimber, called Metellus in Plutarch's *Caesar*, Tullius in the *Brutus*)	*Caesar*
CINNA	(Lucius Cornelius Cinna)	
FLAVIUS	(Lucius Caesetius Flavus)	*Tribunes*
MURELLUS	(Caius Epidius Marullus)	
ARTEMIDORUS OF CNIDOS, *a Doctor of Rhetoric*		
SOOTHSAYER		
CINNA, A POET	(Caius Helvius Cinna)	
ANOTHER POET	(Marcus Favonius in Plutarch, erroneously Phaonius in North)	
LUCILIUS	no further identification possible	*Friends to*
TITINIUS		*Brutus and*
MESSALA	(Marcus Valerius Messala Corvinus)	*Cassius*
YOUNG CATO	(Marcus Porcius Cato)	
VOLUMNIUS	(Publius Volumnius)	
STATILIUS	(non-speaking)	

FLAVIUS	(non-speaking)	
LABEO	(non-speaking)	
VARRUS	(Varro)	
CLAUDIO	(Claudius)	*Officers or*
CLITUS	(Cleitus)	*Servants to*
STRATO	(Straton)	*Brutus*
LUCIUS	(not in Plutarch)	
DARDANIUS	(Dardanus)	

PINDARUS, *servant to Cassius*

CALPURNIA, *wife to Caesar*

PORTIA, *wife to Brutus*

CARPENTER, COBBLER, MESSENGER, PLEBEIANS, SENATORS, SERVANTS, SOLDIERS

SCENE: Rome, near Sardis, fields of Philippi

Notes

As is often the case in Shakespeare there is inaccuracy and confusion in the names of the characters: historical names are garbled or misunderstood, others are invented or ghosts. The perpetrator, intentional or not, may well be Shakespeare or a compositor or an editorial tradition. Thus, F's spelling of the name of the tribune Murellus has been changed by almost all editors since Theobald to Marullus, the authentic name and the spelling to be found in North's translation and in Plutarch. F's spelling of the name of the conspirator Decius Brutus is retained in all editions, however, although the authentic name is Decimus Brutus, the spelling to be found in Plutarch, Suetonius, Appian, and in one of the two instances in North's translation (the other has Decius). Similarly, other perversions in F of historical names are retained in all editions: the tribune Flavus is called Flavius, presumably because North and Plutarch spell it so; Brutus's shield-bearer Dardanus is called Dardanius, however, although North and Plutarch employ the former. Varrus and Claudio – F's spellings – are changed by almost all editions to Varro and Claudius, forms which do not appear in Plutarch, North, Suetonius, or Appian but which are presumably held to be Roman rather than Italian.

Under the circumstances, it seems best to retain F spellings, followed by the full historical names and remarks about their authenticity. Other information may also be found in the commentary. Small alterations, usually of only a single letter, designed to bring the name up to the received standard, are made silently: for example Labeo (for Labio), Calpurnia (for Calphurnia); others, for general recognisability, are unchanged: Clitus (for Cleitus), Portia (for Porcia), and Sardis (for Sardes).

JULIUS CAESAR

1.1 *Enter* FLAVIUS, MURELLUS, *and certain* COMMONERS *over the stage*

FLAVIUS Hence! Home, you idle creatures, get you home!
      Is this a holiday? What, know you not,
      Being mechanical, you ought not walk
      Upon a labouring day without the sign
      Of your profession? Speak, what trade art ~~thou?~~ *you*   5
CARPENTER Why, sir, a carpenter.
MURELLUS Where is thy leather apron and thy rule?
      What dost thou with thy best apparel on?
      You, sir, what trade are you?
COBBLER Truly, sir, in respect of a fine workman, I am but, as you would   10
  say, a cobbler.
MURELLUS But what trade art thou? Answer me directly.
COBBLER A trade, sir, that I hope I may use with a safe conscience, which
  is indeed, sir, a mender of bad soles.
FLAVIUS What trade, thou knave? Thou naughty knave, what trade?   15
COBBLER Nay, I beseech you, sir, be not out with me; yet if you be out, sir,
  I can mend you.

Act 1, Scene 1 1.1] *Actus Primus. Scoena Prima.* F   Location] *Theobald (after Rowe)* 0 SD MURELLUS] F *(throughout);*
Marullus *Theobald (after Plutarch)* 14 soles] Q (1684); soules F 15 SH FLAVIUS] F; *MUR.* / Capell *(Capell MS.)*
15] *As verse, Johnson; as prose,* F

Act 1, Scene 1
Location Rome. A street. Unless otherwise indicated, the location or place of the action is modern,
as supplied by the editors mentioned in the
collation.
  0 SD over the stage 'A conventional phrase
indicating that the actors enter and cross the
stage before they come to a halt' (Kittredge).
Although the persons are named, according to
convention, in descending order of rank, it is
obvious that the Commoners enter first. Compare
F's SD in *Oth.* 2.3.144: *Enter Cassio pursuing
Rodorigo.*
  3 mechanical of the artisan or labouring
classes.
  10–11 as you would say, a cobbler
The cobbler is literally a cobbler, i.e. one who
mends shoes, but he plays upon the word *cobble*'s
meaning 'to mend or repair roughly or clumsily' (as
in the modern phrase *cobble together*). He assumes
that the tribunes see him not as a *fine workman*, but
as incompetent.
  15 naughty worthless (more pejorative than in
modern usage).
  16 out with at variance, frustrated.
  16 be out are out of sorts.
  17 mend you put you right. With a pun on the
sense 'repair your shoes', as at 23–4.

MURELLUS What mean'st thou by that? Mend me, thou saucy fellow?

COBBLER Why, sir, cobble you.

FLAVIUS Thou art a cobbler, art thou?   20

COBBLER Truly, sir, all that I live by is with the awl. I meddle with no
    tradesman's matters, nor women's matters; but withal I am indeed,
    sir, a surgeon to old shoes: when they are in great danger I recover
    them. As proper men as ever trod upon neat's leather have gone upon
    my handiwork.   25

FLAVIUS But wherefore art not in thy shop today?
    Why dost thou lead these men about the streets?

COBBLER Truly, sir, to wear out their shoes, to get myself into more work.
    But indeed, sir, we make holiday to see Caesar and to rejoice in his   30
    triumph.

MURELLUS Wherefore rejoice? What conquest brings he home?
    What tributaries follow him to Rome
    To grace in captive bonds his chariot wheels?
    You blocks, you stones, you worse than senseless things!
    O you hard hearts, you cruel men of Rome,   35
    Knew you not Pompey? Many a time and oft

---

18 SH MURELLUS] *Mur.* F; *Flav. / Theobald*   18] *As verse, Capell; as prose,* F   22 tradesman's] Tradesmans F; tradesmen's *Warburton (Folger MS.)*; man's *Hanmer;* trade, – man's *Steevens² (conj. Farmer apud Steevens²)*; trades, man's *conj.
Staunton*   22 women's] womens F; womans F2   22 matters; . . . withal] F; matters; . . . with all. *Capell;* matters, . . . with
awl. *Jennens (conj. Farmer apud Steevens)*   31] *Rowe;* Wherefore reioyce? / . . . home? F   36 Pompey? . . . oft] *Rowe³
(Folger MS.); Pompey . . . oft?* F

21 **awl** a pointed metal tool used by shoemakers
for piercing holes in leather. The cobbler puns on
all in the first part of the line. The shape and
function of the awl are part of the sexual innuendo
in the subsequent phrase *women's matters*.

21 **meddle ... women's matters** A *tradesman* is a shopkeeper, as distinct from a labourer.
Meddle takes on a comic sexual sense (see *OED*
4) when the cobbler begins talking about
women's matters.

22 **withal** nevertheless.

23 **recover** save, with a pun on the sense of
'repair'.

24 **proper** fine.

24 **neat's leather** leather made from cowhide.
The cobbler is adapting the proverbial expression
'As good a man as ever trod on shoe (neat's) leather'
(Dent M66).

30 **triumph** the entrance of a victorious com-
mander with his army and spoils in solemn proces-
sion into Rome. The triumph marking Caesar's
victory over Pompey actually happened in October
45 BC. Shakespeare overlaps it with the Feast of
Lupercal in February 44 BC (see 66 n.).

32 **tributaries** foreign captives who will pay
tribute to Rome.

33 **grace ... wheels** Prisoners-of-war were tied
to chariot wheels.

34 **senseless** incapable of sensation or
perception.

36 **Pompey** Cneius Pompeius (106–48 BC), called
Magnus ('the Great') after 81 BC, allied with Caesar
and Crassus in the First Triumvirate in 60 BC.
Pompey was defeated by Caesar at Pharsalus on
9 August 48 BC. He fled to Egypt, but was stabbed
to death upon his arrival there on 28 September.

Have you climbed up to walls and battlements,
To towers and windows, yea, to chimney tops,
Your infants in your arms, and there have sat
The livelong day, with patient expectation,   40
To see great Pompey pass the streets of Rome.
And when you saw his chariot but appear
Have you not made an universal shout,
That Tiber trembled underneath her banks
To hear the replication of your sounds   45
Made in her concave shores?
And do you now put on your best attire?
And do you now cull out a holiday?
And do you now strew flowers in his way,
That comes in triumph over Pompey's blood?   50
Be gone!
Run to your houses, fall upon your knees,
Pray to the gods to intermit the plague
That needs must light on this ingratitude.
FLAVIUS Go, go, good countrymen, and for this fault   55
Assemble all the poor men of your sort,
Draw them to Tiber banks, and weep your tears
Into the channel till the lowest stream
Do kiss the most exalted shores of all.

Exeunt all the Commoners

See where their basest metal be not moved: 60
They vanish tongue-tied in their guiltiness.
Go you down that way towards the Capitol,
This way will I. Disrobe the images
If you do find them decked with ceremonies.

---

60 where] F; whether *Thomas Johnson*   60 metal] *Theobald*³; mettle F

45 replication ... sounds echoes of your shouts.

48 cull out decide to select today as.

50 blood blood-relations. The word combines Caesar's victory over Pompey in 48 BC with his victory over Pompey's sons, Cneius and Sextus Magnus Pius, at the battle of Munda in Spain in 45 BC.

53 Pray ... intermit pray the gods do not send.

59 most exalted highest.

60 where whether.

60 metal A pun on *mettle*, i.e. spirit or worth. Like lead, a base metal that melts rapidly, the spiritless commoners yield quickly to the tribunes.

63–4 Disrobe ... ceremonies remove the festive ornaments (*ceremonies*) that have been hung upon statues (*images*) throughout the city in honour of Caesar's triumph. The word *ceremonies* could also refer to accessories of worship, as is indicated by Murellus's question at 65–6.

MURELLUS May we do so?   65
    You know it is the feast of Lupercal.
FLAVIUS It is no matter; let no images
    Be hung with Caesar's trophies. I'll about
    And drive away the vulgar from the streets;
    So do you too, where you perceive them thick.   70
    These growing feathers plucked from Caesar's wing
    Will make him fly an ordinary pitch,
    Who else would soar above the view of men
    And keep us all in servile fearfulness.   *Exeunt*

1.2 *Enter* CAESAR, ANTONY *for the course,* CALPURNIA, *Portia, Decius, Cicero,*
BRUTUS, CASSIUS, CASCA, *a* SOOTHSAYER, [*a great crowd following*]; *after them*
Murellus and Flavius

CAESAR Calpurnia.
CASCA   Peace ho, Caesar speaks.
CAESAR   Calpurnia.
CALPURNIA Here, my lord.
CAESAR Stand you directly in Antonio's way
    When he doth run his course. Antonio.
ANTONY Caesar, my lord.   5
CAESAR Forget not in your speed, Antonio,
    To touch Calpurnia, for our elders say
    The barren, touchèd in this holy chase,

Act 1, Scene 2 1.2] *Pope (after Folger MS.)* Location] *Capell (Capell MS.)* 0 SD *a … following*]
Capell 3 Antonio's] F; *Antonius.'* / *Pope* 4, 6 Antonio] F; *Antonius* / *Pope*

66 feast of Lupercal Roman festival in honour
of Lupercus, protector of flocks against wolves and
a patron of agriculture, held on 15 February at the
Lupercal, a cave below the western corner of the
Palatine. Young men – called Luperci – 'naked
except for girdles made from the skins of [sacrificial
goats] ran about the bounds of the Palatine settle-
ment, striking those whom they met, especially
women, with strips of the goat-skins, a form of
fertility magic combined with the ritual beating of
the bounds and with purificatory rites' (*OCD*
Lupercalia).
68 trophies arms or other spoils taken from the
enemy as a memorial of victory.
69 vulgar common people.
72 pitch elevation or altitude. In hunting

parlance, it is the height to which a falcon soars
before swooping down on its prey.

Act 1, Scene 2
Location Rome. A public place.
   0 SD for the course dressed for the race (see
1.1.66 n.).
   3 Antonio's Steevens[2] suggests that this spelling, as well as 'Octavio' (3.1.275 SD, 5.2.4), and
'Flavio' (5.3.108) arose from the fact that the
'players were more accustomed to Italian than
Roman terminations, on account of the many versions from Italian novels, and the many Italian
characters in dramatic pieces formed on the same
originals'. Nevertheless, the spellings 'Antony' and
'Octavius' are also (and more frequently) used.

Shake off their sterile curse.

ANTONY   I shall remember:
When Caesar says, 'Do this', it is performed.   10

CAESAR Set on, and leave no ceremony out.

SOOTHSAYER Caesar!

CAESAR Ha? Who calls?

CASCA Bid every noise be still – peace yet again!

CAESAR Who is it in the press that calls on me?   15
I hear a tongue shriller than all the music
Cry 'Caesar!' Speak, Caesar is turned to hear.

SOOTHSAYER Beware the Ides of March.

CAESAR   What man is that?

BRUTUS A soothsayer bids you beware the Ides of March.

CAESAR Set him before me, let me see his face.   20

CASSIUS Fellow, come from the throng, look upon Caesar.

CAESAR What say'st thou to me now? Speak once again.

SOOTHSAYER Beware the Ides of March.

CAESAR He is a dreamer, let us leave him. Pass.

               Sennet. Exeunt [all but] Brutus and Cassius

CASSIUS Will you go see the order of the course?   25

BRUTUS Not I.

CASSIUS I pray you, do.

BRUTUS I am not gamesome: I do lack some part
Of that quick spirit that is in Antony.
Let me not hinder, Cassius, your desires;   30
I'll leave you.

CASSIUS Brutus, I do observe you now of late:
I have not from your eyes that gentleness
And show of love as I was wont to have.
You bear too stubborn and too strange a hand   35

---

9 curse] F; Course *Rowe*³   21 SH CASSIUS] *Cassi.* F; *Casca* / *Theobald*⁴

9 **sterile curse** i.e. curse of sterility.
11 **ceremony** appropriate ritualistic action.
15 **press** crowd.
18 **Ides** In the old Roman calendar the Ides was the fifteenth of March, as well as of May, July, and October, but the thirteenth day of the other months.
24 SD **Sennet** a fanfare played on a trumpet or cornet. Typically used to announce the

entrance or exit of important figures (Dessen and Thomson).
25 **order** ritualistic proceeding.
28 **gamesome** 'full of the spirit of game or play' (*OED*).
35 **bear … a hand** assert yourself in too stubborn and too unfriendly a manner. See *OED* Bear *v*¹ 3e 'maintain or assert to or against (a person)'.
35 **strange** unfriendly, unfamiliar, distant.

      Over your friend that loves you.
BRUTUS   Cassius,
      Be not deceived. If I have veiled my look
      I turn the trouble of my countenance
      Merely upon myself. Vexèd I am
      Of late with passions of some difference,   40
      Conceptions only proper to myself,
      Which give some soil, perhaps, to my behaviours.
      But let not therefore my good friends be grieved
      (Among which number, Cassius, be you one)
      Nor construe any further my neglect   45
      Than that poor Brutus, with himself at war,
      Forgets the shows of love to other men.
CASSIUS Then, Brutus, I have much mistook your passion,
      By means whereof this breast of mine hath buried
      Thoughts of great value, worthy cogitations.   50
      Tell me, good Brutus, can you see your face?
BRUTUS No, Cassius, for the eye sees not itself
      But by reflection, by some other things.
CASSIUS 'Tis just,
      And it is very much lamented, Brutus,   55
      That you have no such mirrors as will turn
      Your hidden worthiness into your eye
      That you might see your shadow. I have heard
      Where many of the best respect in Rome
      (Except immortal Caesar), speaking of Brutus   60
      And groaning underneath this age's yoke,
      Have wished that noble Brutus had his eyes.
BRUTUS Into what dangers would you lead me, Cassius,
      That you would have me seek into myself
      For that which is not in me?   65

52–3] *Rowe;* No *Cassius: / . . .* reflection, / . . . things. F   53 reflection, by] F; reflection from *Pope*   58] *Rowe;* That . . .
shadow: / . . . heard, F   62 his] F; their *conj. Thirlby*   63] *Rowe (Folger MS.);* Into . . . you / . . . *Cassius?* F

39 **Merely** entirely.   45 Nor think my distance means anything
40 **passions ... difference** conflicting   more.
emotions.   49 **By means whereof** As a result of which.
  41 **only proper to** belonging only to.   52–3 The phrase 'The eye sees not itself but by
  42 **soil** ill appearance; moral stain or tarnish. reflection' was proverbial (Dent E231a).
  43 **be grieved** take offence.   58 **shadow** reflection.

CASSIUS Therefore, good Brutus, be prepared to hear.
   And since you know you cannot see yourself
   So well as by reflection, I, your glass,
   Will modestly discover to yourself
   That of yourself which you yet know not of.   70
   And be not jealous on me, gentle Brutus,
   Were I a common laughter, or did use
   To stale with ordinary oaths my love
   To every new protester. If you know
   That I do fawn on men and hug them hard   75
   And after scandal them, or if you know
   That I profess myself in banqueting
   To all the rout, then hold me dangerous.
                           Flourish and shout
BRUTUS What means this shouting? I do fear the people
   Choose Caesar for their king.
CASSIUS   Ay, do you fear it?   80
   Then must I think you would not have it so.
BRUTUS I would not, Cassius, yet I love him well.
   But wherefore do you hold me here so long?
   What is it that you would impart to me?
   If it be aught toward the general good,   85
   Set honour in one eye and death i'th'other
   And I will look on both indifferently.

---

72 laughter] F; Laughter *Rowe;* lover *conj. Herr;* loffer [*obsolete form of* love *and* laugh] *conj. Wilson*   79–80] *Steevens³*
(Capell MS.); Bru. … Showting? / … *Caesar* / … King. F; *Bru.* … People / … King. / … it? *Rowe*   87 both] F;
Death *Theobald (conj. Warburton apud Theobald)*

68 **glass** mirror.
69 **discover** uncover, expose to view. See also 2.1.75.
71 **jealous on** mistrustful of.
71 **gentle** well-born, noble (the dominant sense in the play).
72 **Were I** as though I were.
72 **common laughter** laughing stock.
72–4 **did use… protester** made a habit of professing love to anyone who professed love to me. *To stale* means 'to make stale', and *ordinary oaths* suggests 'oaths that are empty because they are so readily made'. The latter phrase also suggests 'oaths made in a tavern', since *ordinary* was in Shakespeare's time another word for *inn* or *tavern*

(*OED* 12 c).
74 **If you know** when you know. Or, perhaps, 'Should you find out'.
77–8 **That I … rout** that, during a banquet, I give my friendship to the entire table. The word *rout* (gathering) is used pejoratively.
78 SD **Flourish** A fanfare played on a trumpet or cornet. Typically used to announce the entrance or exit of important figures, or to signal the beginning of an event such as an entertainment or the reading of a proclamation (Dessen and Thomson).
85 **aught** anything.
87 **indifferently** dispassionately; without preferring one to the other.

For let the gods so speed me as I love
The name of honour more than I fear death.
CASSIUS I know that virtue to be in you, Brutus,   90
As well as I do know your outward favour.
Well, honour is the subject of my story:
I cannot tell what you and other men
Think of this life, but for my single self
I had as lief not be as live to be   95
In awe of such a thing as I myself.
I was born free as Caesar, so were you;
We both have fed as well, and we can both
Endure the winter's cold as well as he.
For once, upon a raw and gusty day,   100
The troubled Tiber chafing with her shores,
Caesar said to me, 'Dar'st thou, Cassius, now
Leap in with me into this angry flood
And swim to yonder point?' Upon the word,
Accoutred as I was, I plungèd in   105
And bade him follow; so indeed he did.
The torrent roared, and we did buffet it
With lusty sinews, throwing it aside
And stemming it with hearts of controversy.
But ere we could arrive the point proposed,   110
Caesar cried, 'Help me, Cassius, or I sink!'
Ay, as Aeneas, our great ancestor,
Did from the flames of Troy upon his shoulder
The old Anchises bear, so from the waves of Tiber
Did I the tired Caesar. And this man   115
Is now become a god, and Cassius is
A wretched creature and must bend his body
If Caesar carelessly but nod on him.

---

101 chafing] F; chasing F2   105 Accoutred] F; Accounted F2   107–8 it … sinews,] F; it, … sinews
Bevington   112 Ay] *Bevington*; I F

88 speed me cause me to succeed or prosper.
See also 2.4.41.
  91 favour appearance. See also 1.3.129, 2.1.76.
  95 had as lief would as gladly.
  105 Accoutred as I was without undressing
  107 buffet it beat back the water.

109 And fighting with contentious hearts.
  112–14 Aeneas The hero of Virgil's *Aeneid*
who, escaping from the sack of Troy, went on to
found Rome. At the end of *Aeneid* Book II, Aeneas
takes his aged father Anchises upon his back in
order to carry him out of the burning city.

He had a fever when he was in Spain,
And when the fit was on him I did mark   120
How he did shake. 'Tis true, this god did shake,
His coward lips did from their colour fly,
And that same eye whose bend doth awe the world
Did lose his lustre. I did hear him groan,
Ay, and that tongue of his that bade the Romans   125
Mark him and write his speeches in their books,
'Alas', it cried, 'give me some drink, Titinius',
As a sick girl. Ye gods, it doth amaze me
A man of such a feeble temper should
So get the start of the majestic world   130
And bear the palm alone.

Shout. Flourish

BRUTUS Another general shout!
    I do believe that these applauses are
    For some new honours that are heaped on Caesar.
CASSIUS Why, man, he doth bestride the narrow world   135
    Like a Colossus, and we petty men
    Walk under his huge legs and peep about
    To find ourselves dishonourable graves.
    Men at some time are masters of their fates:
    The fault, dear Brutus, is not in our stars   140
    But in ourselves, that we are underlings.

---

123 bend] F; beam *conj. Daniel*   125 Ay] *Rowe;* I F   127 'Alas'] *Quotation marks, Hudson*   131–2] *As one line, Collier (Capell MS.)*   132 shout!] *Pope;* shout? F

119–31 Plutarch reports that Caesar 'was often subject to headache, and otherwise to the falling sickness (the which took him the first time … in Corduba, a city of Spain)'. Contrary to Shakespeare's Cassius, he also says that Caesar 'yielded not to the disease of his body, to make it a cloak to cherish him withal, but, contrarily, took the pains of war as a medicine to cure his sick body, fighting always with his disease'. See *Caesar* (Bullough, p. 66).

122 His lips grew white. The metaphor is of cowardly soldiers (here the *lips*) fleeing from their own flag (*colour*) when facing adversity in battle.

123 bend glance.

124 his its.

125–6 According to Plutarch (*Caesar*, Bullough, p. 60), 'it is reported that Caesar had an excellent natural gift to speak well before the

people; and, besides that rare gift, he was excellently well studied, so that doubtless he was counted the second man [to Cicero] for eloquence in his time'.

130 get the start outstrip; rapidly attain an advantageous position, as in a race.

131 palm leaf or branch as sign of victory.

136 Colossus a huge statue. Shakespeare is most likely thinking of the Colossus at Rhodes, one of the seven wonders of the ancient world. This was a bronze statue of the sun god Helios, erected on the Greek island of Rhodes early in the third century BC. Standing about 100 feet tall, the Colossus collapsed in an earthquake in 226 BC. Medieval and Renaissance writers imagined (almost certainly incorrectly) that the statue's enormous legs straddled the harbour of Rhodes; this is the image suggested when Cassius talks of walking 'under his huge legs'.

Brutus and Caesar: what should be in that 'Caesar'?
Why should that name be sounded more than yours?
Write them together, yours is as fair a name;
Sound them, it doth become the mouth as well;   145
Weigh them, it is as heavy; conjure with 'em,
'Brutus' will start a spirit as soon as 'Caesar'.
Now in the names of all the gods at once,
Upon what meat doth this our Caesar feed
That he is grown so great? Age, thou art shamed!   150
Rome, thou hast lost the breed of noble bloods!
When went there by an age since the great flood
But it was famed with more than with one man?
When could they say, till now, that talked of Rome,
That her wide walks encompassed but one man?   155
Now is it Rome indeed and room enough
When there is in it but one only man.
O, you and I have heard our fathers say
There was a Brutus once that would have brooked
Th'eternal devil to keep his state in Rome   160
As easily as a king.
BRUTUS That you do love me, I am nothing jealous;
What you would work me to, I have some aim.
How I have thought of this, and of these times,
I shall recount hereafter. For this present,   165
I would not (so with love I might entreat you)
Be any further moved. What you have said
I will consider; what you have to say
I will with patience hear and find a time
Both meet to hear and answer such high things.   170
Till then, my noble friend, chew upon this:
Brutus had rather be a villager

---

155 walks] F; Walls *Rowe²* (Folger MS.)   160 eternal] F; infernal *conj. Thirlby*   166 (so with] *Thomas Johnson;* so (with
F   170 Both] F; But *Rowe²*

145 **Sound** speak.
147 **start** startle so as to raise – as by a magic word.
152 **great flood** brought about by Zeus to destroy all mankind for the sins of the Bronze Age.
155 **walks** avenues, paths.
156 **room** A homophonic pun on 'Rome' earlier in the line. See also 3.1.288.
159 **a Brutus once** Lucius Junius Brutus,

traditionally thought to be the founder of the Roman Republic in the sixth century BC. See also 2.1.54 n.
159 **brooked** tolerated.
160 **keep ... state** observe the pomp and ceremony befitting a high position; maintain his place.
162 **I am nothing jealous** I am not at all doubtful.
163 **aim** idea, guess.
170 **meet** suitable.

> Than to repute himself a son of Rome
> Under these hard conditions as this time
> Is like to lay upon us.   175
>
> CASSIUS I am glad that my weak words
> Have struck but thus much show of fire from Brutus.

Enter CAESAR *and his* TRAIN

> BRUTUS The games are done and Caesar is returning.
> CASSIUS As they pass by, pluck Casca by the sleeve
> And he will (after his sour fashion) tell you   180
> What hath proceeded worthy note today.
> BRUTUS I will do so. But look you, Cassius,
> The angry spot doth glow on Caesar's brow
> And all the rest look like a chidden train:
> Calpurnia's cheek is pale, and Cicero   185
> Looks with such ferret and such fiery eyes
> As we have seen him in the Capitol,
> Being crossed in conference by some senators.
> CASSIUS Casca will tell us what the matter is.
> CAESAR Antonio.   190
> ANTONY Caesar.
> CAESAR Let me have men about me that are fat,
> Sleek-headed men and such as sleep a-nights.
> Yond Cassius has a lean and hungry look,
> He thinks too much: such men are dangerous.   195
> ANTONY Fear him not, Caesar, he's not dangerous,
> He is a noble Roman and well given.
> CAESAR Would he were fatter! But I fear him not.
> Yet if my name were liable to fear
> I do not know the man I should avoid   200
> So soon as that spare Cassius. He reads much,

175–7 F; Is . . . words [*omitting* that *and* weak]/ . . . Brutus. *conj. Ritson (apud Steevens*[3]*)*; Is . . . words / . . . Brutus. *Collier*; Is . . . glad, / . . . shew / . . . Brutus. *White (conj. Walker)*   178] *Rowe*; The . . . done, / . . . returning. F   179] *Rowe*; As . . . by, / . . . Sleeue, F   183 glow] F; *blow* F3 (hlow F2*)*; grow *Folger MS.*   188 senators] F; *senator Dyce*[2] *(conj. Walker)*   190 Antonio] F; *Antonius / Pope*

177 **but . . . fire** even this small spark. Cassius thinks of Brutus as a flint-stone, which gives off a spark when struck.

177 SD TRAIN followers.

186 **ferret** perhaps 'red' (since some ferrets have red eyes), and perhaps also 'fierce' (since ferrets were used to hunt rats).

188 **crossed** opposed.

188 **conference** discussion or debate.

193 **Sleek-headed** agreeable (i.e. 'smooth'). Plutarch reports (*Caesar*, Bullough, p. 61) that Cicero observed 'how finely he [Caesar] combeth his fair bush of hair, and how smooth it lieth' and thus 'should not have so wicked a thought in his head as to overthrow the state of the commonwealth'.

He is a great observer, and he looks
Quite through the deeds of men. He loves no plays,
As thou dost, Antony, he hears no music;
Seldom he smiles, and smiles in such a sort   205
As if he mocked himself and scorned his spirit
That could be moved to smile at any thing.
Such men as he be never at heart's ease
Whiles they behold a greater than themselves,
And therefore are they very dangerous.   210
I rather tell thee what is to be feared
Than what I fear: for always I am Caesar.
Come on my right hand, for this ear is deaf,
And tell me truly what thou think'st of him.

Sennet. Exeunt Caesar and his train

CASCA You pulled me by the cloak, would you speak with me?   215
BRUTUS Ay, Casca, tell us what hath chanced today
That Caesar looks so sad.
CASCA Why, you were with him, were you not?
BRUTUS I should not then ask, Casca, what had chanced.
CASCA Why, there was a crown offered him, and being offered him he put   220
it by with the back of his hand thus, and then the people fell
a-shouting.
BRUTUS What was the second noise for?
CASCA Why, for that too.
CASSIUS They shouted thrice; what was the last cry for?   225
CASCA Why, for that too.
BRUTUS Was the crown offered him thrice?
CASCA Ay, marry, was't, and he put it by thrice, every time gentler than
other; and at every putting-by mine honest neighbours shouted.

215–16] *As prose,* F; *as verse,* Pope²   219 ask, Casca,] Q (1691); aske *Caska* F

206 scorned his spirit scorned the spirit of anyone.

213 deaf The historical Caesar was not deaf in one ear. It is possible that Shakespeare intended *deaf* to be understood literally, and connected to the historical fact of Caesar's epilepsy (see 119–31 n.) and the physical weaknesses detailed by Cassius at 1.2.119–31. It is also possible that Shakespeare did not mean *deaf* literally, but rather meant Caesar to express disbelief in Antony's first opinion of Cassius (196–7), and to ask him to tell him the truth: 'Your words have fallen on deaf ears; now tell me what you *really* think of him.' For this

argument, see Douglas L. Peterson, '"Wisdom consumed in confidence": an examination of Shakespeare's Julius Caesar', *SQ* 16 (1965), 19–28.

217 sad grave, serious. See also 2.1.308.

221 fell began.

225 thrice According to the stage directions (78 and 131), the crowd shouts only twice. It is possible that Shakespeare wrote a third such direction which did not find its way into the printed text.

228 marry An interjection meaning 'Why, to be sure'. Originally the name of the Virgin Mary used as an oath (i.e. 'By Mary').

CASSIUS Who offered him the crown?   230
CASCA Why, Antony.
BRUTUS Tell us the manner of it, gentle Casca.
CASCA I can as well be hanged as tell the manner of it. It was mere foolery,
  I did not mark it. I saw Mark Antony offer him a crown – yet 'twas not
  a crown neither, 'twas one of these coronets – and, as I told you, he   235
  put it by once; but for all that, to my thinking he would fain have had
  it. Then he offered it to him again; then he put it by again; but to my
  thinking he was very loath to lay his fingers off it. And then he offered
  it the third time; he put it the third time by, and still as he refused it,
  the rabblement hooted, and clapped their chopped hands, and threw   240
  up their sweaty nightcaps, and uttered such a deal of stinking breath
  because Caesar refused the crown that it had, almost, choked Caesar,
  for he swounded and fell down at it. And for mine own part I durst not
  laugh for fear of opening my lips and receiving the bad air.
CASSIUS But soft, I pray you; what, did Caesar swound?   245
CASCA He fell down in the market-place, and foamed at mouth, and was
  speechless.
BRUTUS 'Tis very like, he hath the falling sickness.
CASSIUS No, Caesar hath it not, but you, and I,
          And honest Casca, we have the falling sickness.   250
CASCA I know not what you mean by that, but I am sure Caesar fell down.
  If the tag-rag people did not clap him and hiss him according as he
  pleased and displeased them, as they use to do the players in the theatre,
  I am no true man.
BRUTUS What said he when he came unto himself?   255
CASCA Marry, before he fell down, when he perceived the common herd
  was glad he refused the crown, he plucked me ope his doublet and

---

230–1] F; *as one line, Mason 1919*   240 hooted] howted F; shouted *Hanmer*   248 like,] *Rowe;* like F

234 **mark it** pay very close attention.

235 **coronet** a small crown 'denoting a dignity inferior to that of a sovereign' (*OED* 1a). Perhaps Caesar's idea is that, since a coronet is more humble than a crown, to wear it will not be to suggest that he seeks absolute power. In Plutarch, Antony offers Caesar 'a diadem wreathed about with laurel' (Appendix, p. 141), which might primarily symbolise his victory over Pompey.

236 **fain** gladly.

239 **still as** whenever.

240 **chopped** chapped.

243 **swounded** swooned.

248 **falling sickness** epilepsy. See 119–31 n.

250 **we … sickness** we are in danger of being cut down (i.e. by Caesar).

252 **tag-rag people** i.e. rabble (from 'dressed in tags and rags').

257 **plucked me ope** plucked open. The *me* here is an emphatic colloquialism intended to call attention to the speaker himself and his mocking tone. For a similar instance in Shakespeare, see *1 Henry IV* 2.4.89–90, where Hal mockingly describes Hotspur's fierceness: 'he that kills me some six or seven dozen of Scots at a breakfast … ' See Abbott 220.

offered them his throat to cut. And I had been a man of any
occupation, if I would not have taken him at a word I would I might go
to hell among the rogues. And so he fell. When he came to himself   260
again, he said if he had done or said anything amiss, he desired their
worships to think it was his infirmity. Three or four wenches where I
stood cried, 'Alas, good soul', and forgave him with all their hearts.
But there's no heed to be taken of them: if Caesar had stabbed their
mothers they would have done no less.   265

BRUTUS And after that he came thus sad away?

CASCA Ay.

CASSIUS Did Cicero say anything?

CASCA Ay, he spoke Greek.

CASSIUS To what effect?   270

CASCA Nay, and I tell you that, I'll ne'er look you i'th'face again. But those
that understood him smiled at one another and shook their heads;
but for mine own part it was Greek to me. I could tell you more
news too. Murellus and Flavius, for pulling scarves off Caesar's
images, are put to silence. Fare you well. There was more foolery yet, 275
if I could remember it.

CASSIUS Will you sup with me tonight, Casca?

CASCA No, I am promised forth.

CASSIUS Will you dine with me tomorrow?

CASCA Ay, if I be alive, and your mind hold, and your dinner worth the   280
eating.

CASSIUS Good, I will expect you.

CASCA Do so. Farewell both.   *Exit*

BRUTUS What a blunt fellow is this grown to be!
He was quick mettle when he went to school.   285

CASSIUS So is he now in execution
Of any bold or noble enterprise,
However he puts on this tardy form.
This rudeness is a sauce to his good wit,

---

266 away?] *Theobald;* away. F

258 And if.
258–9 a man … occupation a man of action.
Or, possibly, a tradesman (such as those to whom
Caesar offered his throat).
266 sad solemnly.
270 effect purpose.
275 put to silence This phrase implies that the
tribunes have been executed, and perhaps this is what
Shakespeare wanted his audience to think. Cassius

certainly thinks that Caesar has marked him out for
death (see 249–50). Plutarch, however, simply says
that Murellus and Flavius were 'deprived … of their
Tribuneships' (Appendix, p. 141).
278 I … forth I have a previous engagement.
285 was quick mettle was known for his energetic spirit.
288 However even though.
288 tardy slow, uncooperative.

> Which gives men stomach to digest his words   290
> With better appetite.

BRUTUS And so it is. For this time I will leave you.
> Tomorrow if you please to speak with me,
> I will come home to you; or if you will,
> Come home to me and I will wait for you.   295

CASSIUS I will do so. Till then, think of the world.

Exit Brutus

> Well, Brutus, thou art noble; yet I see
> Thy honourable metal may be wrought
> From that it is disposed. Therefore it is meet
> That noble minds keep ever with their likes;   300
> For who so firm that cannot be seduced?
> Caesar doth bear me hard, but he loves Brutus.
> If I were Brutus now and he were Cassius,
> He should not humour me. I will this night,
> In several hands, in at his windows throw,   305
> As if they came from several citizens,
> Writings, all tending to the great opinion
> That Rome holds of his name, wherein obscurely
> Caesar's ambition shall be glancèd at.
> And after this let Caesar seat him sure,   310
> For we will shake him, or worse days endure.   *Exit*

1.3 *Thunder and lightning. Enter [from opposite sides]* CASCA *and* CICERO

CICERO Good even, Casca, brought you Caesar home?
> Why are you breathless, and why stare you so?

CASCA Are not you moved when all the sway of earth

291–2] *Rowe;* With . . . Appetite. / . . . is: / . . . you: F   297 art noble;] F; art: Noble F2   298 metal] F2; Mettle F   Act 1, Scene 3   1.3] *Capell*   Location] *Capell (Capell MS.)*   0 SD *from opposite sides] Capell (Capell MS.)*

290 **stomach** the inclination.
298 **metal** with a pun on *mettle*. See 1.1.60 n.
299 **that it is disposed** that to which it is naturally inclined – i.e. Brutus may be persuaded to dishonourable, or rebellious, action in spite of being naturally honourable.
300 **their likes** minds that are similarly noble.
302 **bear me hard** resent me (see *OED* Bear v¹ 16). See also 2.1.215, 3.1.157.
304 **humour** influence (by indulging my *humour* – i.e. my peculiar nature).
305 **hands** handwritings.

307 **tending to** giving attention to (see *OED* v¹ 2 c).
308 **obscurely** indirectly.
308 **glancèd at** pointed out, noted.
310 **let . . . sure** Caesar had better get ready to hold on to the throne very tightly.

Act 1, Scene 3
Location Rome. A street.
3 **sway** the motion of a rotating body, i.e. the earth's natural motion.

Shakes like a thing unfirm? O Cicero,
I have seen tempests when the scolding winds   5
Have rived the knotty oaks, and I have seen
Th'ambitious ocean swell, and rage, and foam,
To be exalted with the threatening clouds;
But never till tonight, never till now,
Did I go through a tempest dropping fire.   10
Either there is a civil strife in heaven,
Or else the world, too saucy with the gods,
Incenses them to send destruction.
CICERO Why, saw you anything more wonderful?
CASCA A common slave – you know him well by sight –   15
Held up his left hand, which did flame and burn
Like twenty torches joined, and yet his hand,
Not sensible of fire, remained unscorched.
Besides – I ha' not since put up my sword –
Against the Capitol I met a lion   20
Who glazed upon me and went surly by
Without annoying me. And there were drawn
Upon a heap a hundred ghastly women,
Transformèd with their fear, who swore they saw
Men, all in fire, walk up and down the streets.   25
And yesterday the bird of night did sit
Even at noon-day upon the market-place,
Hooting and shrieking. When these prodigies
Do so conjointly meet let not men say,
'These are their reasons, they are natural',   30
For I believe they are portentous things
Unto the climate that they point upon.

---

15 know] F; knew *conj. Craik*   21 glazed] F; glar'd *Thomas Johnson;* gaz'd Q (1691) *(Folger MS.);* glased [= glazed *or* glassed] *conj. Nicholson*   30 reasons] F; seasons *Collier² (Collier MS.)*

6 **rived** split.
8 **exalted with** raised as high as.
12 **saucy** insolent towards superiors.
14 **wonderful** such as to excite wonder or astonishment.
18 **sensible of** liable to be affected by.
19 **put up** put away.
20 **Against** in front of.
21 **glazed** stared. According to *OED* (Glaze *v²*), Shakespeare is the first to use this word in this sense, and there are no other similar uses before

the nineteenth century. It is possible that Folio's *glazed* is a misprint for *gazed* (see 59 for a comparable use of *gaze*) or *glared*.
22 **annoying** harming.
22–3 **drawn … heap** assembled in a mass.
26 **bird of night** screech-owl.
28 **prodigies** extraordinary sights or occurrences from which omens are drawn.
29 **conjointly meet** appear at the same time.
32 **climate** region of the earth.

CICERO Indeed, it is a strange-disposèd time.
 But men may construe things after their fashion
 Clean from the purpose of the things themselves. 35
 Comes Caesar to the Capitol tomorrow?
CASCA He doth, for he did bid Antonio
 Send word to you he would be there tomorrow.
CICERO Good night then, Casca. This disturbèd sky
 Is not to walk in.
CASCA   Farewell, Cicero. 40

Exit Cicero

Enter CASSIUS

CASSIUS Who's there?
CASCA   A Roman.
CASSIUS   Casca, by your voice.
CASCA Your ear is good. Cassius, what night is this!
CASSIUS A very pleasing night to honest men.
CASCA Who ever knew the heavens menace so?
CASSIUS Those that have known the earth so full of faults. 45
 For my part I have walked about the streets,
 Submitting me unto the perilous night,
 And, thus unbracèd, Casca, as you see,
 Have bared my bosom to the thunderstone;
 And when the cross blue lightning seemed to open 50
 The breast of heaven, I did present myself
 Even in the aim and very flash of it.
CASCA But wherefore did you so much tempt the heavens?
 It is the part of men to fear and tremble
 When the most mighty gods by tokens send 55
 Such dreadful heralds to astonish us.
CASSIUS You are dull, Casca, and those sparks of life
 That should be in a Roman you do want,
 Or else you use not. You look pale, and gaze,

37 Antonio] F; *Antonius /Pope* 39] *Rowe;* Good-night ... *Caska: / ... in.* F 42] *Rowe;* Your ... good. / ... this?
F 42 what] F; what a *Craik* 42 this!] *Johnson;* this? F 57–60] *Rowe;* You ... *Caska: / ... Roman, / ... not. / ...
feare, / ... wonder,* F

34 **after their fashion** in their own way.
35 Completely misunderstanding the true meaning of the things themselves.
48 **unbracèd** with part of my clothing unfastened or loosened. See also 2.1.262.

49 **thunderstone** thunderbolt.
50 **cross** 'criss-crossing' or, perhaps figuratively, 'adverse'.
54 **the part of men** appropriate for men.
58 **want** lack.

And put on fear, and cast yourself in wonder   60
To see the strange impatience of the heavens.
But if you would consider the true cause
Why all these fires, why all these gliding ghosts,
Why birds and beasts from quality and kind,
Why old men, fools, and children calculate,   65
Why all these things change from their ordinance,
Their natures, and preformèd faculties,
To monstrous quality – why, you shall find
That heaven hath infused them with these spirits
To make them instruments of fear, and warning   70
Unto some monstrous state.
Now could I, Casca, name to thee a man
Most like this dreadful night,
That thunders, lightens, opens graves, and roars
As doth the lion in the Capitol –   75
A man no mightier than thyself, or me,
In personal action, yet prodigious grown
And fearful, as these strange eruptions are.

CASCA 'Tis Caesar that you mean, is it not, Cassius?

CASSIUS Let it be who it is, for Romans now   80
Have thews and limbs like to their ancestors'.
But, woe the while, our fathers' minds are dead
And we are governed with our mothers' spirits;
Our yoke and sufferance show us womanish.

CASCA Indeed, they say the senators tomorrow   85
Mean to establish Caesar as a king,
And he shall wear his crown by sea and land,
In every place save here in Italy.

---

60 cast] F; case *White (conj. Jervis)*   65 men, fools] F; men fools *Steevens²* (Folger MS.); men fool *White (conj. Mitford)*   71–3] F; Unto … Casca, / … night; *Hanmer (conj. Thirlby)*   74 roars] F; teares F2   79] *Rowe;* 'Tis … meane: / … *Cassius?* F   81 ancestors'] *This edn;* Ancestors F   85 say] *Blair;* say, F

60 **cast yourself in** throw yourself into; commit yourself resolutely to (see *OED* 34); mould yourself into the form of (see *OED* 50).

64 **from … kind** against their natures.

65 **calculate** reckon, or prophesy – i.e. try to determine the future from signs in the heavens.

66 **ordinance** that which has been ordained by God.

67 **preformèd faculties** characteristics which they were given at their creation.

77 **prodigious** abnormal, ominous. See also 28 n.

78 **fearful** causing fear in others.

81 **thews** bodily proportion, physical strength.

84 **sufferance** patient endurance.

88 **every … Italy** Plutarch (Appendix, p. 143) says that on the day of the assassination Decius Brutus told Caesar that he should go to the Capitol because the Senate was ready to 'proclaim him king of all the provinces of the Empire of Rome out of Italy, and that he should wear his diadem in all other places, both by sea and land'.

CASSIUS I know where I will wear this dagger then:
    Cassius from bondage will deliver Cassius.   90
    Therein, ye gods, you make the weak most strong;
    Therein, ye gods, you tyrants do defeat.
    Nor stony tower, nor walls of beaten brass,
    Nor airless dungeon, nor strong links of iron,
    Can be retentive to the strength of spirit;   95
    But life, being weary of these worldly bars,
    Never lacks power to dismiss itself.
    If I know this, know all the world besides,
    That part of tyranny that I do bear
    I can shake off at pleasure.
               Thunder still
CASCA   So can I,   100
    So every bondman in his own hand bears
    The power to cancel his captivity.
CASSIUS And why should Caesar be a tyrant then?
    Poor man, I know he would not be a wolf
    But that he sees the Romans are but sheep;   105
    He were no lion, were not Romans hinds.
    Those that with haste will make a mighty fire
    Begin it with weak straws. What trash is Rome,
    What rubbish and what offal, when it serves
    For the base matter to illuminate   110
    So vile a thing as Caesar? But, O grief,
    Where hast thou led me? I perhaps speak this
    Before a willing bondman, then I know
    My answer must be made. But I am armed,
    And dangers are to me indifferent.   115
CASCA You speak to Casca, and to such a man
    That is no fleering tell-tale. Hold, my hand.

---

111 Caesar?] F *(question mark after* offal *at 109); Caesar! / Jennens*   117 Hold,] F; Hold *Theobald*

91 Therein i.e. in suicide (see 96–7).
95 Can be retentive is able to confine.
100 SD **still** continues.
101 bondman slave.
106 hinds female deer; the word *hind* can also refer to a domestic or agricultural servant, or, more generally, to any lower-class or rustic person.

109 offal residue or waste products (e.g. wood chips or table scraps); also the entrails cut out in the process of preparing an animal for food.

117 fleering laughing coarsely, sneeringly.

Be factious for redress of all these griefs,
And I will set this foot of mine as far
As who goes farthest.

CASSIUS   There's a bargain made.   120
Now know you, Casca, I have moved already
Some certain of the noblest-minded Romans
To undergo with me an enterprise
Of honourable dangerous consequence.
And I do know by this they stay for me   125
In Pompey's Porch. For now, this fearful night,
There is no stir or walking in the streets,
And the complexion of the element
In favour's like the work we have in hand,
Most bloody, fiery, and most terrible.   130

Enter CINNA

CASCA Stand close a while, for here comes one in haste.
CASSIUS 'Tis Cinna, I do know him by his gait.
He is a friend. Cinna, where haste you so?
CINNA To find out you. Who's that? Metellus Cimber?
CASSIUS No, it is Casca, one incorporate   135
To our attempts. Am I not stayed for, Cinna?
CINNA I am glad on't. What a fearful night is this!
There's two or three of us have seen strange sights.
CASSIUS Am I not stayed for? Tell me.

---

124 honourable dangerous] F; *hyphen, Capell*; honourable, dangerous *Collier³*   125 know by this] F; know, by this *Rowe*   129 In favour's] Q (1691); Is Fauors F; is favorous *Folger MS.*; Is Feav'rous *Rowe*; Is favour'd *Capell (conj. Thirlby)*; It favours *Steevens*   130 bloody, fiery] F; *hyphen, Dyce² (conj. Walker)*   130 SD] F; *at 133 after* friend *Dyce*   131] *As verse,* Q (1684); *as prose,* F   134] *As verse,* Q (1684); *as prose,* F   137] *Rowe*; I ... on't. / ... this? F   139–41] *Delius², Singer² (conj. W. S. Walker); Cassi.* ... me. / ... *Cassius,* / ... *Brutus* / ... party – F; *Cas.* ... me. / ... are. / ... *Brutus* / ... *Party – Rowe; Cas.* ... me. / ... could / ... party – *Johnson; CAS.* ... me. [*adding* Cinna *after* for,]/ ... Yes, / ... win / ... party – *Capell (Capell MS.); Cas.* ... me. / ... Yes, / ... win / ... party – *Steevens; Cas.* ... Cassius! / ... party ... *Keightley;* CASSIUS ... Cassius, / ... Brutus / ... party – *Charney*

118 factious ... griefs join the faction that seeks redress for these grievances.
120 As who as anyone who.
126 Pompey's Porch A rectangular court, in which were four parallel rows of columns, built adjoining the *scaena* (stage) of Pompey's Theatre (see 152) to provide shelter for the spectators in case of rain. Pompey had both the Theatre and the Porch constructed in 55 BC. In Plutarch, the Porch (not the Capitol, as in Shakespeare) is the site of Caesar's assassination.
128 complexion visible aspect, condition.
128 element sky.
129 *favour appearance. See also 1.2.91.
131 Stand close stand quietly.
135–6 incorporate ... attempts a part of our conspiracy.
137 on't of it.

CINNA   Yes, you are.
    O Cassius, if you could   140
    But win the noble Brutus to our party –
CASSIUS Be you content. Good Cinna, take this paper
    And look you lay it in the praetor's chair,
    Where Brutus may but find it; and throw this
    In at his window; set this up with wax   145
    Upon old Brutus' statue. All this done,
    Repair to Pompey's Porch, where you shall find us.
    Is Decius Brutus and Trebonius there?
CINNA All but Metellus Cimber, and he's gone
    To seek you at your house. Well, I will hie,   150
    And so bestow these papers as you bade me.
CASSIUS That done, repair to Pompey's Theatre.

                Exit Cinna

    Come, Casca, you and I will yet, ere day,
    See Brutus at his house. Three parts of him
    Is ours already, and the man entire   155
    Upon the next encounter yields him ours.
CASCA O, he sits high in all the people's hearts,
    And that which would appear offence in us
    His countenance, like richest alchemy,
    Will change to virtue and to worthiness.   160
CASSIUS Him and his worth and our great need of him
    You have right well conceited. Let us go,
    For it is after midnight, and ere day
    We will awake him and be sure of him.

                Exeunt

---

144 but] F; best *Hudson* ² *(conj. Craik)*

143 praetor's chair The *praetor's chair* is where
Brutus would have sat when hearing disputes
brought before him. A praetor was an elected
magistrate, a position just below consul. Brutus
was made praetor by Caesar in 44 BC.
 145 set ... wax affix this with wax.
 146 old Brutus' statue the statue of Lucius
Junius Brutus. See 1.2.159 n. Brutus, who consid-
ered himself an ancestor of the founder of the
Republic, kept a bust of Lucius Junius Brutus in
his house.

152 Pompey's Theatre The first permanent
theatre in Rome, built of stone by Pompey in
his second consulship in 55 BC. See 126 n.
 157–60 O ... worthiness Brutus has such a high
reputation among the people that he will, in their
eyes, transform even such a treasonous act as we are
planning into an act of virtue and worthiness – just
as alchemy might transform base metal into gold.
 162 You ... conceited You have correctly
apprehended; you have described him with exactly
the right metaphor (*conceit*).

2.1 *Enter* BRUTUS *in his orchard*

BRUTUS What, Lucius, ho!
        I cannot by the progress of the stars
        Give guess how near to day. Lucius, I say!
        I would it were my fault to sleep so soundly.
        When, Lucius, when? Awake, I say! What, Lucius!   5

                Enter LUCIUS

LUCIUS Called you, my lord?
BRUTUS Get me a taper in my study, Lucius.
        When it is lighted, come and call me here.
LUCIUS I will, my lord.   *Exit*
BRUTUS It must be by his death. And for my part   10
        I know no personal cause to spurn at him
        But for the general. He would be crowned:
        How that might change his nature, there's the question.
        It is the bright day that brings forth the adder
        And that craves wary walking. Crown him that,   15
        And then I grant we put a sting in him
        That at his will he may do danger with.
        Th'abuse of greatness is when it disjoins
        Remorse from power. And to speak truth of Caesar,
        I have not known when his affections swayed   20
        More than his reason. But 'tis a common proof
        That lowliness is young ambition's ladder,
        Whereto the climber-upward turns his face;
        But when he once attains the upmost round
        He then unto the ladder turns his back,   25
        Looks in the clouds, scorning the base degrees

Act 2, Scene 1   2.1] *Actus Secundus.* F; ACT II. SCENE I. *Rowe*   Location] F *(subst.)*   23 climber-upward] *Hyphen.*
Warburton

Act 2, Scene 1
Location Rome. Brutus's garden.
  1, 5 What, When exclamations of impatience.
  7 taper candle.
  11 spurn strike out.
  12 the general the cause (i.e. Caesar's tyranny)
that affects everyone.
  15 craves cries out for.
  15 Crown him that Give him a crown. *That*
seems to be used emphatically here, in the same way
one might use the word *So.*

  18 Th'abuse … is greatness becomes dangerous when.
  19 Remorse compassion, scruple.
  20 affections emotions.
  20 swayed ruled, held sway.
  21 'tis … proof it is well known from
experience.
  24 round rung.
  26 degrees rungs; also increments, with
the additional connotation of social or political
rank.

By which he did ascend. So Caesar may.
Then lest he may, prevent. And since the quarrel
Will bear no colour for the thing he is,
Fashion it thus: that what he is, augmented, 30
Would run to these and these extremities.
And therefore think him as a serpent's egg
(Which, hatched, would as his kind grow mischievous)
And kill him in the shell.

Enter LUCIUS

LUCIUS The taper burneth in your closet, sir. 35
Searching the window for a flint, I found
This paper, thus sealed up, and I am sure
It did not lie there when I went to bed.
Gives him the letter
BRUTUS Get you to bed again, it is not day.
Is not tomorrow, boy, the Ides of March? 40
LUCIUS I know not, sir.
BRUTUS Look in the calendar and bring me word.
LUCIUS I will, sir.   *Exit*
BRUTUS The exhalations whizzing in the air
Give so much light that I may read by them. 45
Opens the letter and reads
'Brutus, thou sleep'st. Awake, and see thyself!
Shall Rome, etc. Speak, strike, redress!'
'Brutus, thou sleep'st. Awake!'
Such instigations have been often dropped
Where I have took them up. 50
'Shall Rome, etc.' Thus must I piece it out:
Shall Rome stand under one man's awe? What, Rome?
My ancestors did from the streets of Rome

---

40 Ides] *Theobald (conj. Warburton apud Theobald);* first F   52 What,] *Rome;* What F

28 **prevent** do something to stop him.
28–9 **And since ... he is** since our complaints about his tyranny will seem unjustified based on what he is now.
31 **these and these** such and such.
33 **as ... mischievous** become dangerous, as is natural to serpents.
35 **closet** private room. See also 3.2.121.
40 **Ides of March** The Folio reading here is *first of March.* Theobald suggests that this was

a misreading of a manuscript contraction *I*ˢ. John Hunter, however, argues that 'Shakspeare must ... have inadvertently quoted from a passage in Plutarch (see Appendix, p. 148) not applicable here, but which refers to Cassius asking Brutus if he intended to be in the senate-house on the first of March.' Many modern editors follow Hunter, though Daniell has recently made a case for retaining *first.*

44 **exhalations** meteors or fiery vapours.

The Tarquin drive when he was called a king.
'Speak, strike, redress!' Am I entreated   55
To speak and strike? O Rome, I make thee promise,
If the redress will follow, thou receivest
Thy full petition at the hand of Brutus.

Enter LUCIUS

LUCIUS Sir, March is wasted fifteen days.
                        Knock within
BRUTUS 'Tis good. Go to the gate, somebody knocks.   60

                        [*Exit Lucius*]

Since Cassius first did whet me against Caesar
I have not slept.
Between the acting of a dreadful thing
And the first motion, all the interim is
Like a phantasma or a hideous dream.   65
The genius and the mortal instruments
Are then in council, and the state of a man,
Like to a little kingdom, suffers then
The nature of an insurrection.

Enter LUCIUS

LUCIUS Sir, 'tis your brother Cassius at the door,   70
Who doth desire to see you.
BRUTUS   Is he alone?

---

56 thee] F; the F2   59 fifteen] F; fourteen *Theobald*   60 SD] *Theobald*   67 a] F; *omitted in* F2

54 Tarquin Tarquinius Superbus, traditionally thought to have lived 534–510 BC, and to have been the last king of Rome. He is believed to have been expelled by Lucius Junius Brutus, the traditional founder of the Roman Republic. See also 1.2.159 n. and 1.3.146 n.

58 Thy full petition all that you ask for.

58 at from.

59 fifteen Since, at 40, Brutus asked whether *tomorrow* was the Ides of March, we might here expect Lucius to say that March has wasted *fourteen* days. Possibly Shakespeare imagined this conversation taking place very early in the morning (i.e. just after midnight) on the fifteenth.

64 motion impulse.

65 phantasma apparition, illusion.

66 genius 'with reference to classical pagan belief: the tutelary god or attendant spirit allotted to every person at his birth, to govern his fortunes and determine his character, and finally to conduct him out of the world' (*OED* 1a).

66 mortal instruments mental and physical faculties – as distinct from (and here in dialogue with) the supernatural influence of the 'genius'.

67 in council deliberating.

70 brother i.e. brother-in-law. Cassius had married Brutus's sister, Junia Tertia (Tertulla). For a similar usage, compare *Ant.* 2.7.119.

72 mo more. Used only with count nouns in the plural. See also 5.3.101.

LUCIUS No, sir, there are mo with him.
BRUTUS   Do you know them?
LUCIUS No, sir, their hats are plucked about their ears
         And half their faces buried in their cloaks,
         That by no means I may discover them   75
         By any mark of favour.
BRUTUS   Let 'em enter.

                                              [*Exit Lucius*]

         They are the faction. O conspiracy,
         Sham'st thou to show thy dang'rous brow by night,
         When evils are most free? O then by day
         Where wilt thou find a cavern dark enough   80
         To mask thy monstrous visage? Seek none, conspiracy,
         Hide it in smiles and affability,
         For if thou path, thy native semblance on,
         Not Erebus itself were dim enough
         To hide thee from prevention.   85

Enter the conspirators, CASSIUS, CASCA, DECIUS, CINNA, METELLUS, *and*
                           TREBONIUS

CASSIUS I think we are too bold upon your rest.
         Good morrow, Brutus, do we trouble you?
BRUTUS I have been up this hour, awake all night.
         Know I these men that come along with you?
CASSIUS Yes, every man of them; and no man here   90
         But honours you, and every one doth wish
         You had but that opinion of yourself
         Which every noble Roman bears of you.
         This is Trebonius.
BRUTUS   He is welcome hither.
CASSIUS This, Decius Brutus.
BRUTUS   He is welcome too.   95
CASSIUS This, Casca; this, Cinna; and this, Metellus Cimber.
BRUTUS They are all welcome.

74 cloaks] F; Cloathes F2   76 of] F; or *Folger MS.*   76 SD] *Rowe*   79 O then] QU1; O then, F; O, then
Globe   83 path,] path F; hath QU3; march, *Pope;* hadst *conj. White;* put *Dyce² (Folger MS.);* pass, *Hudson² (conj.
Cartwright);* parle, *conj. Nicholson;* pall [*replacing* on *with* o'er] *conj. Heraud (apud Cam.);* pace, *conj. Anon. (apud Cam.)*
96] *As verse, Thomas Johnson²; as prose,* F; This ... Cinna; / ... Cimber. / *Rowe*

75 **may** am able to. See Abbott 307.
75 **discover** identify. See 1.2.69 n.
76 **favour** appearance. See 1.2.91.
83 **path** go down the path; pursue your
course.
83 **thy ... on** showing yourself as you are.

84 **Erebus** Son of Chaos and Darkness, he came
to signify the nether world or Darkness itself.
85 **from prevention** from being discovered and
forestalled.
90–1 **no man ... honours you** there is no man
here who does not honour you.

What watchful cares do interpose themselves
Betwixt your eyes and night?
CASSIUS Shall I entreat a word?   100

They whisper

DECIUS Here lies the east, doth not the day break here?
CASCA No.
CINNA O, pardon, sir, it doth, and yon grey lines
        That fret the clouds are messengers of day.
CASCA You shall confess that you are both deceived.   105
        Here, as I point my sword, the sun arises,
        Which is a great way growing on the south,
        Weighing the youthful season of the year.
        Some two months hence, up higher toward the north
        He first presents his fire, and the high east   110
        Stands, as the Capitol, directly here.
BRUTUS [*Advancing with Cassius*] Give me your hands all over, one by
        one.
CASSIUS And let us swear our resolution.
BRUTUS No, not an oath! If not the face of men,
        The sufferance of our souls, the time's abuse –   115
        If these be motives weak, break off betimes,
        And every man hence to his idle bed;
        So let high-sighted tyranny range on,
        Till each man drop by lottery. But if these
        (As I am sure they do) bear fire enough   120
        To kindle cowards and to steel with valour
        The melting spirits of women, then, countrymen,
        What need we any spur but our own cause

99–100] *As one line, Keightley*   **101**] *As verse, Theobald; as prose,* F   **112** SD] *Staunton (subst.)*   **114** not the face] F; *that the face Theobald; that the Fate Warburton (conj. Warburton 1734); not the faith conj. Thirlby; not the faiths conj. Malone; not the fate Singer²*   **118** high-sighted] F; *high-seated conj. Theobald*   **118** range] F; *reign Folger MS.; rage Thomas Johnson*

98 watchful i.e. causing watchfulness. For the *-ful* suffix, see 1.3.78 n.
100 SD Brutus and Cassius most likely move or turn away from the others.
104 fret form a pattern upon.
107 growing advancing.
108 Considering how early it is in the year.
112 all over from all sides, all included.
114 face appearance, i.e. how men look under the threat of tyranny.
115 sufferance suffering.

116 betimes without delay, speedily.
117 idle bed empty (i.e. unused) bed; or, perhaps, 'the bed in which he will be idle' (i.e. since he will not be fighting).
118 range on spread in all directions.
119 drop by lottery die by chance, without any control over his fate. Steevens suggested that Shakespeare may have been thinking of the Roman practice of *decimation*: 'to select by lot and put to death one in every ten' soldiers guilty of mutiny or some other crime (*OED* 3).

To prick us to redress? What other bond
Than secret Romans that have spoke the word   125
And will not palter? And what other oath
Than honesty to honesty engaged
That this shall be or we will fall for it?
Swear priests and cowards and men cautelous,
Old feeble carrions, and such suffering souls   130
That welcome wrongs: unto bad causes swear
Such creatures as men doubt. But do not stain
The even virtue of our enterprise,
Nor th'insuppressive mettle of our spirits,
To think that or our cause or our performance.   135
Did need an oath, when every drop of blood
That every Roman bears, and nobly bears,
Is guilty of a several bastardy
If he do break the smallest particle
Of any promise that hath passed from him.   140
CASSIUS But what of Cicero? Shall we sound him?
          I think he will stand very strong with us.
CASCA Let us not leave him out.
CINNA   No, by no means.
METELLUS O, let us have him, for his silver hairs
          Will purchase us a good opinion   145
          And buy men's voices to commend our deeds.
          It shall be said his judgement ruled our hands;
          Our youths and wildness shall no whit appear,
          But all be buried in his gravity.
BRUTUS O, name him not, let us not break with him,   150
          For he will never follow anything
          That other men begin.

---

126 palter] F; falter *Thomas Johnson*   132 stain] F; strain *conj. Warburton*   152–3] *Steevens*[3]; That ... begin. / ... out. /
... fit. F; That ... begin. / ... fit. *Capell MS.*

125 Than than that of. See also 127.
126 palter shift position (from 'speak indistinctly').
129 Swear ... men Let priests (etc.) swear.
129 cautelous cautious and wary (*OED* 2a) or, perhaps, deceitful and crafty (*OED* 1).
130 carrions carcases. Used contemptuously of a living person.
130 suffering patient, all-enduring.
132 as men doubt of whom other men are suspicious.

133 even impartial, just (from the literal sense 'level').
134 insuppressive not suppressible. According to *OED*, Shakespeare is the first to use this word. A synonym might be *indomitable*.
135 or ... or either ... or.
138 a several bastardy a separate or distinct act of baseness. See also 3.2.232, 5.5.18.
141 sound him try to gauge his commitment to our cause.
150 break with him reveal the plan to him.

CASSIUS   Then leave him out.

CASCA   Indeed he is not fit.

DECIUS   Shall no man else be touched but only Caesar?

CASSIUS   Decius, well urged. I think it is not meet   155
     Mark Antony, so well beloved of Caesar,
     Should outlive Caesar. We shall find of him
     A shrewd contriver. And, you know, his means,
     If he improve them, may well stretch so far
     As to annoy us all, which to prevent,   160
     Let Antony and Caesar fall together.

BRUTUS   Our course will seem too bloody, Caius Cassius,
     To cut the head off and then hack the limbs –
     Like wrath in death and envy afterwards –
     For Antony is but a limb of Caesar.   165
     Let's be sacrificers, but not butchers, Caius.
     We all stand up against the spirit of Caesar,
     And in the spirit of men there is no blood.
     O, that we then could come by Caesar's spirit
     And not dismember Caesar! But, alas,   170
     Caesar must bleed for it. And, gentle friends,
     Let's kill him boldly, but not wrathfully;
     Let's carve him as a dish fit for the gods,
     Not hew him as a carcass fit for hounds.
     And let our hearts, as subtle masters do,   175
     Stir up their servants to an act of rage
     And after seem to chide 'em. This shall make
     Our purpose necessary, and not envious;
     Which so appearing to the common eyes,
     We shall be called purgers, not murderers.   180
     And for Mark Antony, think not of him,
     For he can do no more than Caesar's arm
     When Caesar's head is off.

CASSIUS   Yet I fear him,
     For in the engrafted love he bears to Caesar –

---

166 Caius] F; *Cassius Rowe; omitted in Pope*   177 make] F; mark *Collier² (Collier MS.)*   184 Caesar –] *Rowe; Caesar.* F

158 **contriver** plotter.
158 **means** strength and position.
159 **improve** take advantage of.
160 **annoy** harm. See 1.3.22.
164 **envy** malice.

175 **subtle** wickedly cunning.
176 **their servants** i.e. the servants of 'our hearts' – our passions.
178 **envious** malicious. See also 3.2.166.
181 **for** as for.

BRUTUS Alas, good Cassius, do not think of him. 185
　　　　If he love Caesar, all that he can do
　　　　Is to himself – take thought and die for Caesar;
　　　　And that were much he should, for he is given
　　　　To sports, to wildness, and much company.
TREBONIUS There is no fear in him, let him not die, 190
　　　　For he will live and laugh at this hereafter.

Clock strikes

BRUTUS Peace, count the clock.
CASSIUS 　　　　　　　　　　　The clock hath stricken three.
TREBONIUS 'Tis time to part.
CASSIUS 　　　　　　　　　　　But it is doubtful yet
　　　　Whether Caesar will come forth today or no,
　　　　For he is superstitious grown of late, 195
　　　　Quite from the main opinion he held once
　　　　Of fantasy, of dreams, and ceremonies.
　　　　It may be these apparent prodigies,
　　　　The unaccustomed terror of this night,
　　　　And the persuasion of his augurers 200
　　　　May hold him from the Capitol today.
DECIUS Never fear that. If he be so resolved
　　　　I can o'ersway him, for he loves to hear
　　　　That unicorns may be betrayed with trees,
　　　　And bears with glasses, elephants with holes, 205
　　　　Lions with toils, and men with flatterers.
　　　　But when I tell him he hates flatterers
　　　　He says he does, being then most flatterèd.

---

196 main] F; mean QU4

187 **take thought** '*turn* melancholy' (Johnson).
188 **And that ... should** And even that might be too much for him to do.
190 **no fear** nothing to fear.
193 **doubtful yet** still uncertain.
196 **Quite from** quite contrary to.
197 **fantasy** delusive imagination. See also 3.3.2.
197 **ceremonies** Most typically in this play, *ceremonies* refers to the external accessories of worship (see 1.1.63–4 n.). Here it seems to refer to portents and omens, or to rites of divination – i.e. the portents or omens discovered by a priest or soothsayer through sacrifice or some other ritual (see *OED* 5).

198 **apparent** visible.
198 **prodigies** omens. See 1.3.28 n.
204–6 **unicorns ... toils** Steevens explains these lines as follows: 'Unicorns are said to have been taken by one who, running behind a tree, eluded the violent push the animal was making at him, so that his horn spent its force on the trunk, and stuck fast ... *Bears* are reported to have been surprised by means of a *mirror*, which they would gaze on, affording their pursuers an opportunity of taking the surer aim ... *Elephants* were seduced into pitfalls, lightly covered with hurdles and turf, on which a proper bait to tempt them, was exposed.'
206 **toils** nets.

Let me work:
For I can give his humour the true bent,   210
And I will bring him to the Capitol.

CASSIUS Nay, we will all of us be there to fetch him.

BRUTUS By the eighth hour, is that the uttermost?

CINNA Be that the uttermost, and fail not then.

METELLUS Caius Ligarius doth bear Caesar hard,   215
Who rated him for speaking well of Pompey.
I wonder none of you have thought of him.

BRUTUS Now, good Metellus, go along by him.
He loves me well, and I have given him reasons.
Send him but hither and I'll fashion him.   220

CASSIUS The morning comes upon's. We'll leave you, Brutus,
And, friends, disperse yourselves, but all remember
What you have said and show yourselves true Romans.

BRUTUS Good gentlemen, look fresh and merrily:
Let not our looks put on our purposes,   225
But bear it as our Roman actors do,
With untired spirits and formal constancy.
And so good morrow to you every one.

Exeunt [all but] Brutus

Boy! Lucius! Fast asleep? It is no matter,
Enjoy the honey-heavy dew of slumber.   230
Thou hast no figures nor no fantasies
Which busy care draws in the brains of men,
Therefore thou sleep'st so sound.

Enter PORTIA

PORTIA   Brutus, my lord.

BRUTUS Portia! What mean you? Wherefore rise you now?
It is not for your health thus to commit   235
Your weak condition to the raw cold morning.

---

215 hard] F; Hatred F2   218 by] F; to *Pope*   221] *Rowe*; The … vpon's: / … *Brutus*, F   230 honey-heavy dew]
Q (1684); hony-heauy-Dew F; heavy honey-dew *Collier²* (Collier MS.)

210 I can make him act according to his true
disposition.
212 there i.e. Caesar's house.
213 uttermost latest.
215 bear … hard hold a grudge against Caesar.
216 rated reproved vehemently.
218 go along by go to.

220 fashion him make him one of us.
225 put on reveal.
227 formal constancy self-possession. That is:
'Let us maintain (keep *constant*) our outward (*formal*) composure in spite of the terrible thing we are
about to undertake.'
231 figures imaginary forms, phantasms.

PORTIA Nor for yours neither. Y'have ungently, Brutus,
        Stole from my bed; and yesternight at supper
        You suddenly arose and walked about,
        Musing and sighing, with your arms across,   240
        And when I asked you what the matter was,
        You stared upon me with ungentle looks.
        I urged you further, then you scratched your head
        And too impatiently stamped with your foot.
        Yet I insisted, yet you answered not,   245
        But with an angry wafture of your hand
        Gave sign for me to leave you. So I did,
        Fearing to strengthen that impatience
        Which seemed too much enkindled, and withal
        Hoping it was but an effect of humour   250
        Which sometime hath his hour with every man.
        It will not let you eat nor talk nor sleep;
        And could it work so much upon your shape
        As it hath much prevailed on your condition,
        I should not know you, Brutus. Dear my lord,   255
        Make me acquainted with your cause of grief.
BRUTUS I am not well in health, and that is all.
PORTIA Brutus is wise, and were he not in health
        He would embrace the means to come by it.
BRUTUS Why, so I do. Good Portia, go to bed.   260
PORTIA Is Brutus sick? And is it physical
        To walk unbracèd and suck up the humours
        Of the dank morning? What, is Brutus sick?
        And will he steal out of his wholesome bed
        To dare the vile contagion of the night   265
        And tempt the rheumy and unpurgèd air
        To add unto his sickness? No, my Brutus,
        You have some sick offence within your mind,

---

255 you,] Q (1684); you F   263 dank] F; darke F2   267 his] F2; hit F

240 **across** crossed, folded (denoting melancholy).

246 **wafture** *OED* cites this line as the first instance of the word. In the Folio, the word is *wafter*. If this was Shakespeare's own coinage, he seems to have derived it from *waft*: 'to signal … by waving the hand or something held in the hand' (*OED* 1b).

250 **effect of humour** passing mood.

251 **his** its.

253 **your shape** appearance of your body.

254 **condition** mental disposition.

261 **physical** beneficial to health. *Physic* in Shakespeare's time was the practice of medicine.

262 **suck … humours** inhale the damp vapours.

266 **rheumy and unpurgèd** damp and impure.

Which by the right and virtue of my place
I ought to know of. And upon my knees   270
I charm you, by my once commended beauty,
By all your vows of love, and that great vow
Which did incorporate and make us one,
That you unfold to me, your self, your half,
Why you are heavy and what men tonight   275
Have had resort to you, for here have been
Some six or seven who did hide their faces
Even from darkness.
BRUTUS   Kneel not, gentle Portia.
PORTIA   I should not need if you were gentle Brutus.
Within the bond of marriage, tell me, Brutus,   280
Is it excepted I should know no secrets
That appertain to you? Am I your self
But, as it were, in sort or limitation,
To keep with you at meals, comfort your bed,
And talk to you sometimes? Dwell I but in the suburbs   285
Of your good pleasure? If it be no more
Portia is Brutus' harlot, not his wife.
BRUTUS   You are my true and honourable wife,
As dear to me as are the ruddy drops
That visit my sad heart.   290
PORTIA   If this were true, then should I know this secret.
I grant I am a woman, but withal
A woman that Lord Brutus took to wife.
I grant I am a woman, but withal
A woman well reputed, Cato's daughter.   295
Think you I am no stronger than my sex,
Being so fathered and so husbanded?

---

271 charm] F; charge *Thomas Johnson*   274, 282 your self] F; yourself *Theobald*⁴   279 gentle] F; gentle,
Staunton   284 comfort] F; consort *Theobald (conj. Theobald 1730)*   295 reputed,] reputed: F; reputed *Warburton*

269 **virtue** power.
271 **charm** 'overcome or subdue, as if by magic power' (OED v^1 4).
273 **incorporate** combine into one body.
274 **unfold** make known.
274 **half** other half.
275 **heavy** sorrowful, preoccupied.
280 **bond** legal contract.
283 **in sort or limitation** in a limited way, or for a limited time. This is a legal phrase, perhaps suggested by 'bond' a few lines earlier (Wilson).

284 **keep with you** keep you company.
285 **suburbs** outlying districts. In Shakespeare's time the suburbs, outside of city jurisdiction, were notorious as the site of brothels, theatres, and other dubious forms of London entertainment.
295 **Cato** Marcus Porcius Cato Uticensis (95–46 BC). Roman senator who vigorously opposed Caesar's rise to power and fought on the side of Pompey in the civil war. He committed suicide in 46 BC to avoid being taken by Caesar after the battle of Thaspus. See also 5.1.101.

Tell me your counsels, I will not disclose 'em.
I have made strong proof of my constancy,
Giving myself a voluntary wound   300
Here, in the thigh. Can I bear that with patience
And not my husband's secrets?
BRUTUS   O ye gods,
Render me worthy of this noble wife!
                              Knock
Hark, hark, one knocks. Portia, go in a while,
And by and by thy bosom shall partake   305
The secrets of my heart.
All my engagements I will construe to thee,
All the charactery of my sad brows.
Leave me with haste.

                                                  Exit Portia
                    Lucius, who's that knocks?

                    Enter LUCIUS *and* LIGARIUS

LUCIUS Here is a sick man that would speak with you.   310
BRUTUS Caius Ligarius, that Metellus spake of.
        Boy, stand aside.

                                                  [*Exit Lucius*]
                    Caius Ligarius, how?
LIGARIUS Vouchsafe good morrow from a feeble tongue.
BRUTUS O, what a time have you chose out, brave Caius,
        To wear a kerchief! Would you were not sick!   315

---

309 who's] F; who's there *Pope;* who's that *Capell (conj. Thirlby);* who is *Steevens;* who is't *Rann (conj. Thirlby)*   312 SD] *Capell (Capell MS.)*   313 SH LIGARIUS] *Hanmer; Cai.* F *(throughout)*

298 counsels private or secret purposes, designs or opinions.

299 constancy fidelity (i.e. to Brutus); steadfastness, endurance, fortitude (*OED* 1a – and see 300–1 n.).

300–1 In Plutarch (Appendix, p. 150) Portia decides that she 'would not ask her husband what he ailed before she made some proof by herself'. She therefore deliberately gashes her thigh with a razor blade (this is the *voluntary wound* of 300), and suffers the subsequent infection in stoical silence, in order to show Brutus that 'no pain nor grief whatsoever can overcome her' – i.e. his secrets will be safe with her.

307 All my engagements all the acts to which I have committed myself.

307 construe explain.

308 charactery expression of thought by characters or symbols.

308 sad grave, serious; as at 1.2.217.

313 Vouchsafe receive graciously.

314 brave worthy, good (a general epithet of admiration or praise; the dominant sense in the play).

315 kerchief a head-covering (commonly worn by the sick).

LIGARIUS I am not sick if Brutus have in hand
          Any exploit worthy the name of honour.
BRUTUS Such an exploit have I in hand, Ligarius,
          Had you a healthful ear to hear of it.
LIGARIUS By all the gods that Romans bow before,   320
          I here discard my sickness!
                    [*He pulls off his kerchief*]
                                        Soul of Rome,
          Brave son, derived from honourable loins,
          Thou, like an exorcist, hast conjured up
          My mortifièd spirit. Now bid me run
          And I will strive with things impossible,   325
          Yea, get the better of them. What's to do?
BRUTUS A piece of work that will make sick men whole.
LIGARIUS But are not some whole that we must make sick?
BRUTUS That must we also. What it is, my Caius,
          I shall unfold to thee as we are going   330
          To whom it must be done.
LIGARIUS   Set on your foot,
          And with a heart new fired I follow you
          To do I know not what; but it sufficeth
          That Brutus leads me on.
                              Thunder
BRUTUS   Follow me then.
                                                    Exeunt

2.2 *Thunder and lightning. Enter* JULIUS CAESAR *in his nightgown*

CAESAR Nor heaven nor earth have been at peace tonight.
          Thrice hath Calpurnia in her sleep cried out,
          'Help ho, they murder Caesar!' Who's within?

                    Enter a SERVANT

321 SD] *Collier²* (subst.) (*Collier MS.*)   326 Yea] F; Yet *Rowe²*   327] *Row;* A . . . worke, / . . . whole. F   330 going]
Capell; going, F   Act 2, Scene 2   2.2] *Rowe*   Location] *Globe (after Rowe)*   1] *Rowe (Folger MS.);* Nor . . . Earth, /
. . . night: F

323–4 **Thou … spirit** *Exorcist* here has the   331 **Set on** advance.
sense 'conjurer' more than 'one who drives out
evil spirits'. Brutus is imagined to be *raising* ('con-   **Act 2, Scene 2**
juring up') the spirit of one who is dead (*mortified*).   **Location** Rome. Caesar's house.
    327 **whole** hale.   0 SD **nightgown** dressing-gown.

SERVANT My lord?

CAESAR Go bid the priests do present sacrifice   5
        And bring me their opinions of success.

SERVANT I will, my lord.   *Exit*

Enter CALPURNIA

CALPURNIA What mean you, Caesar, think you to walk forth?
        You shall not stir out of your house today.

CAESAR Caesar shall forth. The things that threatened me   10
        Ne'er looked but on my back; when they shall see
        The face of Caesar they are vanishèd.

CALPURNIA Caesar, I never stood on ceremonies,
        Yet now they fright me. There is one within,
        Besides the things that we have heard and seen,   15
        Recounts most horrid sights seen by the watch.
        A lioness hath whelpèd in the streets,
        And graves have yawned and yielded up their dead;
        Fierce fiery warriors fight upon the clouds
        In ranks and squadrons and right form of war,   20
        Which drizzled blood upon the Capitol;
        The noise of battle hurtled in the air,
        Horses did neigh and dying men did groan,
        And ghosts did shriek and squeal about the streets.
        O Caesar, these things are beyond all use,   25
        And I do fear them.

CAESAR   What can be avoided
        Whose end is purposed by the mighty gods?
        Yet Caesar shall go forth, for these predictions
        Are to the world in general as to Caesar.

CALPURNIA When beggars die there are no comets seen,   30

---

19 fight] F; fought *White (conj. Thirlby)*   22 hurtled] F; hurried F2   23 did] F2; do F

5 **present** immediate.
5 **sacrifice** The priests will look for omens in the entrails of a slaughtered beast. See also 38–40.
6 **opinions of success** judgement of the result (i.e. of the sacrifice).
13 **stood on ceremonies** attached importance to sacrifices or omens. See 2.1.197 n.

20 **squadrons** soldiers arranged in square formation.
20 **right** appropriate, regular (from the literal meaning 'straight').
20 **form** formation.
22 **hurtled** crashed.
25 **use** usual experience.

The heavens themselves blaze forth the death of princes.
CAESAR Cowards die many times before their deaths,
The valiant never taste of death but once.
Of all the wonders that I yet have heard
It seems to me most strange that men should fear,   35
Seeing that death, a necessary end,
Will come when it will come.

Enter a SERVANT

                            What say the augurers?
SERVANT They would not have you to stir forth today.
Plucking the entrails of an offering forth,
They could not find a heart within the beast.   40
CAESAR The gods do this in shame of cowardice.
Caesar should be a beast without a heart
If he should stay at home today for fear.
No, Caesar shall not. Danger knows full well
That Caesar is more dangerous than he: 45
We are two lions littered in one day,
And I the elder and more terrible.
And Caesar shall go forth.
CALPURNIA   Alas, my lord,
Your wisdom is consumed in confidence.
Do not go forth today. Call it my fear   50
That keeps you in the house, and not your own.
We'll send Mark Antony to the Senate House
And he shall say you are not well today.
Let me, upon my knee, prevail in this.
CAESAR Mark Antony shall say I am not well,   55
And for thy humour I will stay at home.

Enter DECIUS

Here's Decius Brutus, he shall tell them so.
DECIUS Caesar, all hail! Good morrow, worthy Caesar,

---

37 augurers] F; augures QUI   46 We are] *Capell (conj. Thirlby);* We heare F; We heard *Rowe (Folger MS.);* We were
Theobald (conj. Thirlby); Here are *Sampath Thathachariar (privately)*

31 **blaze forth** shine brightly (like a *comet*, 30) with the news of. Also, proclaim, as with a trumpet; this sense comes from *blaze* = 'blow (e.g. with a musical instrument)' (*OED* Blaze v^2 1).

32–3 Proverbial (Dent C774): 'A coward dies many deaths, a brave man but one.'
41 **in shame of cowardice** to shame cowardice.
46 **littered in one day** born on the same day.
56 **humour** mood.

          I come to fetch you to the Senate House.

CAESAR And you are come in very happy time   60
          To bear my greeting to the senators
          And tell them that I will not come today.
          Cannot is false, and that I dare not, falser:
          I will not come today. Tell them so, Decius.

CALPURNIA Say he is sick.

CAESAR   Shall Caesar send a lie?   65
          Have I in conquest stretched mine arm so far
          To be afeard to tell greybeards the truth?
          Decius, go tell them Caesar will not come.

DECIUS Most mighty Caesar, let me know some cause,
          Lest I be laughed at when I tell them so.   70

CAESAR The cause is in my will. I will not come:
          That is enough to satisfy the Senate.
          But for your private satisfaction,
          Because I love you, I will let you know:
          Calpurnia here, my wife, stays me at home.   75
          She dreamt tonight she saw my statue,
          Which like a fountain with an hundred spouts
          Did run pure blood, and many lusty Romans
          Came smiling and did bathe their hands in it.
          And these does she apply for warnings and portents   80
          And evils imminent, and on her knee
          Hath begged that I will stay at home today.

DECIUS This dream is all amiss interpreted,
          It was a vision fair and fortunate.
          Your statue spouting blood in many pipes,   85
          In which so many smiling Romans bathed,
          Signifies that from you great Rome shall suck
          Reviving blood and that great men shall press
          For tinctures, stains, relics, and cognisance.

---

81 And] F; Of *Hanmer (conj. Thirlby)*

60 in ... time at just the right time.
67 greybeards often used contemptuously of old men.
75 stays me makes me stay.
76 tonight last night.
80 apply for interpret as.
89 tinctures ... cognisance The main idea is that the Romans seek to be marked, honourably, with the colour of Caesar's blood.

Tinctures, stains, and *cognisance* are all (as Johnson noted) words pertaining to heraldry, i.e. the colours and designs with which gentle and noble men adorned their coats of arms. See *OED tincture* 2b, *stain* 4, and *cognisance* 5a. *Relics* is a different metaphor: we are to imagine the Romans seeking tokens from Caesar's body such as a Christian worshipper might seek from a saint or martyr.

This by Calpurnia's dream is signified.   90
CAESAR And this way have you well expounded it.
DECIUS I have, when you have heard what I can say.
        And know it now: the Senate have concluded
        To give this day a crown to mighty Caesar.
        If you shall send them word you will not come,   95
        Their minds may change. Besides, it were a mock
        Apt to be rendered for someone to say,
        'Break up the Senate till another time,
        When Caesar's wife shall meet with better dreams.'
        If Caesar hide himself, shall they not whisper,   100
        'Lo, Caesar is afraid'?
        Pardon me, Caesar, for my dear dear love
        To your proceeding bids me tell you this,
        And reason to my love is liable.
CAESAR How foolish do your fears seem now, Calpurnia!   105
        I am ashamèd I did yield to them.
        Give me my robe, for I will go.

        Enter BRUTUS, *Ligarius, Metellus, Casca,* TREBONIUS, *Cinna, and*
                                PUBLIUS

        And look where Publius is come to fetch me.
PUBLIUS Good morrow, Caesar.
CAESAR   Welcome, Publius.
        What, Brutus, are you stirred so early too?   110
        Good morrow, Casca. Caius Ligarius,
        Caesar was ne'er so much your enemy
        As that same ague which hath made you lean.
        What is't o'clock?
BRUTUS   Caesar, 'tis strucken eight.
CAESAR I thank you for your pains and courtesy.   115

                        Enter ANTONY

---

103 proceeding] F; proceedings QUI *(Folger MS.)*   107 SD] *Wells and Taylor add Cassius*

96–7 **it were … to say** someone might well say mockingly.
103 **proceeding** advancement.
104 **reason … liable** my love makes me act against my better judgement (i.e. normally I would not dare to contradict Caesar).

111–13 **Caius Ligarius … lean** Caesar makes a joke about the fact that Ligarius was recently his *enemy* in the civil war against Pompey; having been pardoned by Caesar, the most Ligarius has to worry about now is a recent fever (*ague*) that caused him to lose weight.

See, Antony, that revels long a-nights,
Is notwithstanding up. Good morrow, Antony.
ANTONY   So to most noble Caesar.
CAESAR [*To Calpurnia*]   Bid them prepare within,
                                        [*Exit Calpurnia*]
I am to blame to be thus waited for.
Now, Cinna, now, Metellus. What, Trebonius,   120
I have an hour's talk in store for you.
Remember that you call on me today;
Be near me that I may remember you.
TREBONIUS   Caesar, I will. [*Aside*] And so near will I be
That your best friends shall wish I had been further.   125
CAESAR   Good friends, go in and taste some wine with me,
And we, like friends, will straightway go together.
BRUTUS [*Aside*] That every like is not the same, O Caesar,
The heart of Brutus earns to think upon.

                                        Exeunt

2.3 *Enter* ARTEMIDORUS [*reading a paper*]

ARTEMIDORUS   'Caesar, beware of Brutus, take heed of Cassius, come
not near Casca, have an eye to Cinna, trust not Trebonius, mark well
Metellus Cimber, Decius Brutus loves thee not, thou hast wronged
Caius Ligarius. There is but one mind in all these men, and it is bent
against Caesar. If thou beest not immortal look about you: security   5
gives way to conspiracy. The mighty gods defend thee!
                                        Thy lover,
                                        Artemidorus.'

117–18] Boswell (Capell MS.); Is … Antony. / … Caesar. / … within: F; Is … up:- / … Caesar. / … within: –
Steevens³ 118 SD.1] Wilson; to an Att[endant]/Capell (Capell MS.) 118 SD.2] Wilson (subst.); at 119,
Humphreys 124 SD] Rowe (Douai MS.) 128 SD] Pope (Douai MS.) Act 2, Scene 3 2.3] Rowe Location] Rowe 0 SD
reading a paper] Rowe 1 SH ARTEMIDORUS] Capell (Capell MS.)

128 Brutus ruefully notes that when Caesar says
'*like* friends', he means the word differently (i.e. without implying falsehood) from how the conspirators
might hear it (i.e. they will *act like*, but not *be*, Caesar's
friends). Brutus is modifying a proverbial phrase
(Dent A167): 'All that is alike is not the same.'
129 earns grieves.

Act 2, Scene 3
Location Rome. A street.
5 security the belief that you are secure (with
the implication that Caesar is carelessly over-
confident).
7 lover friend.

Here will I stand till Caesar pass along,
And as a suitor will I give him this.   10
My heart laments that virtue cannot live
Out of the teeth of emulation.
If thou read this, O Caesar, thou mayst live;
If not, the fates with traitors do contrive.   *Exit*

2.4 *Enter* PORTIA *and* LUCIUS

PORTIA I prithee, boy, run to the Senate House.
        Stay not to answer me but get thee gone.
        Why dost thou stay?
LUCIUS   To know my errand, madam.
PORTIA I would have had thee there and here again
        Ere I can tell thee what thou shouldst do there.   5
        [*Aside*] O constancy, be strong upon my side,
        Set a huge mountain 'tween my heart and tongue!
        I have a man's mind, but a woman's might.
        How hard it is for women to keep counsel! –
        Art thou here yet?
LUCIUS   Madam, what should I do?   10
        Run to the Capitol, and nothing else?
        And so return to you, and nothing else?
PORTIA Yes, bring me word, boy, if thy lord look well,
        For he went sickly forth, and take good note
        What Caesar doth, what suitors press to him.   15
        Hark, boy, what noise is that?
LUCIUS I hear none, madam.
PORTIA   Prithee listen well:
        I heard a bustling rumour, like a fray,

Act 2, Scene 4 2.4] *Capell* Location] *Capell* 3 my] thy *Macmillan (Folger MS.)* 6 SD] *Capell* 16–17] *Steevens*[3]
(Capell MS.); Hearke ... that? / ... Madam. / ... well: F; Hark ... Madam./ ... well; *Keightley*

12 **Out of the teeth** away from the dangers.
12 **emulation** envious rivalry.

Act 2, Scene 4
Location Rome. Before Brutus's house.
  6 **constancy** i.e. constancy in her vow not to
reveal Brutus's secrets.
  9 **keep counsel** keep a matter secret or confidential.
  18 **rumour** noise, clamour.
  18 **fray** noisy quarrel, brawl.

And the wind brings it from the Capitol.
LUCIUS Sooth, madam, I hear nothing.   20

Enter the SOOTHSAYER

PORTIA Come hither, fellow, which way hast thou been?
SOOTHSAYER At mine own house, good lady.
PORTIA What is't o'clock?
SOOTHSAYER   About the ninth hour, lady.
PORTIA Is Caesar yet gone to the Capitol?
SOOTHSAYER Madam, not yet. I go to take my stand   25
    To see him pass on to the Capitol.
PORTIA Thou hast some suit to Caesar, hast thou not?
SOOTHSAYER That I have, lady, if it will please Caesar
    To be so good to Caesar as to hear me:
    I shall beseech him to befriend himself.   30
PORTIA Why, know'st thou any harm's intended towards him?
SOOTHSAYER None that I know will be, much that I fear may chance.
    Good morrow to you. Here the street is narrow:
    The throng that follows Caesar at the heels,
    Of senators, of praetors, common suitors,   35
    Will crowd a feeble man almost to death.
    I'll get me to a place more void, and there
    Speak to great Caesar as he comes along.   *Exit*
PORTIA I must go in. [*Aside*] Ay me, how weak a thing
    The heart of woman is! O Brutus,   40
    The heavens speed thee in thine enterprise!
    Sure the boy heard me. Brutus hath a suit
    That Caesar will not grant. O, I grow faint. –
    Run, Lucius, and commend me to my lord,
    Say I am merry. Come to me again   45
    And bring me word what he doth say to thee.

Exeunt [*severally*]

20 SD SOOTHSAYER] F; *Artemidorus Rowe*   **20–3**] *Delius²; Luc. . . . nothing./ . . . Soothsayer. / . . . bin?/ . . . good Lady./
. . . clocke?/ . . . Lady.* F; *LUC. . . . fellow: / . . . good lady./ . . . lady. Steevens³ (Capell MS.); [at 22–3] Art. At . . . clock?
White*   **28–9** *if . . . me:*] F; *If . . . me, Johnson*   **30** *befriend*] F; *defend Rowe³*   **31**] *As verse, Theobald; as prose,* F   **31**
harm's] F; *harms* QU2; *harm Pope*   **32**] *Capell;* None . . . be, / . . . chance: F; None . . . fear, [*omitting* may chance]
Pope   **39**] *Rowe;* I . . . in: / . . . thing F   **39** SD] *Dyce² (after Rowe)*   **46** SD *severally*] *Theobald*

35 praetors administrators of justice. See
1.3.143 n.
37 a place more void a less crowded
place.

44 commend me remember me kindly, present
my kind regards.
46 SD *severally* i.e. at separate doors. See also
3.2.10 n.

3.1 *Flourish. Enter* CAESAR, BRUTUS, CASSIUS, CASCA, DECIUS, METELLUS, TREBONIUS, CINNA, ANTONY, *Lepidus,* ARTEMIDORUS, PUBLIUS, [POPILLIUS, *Ligarius,*] *and the* SOOTHSAYER

CAESAR The Ides of March are come.
SOOTHSAYER Ay, Caesar, but not gone.
ARTEMIDORUS Hail, Caesar! Read this schedule.
DECIUS Trebonius doth desire you to o'er-read
    (At your best leisure) this his humble suit.   5
ARTEMIDORUS O Caesar, read mine first, for mine's a suit
    That touches Caesar nearer. Read it, great Caesar.
CAESAR What touches us ourself shall be last served.
ARTEMIDORUS Delay not, Caesar, read it instantly.
CAESAR What, is the fellow mad?
PUBLIUS   Sirrah, give place.   10
CASSIUS What, urge you your petitions in the street?
    Come to the Capitol.
        [*Caesar enters the Capitol, the rest following*]
POPILLIUS I wish your enterprise today may thrive.
CASSIUS What enterprise, Popillius?
POPILLIUS   Fare you well.
        [*Leaves him and joins Caesar*]
BRUTUS What said Popillius Lena?   15
CASSIUS He wished today our enterprise might thrive.
    I fear our purpose is discoverèd.
BRUTUS Look how he makes to Caesar, mark him.
CASSIUS Casca, be sudden, for we fear prevention.
    Brutus, what shall be done? If this be known   20

Act 3, Scene 1 3.1] *Actus Tertius.* F; ACT III. SCENE I. *Rowe*   Location] *Rowe*   0 SD POPILLIUS] F2   0 SD Ligarius]
This edn   8 us ourself] F; us? ourself *Collier²* (Collier MS.)   12 SD] *Steevens (after Capell)*   14] *Reed (Capell MS.);*
Cassi. . . . Popillius? / . . . well. F   14 SD] *Capell (Capell MS.)*

Act 3, Scene 1
Location Rome. The Capitol.
  0 SD Lepidus does not speak in this scene but is named in the entrance direction. Ligarius, who does not speak but is probably present (he is mentioned in Artemidorus's 'paper' at 2.3.4), is not named in the direction. Some critics have suggested that the Folio compositor misread 'Li' as 'Le' and then improperly expanded the abbreviation to 'Lepidus' instead of 'Ligarius'. But mutes are not uncommon in crowd scenes

and Plutarch does mention Lepidus's fleeing the Capitol with Antony after Caesar's assassination.
  3 schedule 'A slip or scroll of parchment or paper containing writing' (*OED* 1).
  10 Sirrah a term of contempt, usually used to address a servant or to assert the speaker's authority.
  10 give place stand aside.
  18 makes to moves towards.
  19 sudden swift of action.
  19 prevention being forestalled.

Cassius or Caesar never shall turn back,
For I will slay myself.

BRUTUS   Cassius, be constant.
Popillius Lena speaks not of our purposes,
For look he smiles, and Caesar doth not change.

CASSIUS Trebonius knows his time, for look you, Brutus,   25
He draws Mark Antony out of the way.

                          [*Exeunt Antony and Trebonius*]

DECIUS Where is Metellus Cimber? Let him go
And presently prefer his suit to Caesar.

BRUTUS He is addressed, press near and second him.

CINNA Casca, you are the first that rears your hand.   30

CAESAR Are we all ready? What is now amiss
That Caesar and his Senate must redress?

METELLUS Most high, most mighty, and most puissant Caesar,
Metellus Cimber throws before thy seat
An humble heart.

CAESAR   I must prevent thee, Cimber.   35
These couchings and these lowly courtesies
Might fire the blood of ordinary men
And turn preordinance and first decree
Into the law of children. Be not fond
To think that Caesar bears such rebel blood   40
That will be thawed from the true quality
With that which melteth fools – I mean sweet words,
Low-crookèd curtsies, and base spaniel fawning.
Thy brother by decree is banishèd:
If thou dost bend, and pray, and fawn for him,   45

21 or] F; on *Craik (conj. Malone)*   26 SD] *Capell (Capell MS.)*   31 Are ... ready?] *Assigned to Cassius,* QUI; *to Cinna, conj. Ritson (apud Steevens³); to Casca, Collier² (conj. Thirlby, reading* We are all ready)   36 couchings] F; crouchings *Hanmer (conj. Thirlby)*   38 first] F; fixt *conj. Craik*   39 law] *Malone (conj. Johnson);* lane F; love *conj. Thirlby;* line *conj. Thirlby;* play *Hudson² (conj. Mason);* lune *conj. Macmillan*   43 Low-crookèd] F; Low-crouched *Collier²*

21 **turn back** return alive.

22 **constant** resolute, firm of purpose.

25 **knows his time** is acting right on cue.

28 **prefer** put forward, present (for acceptance). See also 5.5.62.

29 **addressed** ready.

36 **couchings** reverent or subservient bows.

37 **fire the blood of** have a powerful effect upon.

38 **preordinance and first decree** laws established since the beginning of time.

39 ***law of children** laws that can be overturned as easily as if they were made by children.

39 **fond** foolish.

41–2 **thawed ... With** lose its integrity in the face of.

43 **low-crookèd** low-bending, i.e. obsequious.

44 Plutarch (Appendix, p. 152) notes that the banishment of Cimber's brother was the pretence under which the conspirators approached Caesar, but he does not say what the reason for his banishment was.

I spurn thee like a cur out of my way.
Know Caesar doth not wrong, nor without cause
Will he be satisfied.

METELLUS Is there no voice more worthy than my own
To sound more sweetly in great Caesar's ear   50
For the repealing of my banished brother?

BRUTUS I kiss thy hand, but not in flattery, Caesar,
Desiring thee that Publius Cimber may
Have an immediate freedom of repeal.

CAESAR What, Brutus?

CASSIUS   Pardon, Caesar! Caesar, pardon!   55
As low as to thy foot doth Cassius fall
To beg enfranchisement for Publius Cimber.

CAESAR I could be well moved, if I were as you;
If I could pray to move, prayers would move me.
But I am constant as the northern star,   60
Of whose true-fixed and resting quality
There is no fellow in the firmament.
The skies are painted with unnumbered sparks,
They are all fire, and every one doth shine;
But there's but one in all doth hold his place.   65
So in the world: 'tis furnished well with men,
And men are flesh and blood, and apprehensive;
Yet in the number I do know but one
That unassailable holds on his rank,
Unshaked of motion, and that I am he   70
Let me a little show it, even in this:
That I was constant Cimber should be banished,
And constant do remain to keep him so.

CINNA O Caesar –

CAESAR   Hence! Wilt thou lift up Olympus?

47–8 wrong ... satisfied] F; wrong, but with just cause, / Nor ... satisfied. *conj. Pope after* wrong *at* 3.2.102; *Hudson*[2] *(conj. Tyrwhitt apud Steevens*[2]*)*   61 true-fixed] *Hyphen, Capell (Capell MS.); true fixt,* F; *true, fixt, Rowe*   69 rank] F; race [*i.e.* course] *conj. Johnson*   74–5] *Steevens*[3] *(Capell MS.); Cinna ... Caesar. / ... Olympus? / ... Caesar. / ... kneele?* F; *Cin. ... Olympus? / ... Caesar, – / ... kneel? Hudson*

46 **spurn** kick.
51 **repealing** recalling from exile.
54 **freedom of repeal** permission to be recalled from banishment.
57 **enfranchisement** restoration of the rights of citizenship.
59 **pray to move** entreat others to do what I ask.
61 **true** sure, secure.
61 **resting** remaining stationary.
62 **no fellow** no comparable star.

63 **unnumbered** innumerable.
65 **his** its.
67 **apprehensive** susceptible to mental or sensuous impressions, i.e. capable of being affected by arguments or emotions.
70 **of** by.
70 **motion** impulses or external forces.
74 **Olympus** Mount Olympus, the highest mountain in Greece. In Greek mythology, Olympus was home to the gods.

DECIUS Great Caesar –
CAESAR   Doth not Brutus bootless kneel?   75
CASCA Speak hands for me!

They stab Caesar

CAESAR *Et tu, Brute?* – Then fall, Caesar!   *Dies*
CINNA Liberty! Freedom! Tyranny is dead!
    Run hence, proclaim, cry it about the streets.
CASSIUS Some to the common pulpits, and cry out,   80
    'Liberty, freedom, and enfranchisement!'
BRUTUS People and senators, be not affrighted,
    Fly not, stand still! Ambition's debt is paid.
CASCA Go to the pulpit, Brutus.
DECIUS   And Cassius too.
BRUTUS Where's Publius?   85
CINNA Here, quite confounded with this mutiny.
METELLUS Stand fast together lest some friend of Caesar's
    Should chance –
BRUTUS Talk not of standing. Publius, good cheer,
    There is no harm intended to your person,   90
    Nor to no Roman else. So tell them, Publius.
CASSIUS And leave us, Publius, lest that the people,
    Rushing on us, should do your age some mischief.
BRUTUS Do so, and let no man abide this deed
    But we the doers.   95

                  [*Exeunt all but the conspirators*]

Enter TREBONIUS

CASSIUS Where is Antony?
TREBONIUS   Fled to his house amazed.
    Men, wives, and children stare, cry out, and run
    As it were doomsday.

---

75 Doth] F; Do F2   76–7] *As one line, Keightley*   76 Speak hands] F; Speak, hands, *Capell (Capell MS.)*   77 fall,]
QU4; fall F   84–5] *Steevens³; Cask. ... Brutus. / ... too. / ... Publius? F;* CASCA ... Brutus. / ... Publius?
Bevington   95 SD.1] *Capell; at 77, Knight; at 82, Wells and Taylor*   95–6] *Steevens³;* But ... Doers. / ... Trebonius. /
... Antony?/ ... amaz'd: F; But ... Antony? / ... amaz'd: *Knight*

  75 **bootless** uselessly.
  77 *Et tu, Brute?* Latin: 'You too, Brutus?'
  80 **common** public.
  80 **pulpits** scaffolds, stages, or platforms for

public representations, speeches, or disputations.
  86 **confounded with** thrown into confusion by.
  94 **abide** suffer the consequences for (see
OED 17).

BRUTUS   Fates, we will know your pleasures.
        That we shall die we know: 'tis but the time,
        And drawing days out, that men stand upon.   100
CASCA Why, he that cuts off twenty years of life
        Cuts off so many years of fearing death.
BRUTUS Grant that, and then is death a benefit.
        So are we Caesar's friends, that have abridged
        His time of fearing death. Stoop, Romans, stoop,   105
        And let us bathe our hands in Caesar's blood
        Up to the elbows and besmear our swords.
        Then walk we forth, even to the market-place,
        And waving our red weapons o'er our heads
        Let's all cry, 'Peace, freedom, and liberty!'   110
CASSIUS Stoop then and wash. How many ages hence
        Shall this our lofty scene be acted over
        In states unborn and accents yet unknown!
BRUTUS How many times shall Caesar bleed in sport,
        That now on Pompey's basis lies along   115
        No worthier than the dust!
CASSIUS   So oft as that shall be,
        So often shall the knot of us be called
        The men that gave their country liberty.
DECIUS What, shall we forth?
CASSIUS   Ay, every man away.
        Brutus shall lead, and we will grace his heels   120
        With the most boldest and best hearts of Rome.

                        Enter a SERVANT

BRUTUS Soft, who comes here? A friend of Antony's.
SERVANT Thus, Brutus, did my master bid me kneel,
        Thus did Mark Antony bid me fall down,
        And, being prostrate, thus he bade me say: 125
        Brutus is noble, wise, valiant, and honest;

---

101 SH CASCA] *Cask.* F; *Cas.* / *Pope*   105–10 Stoop ... liberty] *Assigned to Brutus,* F; *to Casca, Pope*   113 states] F2;
State F   113 accents] F; Nations QU4   114 SH BRUTUS] F; *Casc.* / *Pope*   115 lies] F2; lye F   116 SH CASSIUS] F;
Bru. / *Pope*   118 their] F; our *Malone*

100 **drawing days out** prolonging life.   111 **wash** not 'cleanse' but 'immerse' (hands and
100 **stand upon** attach importance to. See   swords).
2.2.13 n.   115 **Pompey's basis** the pedestal of Pompey's
108 **market-place** i.e. the Forum: the place of   statue.
assembly for all public business.   117 **knot** tightly knit group.

Caesar was mighty, bold, royal, and loving.
Say I love Brutus, and I honour him;
Say I feared Caesar, honoured him, and loved him.
If Brutus will vouchsafe that Antony   130
May safely come to him and be resolved
How Caesar hath deserved to lie in death,
Mark Antony shall not love Caesar dead
So well as Brutus living, but will follow
The fortunes and affairs of noble Brutus   135
Through the hazards of this untrod state
With all true faith. So says my master Antony.

BRUTUS Thy master is a wise and valiant Roman,
I never thought him worse.
Tell him, so please him come unto this place,   140
He shall be satisfied and by my honour
Depart untouched.

SERVANT   I'll fetch him presently.   *Exit Servant*

BRUTUS I know that we shall have him well to friend.

CASSIUS I wish we may. But yet have I a mind
That fears him much, and my misgiving still   145
Falls shrewdly to the purpose.

Enter ANTONY

BRUTUS But here comes Antony. Welcome, Mark Antony!

ANTONY O mighty Caesar! Dost thou lie so low?
Are all thy conquests, glories, triumphs, spoils
Shrunk to this little measure? Fare thee well!   150
I know not, gentlemen, what you intend,
Who else must be let blood, who else is rank.
If I myself, there is no hour so fit

147] *Pope (Folger MS.); But ... Antony: / ... Antony.* F

127 royal Since Caesar was never crowned,
Antony probably intends this word to mean
'noble' or 'generous' in a general way (see *OED*
6a). But the sense 'having the rank of king' (*OED*
4b) is probably present as well, i.e. Antony is implying that Caesar was worthy to be crowned. See also
3.2.234.
　130 vouchsafe grant.
　131 resolved satisfied, convinced. See also
3.2.170.
　136 untrod state unprecedented state of affairs.

143 well to friend as a good friend.
　145–6 my ... purpose my fears usually turn out
to be well founded.
　152 be let blood be put to death. This is
a medical metaphor: physicians in Shakespeare's
time endeavoured to cure a variety of ailments by
draining a quantity of the patient's blood. Antony
imagines the conspirators as doctors trying to purge
an infection.
　152 rank swollen (see *OED adj* 8b) or festering
and rotten (see *OED adj* 12).

As Caesar's death's hour, nor no instrument
Of half that worth as those your swords made rich   155
With the most noble blood of all this world.
I do beseech ye, if you bear me hard,
Now, whilst your purpled hands do reek and smoke,
Fulfil your pleasure. Live a thousand years,
I shall not find myself so apt to die: 160
No place will please me so, no mean of death,
As here by Caesar, and by you cut off,
The choice and master spirits of this age.

BRUTUS O Antony, beg not your death of us.
Though now we must appear bloody and cruel,   165
As by our hands and this our present act
You see we do, yet see you but our hands
And this the bleeding business they have done.
Our hearts you see not, they are pitiful;
And pity to the general wrong of Rome –   170
As fire drives out fire, so pity pity –
Hath done this deed on Caesar. For your part,
To you our swords have leaden points, Mark Antony;
Our arms in strength of malice, and our hearts
Of brothers' temper, do receive you in   175
With all kind love, good thoughts, and reverence.

CASSIUS Your voice shall be as strong as any man's
In the disposing of new dignities.

BRUTUS Only be patient till we have appeased
The multitude, beside themselves with fear,   180
And then we will deliver you the cause

---

154 death's] deaths F; death QU2   174 in strength of malice] F; no strength of malice *Thomas Johnson*; exempt from malice *Pope*; in strength of welcome *Collier² (Collier MS.)*; in strength of manhood *Collier⁴*; in strength of amity *Hudson²* *(conj. Singer apud Hudson²)*; unstrung of malice *Wells and Taylor (after Badham,* unstring their malice*)*

157 bear me hard feel ill will towards me. See 1.2.302 n.

158 purpled blood-stained.

158 reek and smoke Now Antony is imagining the conspirators as having removed the warm entrails from a sacrificial beast. *Reek* is both synonymous with *smoke* (see *OED* 1) and a word descriptive of 'freshly shed blood, or of things stained or soaked with this' (*OED* 2b).

159 Live ... years if I should live a thousand years.

160 apt ready.

161 mean means.

169 pitiful full of pity.

171 Proverbial (Dent F277, P369.1): 'One fire drives out another'; 'Pity destroys pity.'

174 in strength of malice having sufficient power to do harm.

175 Of brothers' temper with the mild feelings brothers might have towards one another. *Temper* is also a word of weapons: the *temper* of a sword is its 'particular degree of hardness and elasticity or resiliency' (*OED* 5).

178 disposing ... dignities conferring of new political offices.

Why I, that did love Caesar when I struck him,
Have thus proceeded.

ANTONY   I doubt not of your wisdom.
Let each man render me his bloody hand.
First, Marcus Brutus, will I shake with you;   185
Next, Caius Cassius, do I take your hand;
Now, Decius Brutus, yours; now yours, Metellus;
Yours, Cinna; and, my valiant Casca, yours;
Though last, not least in love, yours, good Trebonius.
Gentlemen all – alas, what shall I say?   190
My credit now stands on such slippery ground
That one of two bad ways you must conceit me,
Either a coward or a flatterer.
That I did love thee, Caesar, O, 'tis true.
If then thy spirit look upon us now,   195
Shall it not grieve thee dearer than thy death
To see thy Antony making his peace,
Shaking the bloody fingers of thy foes –
Most noble – in the presence of thy corse?
Had I as many eyes as thou hast wounds,   200
Weeping as fast as they stream forth thy blood,
It would become me better than to close
In terms of friendship with thine enemies.
Pardon me, Julius! Here wast thou bayed, brave hart,
Here didst thou fall, and here thy hunters stand,   205
Signed in thy spoil and crimsoned in thy Lethe.
O world! Thou wast the forest to this hart,
And this indeed, O world, the heart of thee.
How like a deer strucken by many princes
Dost thou here lie!   210

CASSIUS Mark Antony –
ANTONY   Pardon me, Caius Cassius,
The enemies of Caesar shall say this;
Then, in a friend, it is cold modesty.

---

204 hart] F; Heart F2   206 Lethe] F; death *Pope*   208 heart] *Theobald*; Hart F

192 **conceit** imagine, think of.
196 **dearer** more deeply.
201 **they** i.e. your wounds.
202 **close** come together.
204 **bayed** brought to bay, i.e. cornered and killed. This is a hunting term, usually referring to a deer being set upon by a pack of dogs.

204 **hart** stag. With a pun on *heart*.
206 **Signed ... spoil** marked with the signs of your slaughter.
206 **Lethe** the river in Hades whose waters, when drunk, caused forgetfulness of the past. It is equated here with Caesar's life-blood.
213 **modesty** moderation.

CASSIUS I blame you not for praising Caesar so,
    But what compact mean you to have with us?   215
    Will you be pricked in number of our friends,
    Or shall we on and not depend on you?
ANTONY Therefore I took your hands, but was indeed
    Swayed from the point by looking down on Caesar.
    Friends am I with you all, and love you all,   220
    Upon this hope, that you shall give me reasons
    Why and wherein Caesar was dangerous.
BRUTUS Or else were this a savage spectacle.
    Our reasons are so full of good regard
    That were you, Antony, the son of Caesar   225
    You should be satisfied.
ANTONY   That's all I seek,
    And am, moreover, suitor that I may
    Produce his body to the market-place,
    And in the pulpit, as becomes a friend,
    Speak in the order of his funeral.   230
BRUTUS You shall, Mark Antony.
CASSIUS   Brutus, a word with you.
    [*Aside to Brutus*] You know not what you do. Do not consent
    That Antony speak in his funeral.
    Know you how much the people may be moved
    By that which he will utter?
BRUTUS [*Aside to Cassius*]   By your pardon,   235
    I will myself into the pulpit first
    And show the reason of our Caesar's death.
    What Antony shall speak, I will protest
    He speaks by leave and by permission,
    And that we are contented Caesar shall   240
    Have all true rites and lawful ceremonies.
    It shall advantage more than do us wrong.

---

225 you,] Q (1691); you F **232** SD] *Rowe* **235** utter?] Q (1684); vtter. F **235** SD] *Capell* **241** true] F; due
Pope **241** ceremonies.] *Rowe (subst.);* Ceremonies, F

215 compact agreement.
216 pricked marked (as by a *prick*, or tick, in a list). See also 4.1.1.
223 Or else were this otherwise this would merely be.

230 order prescribed form of ceremony or rite. See also 'ordered', 5.5.79.
238 protest declare.
242 It shall … more It shall be more to our advantage.

CASSIUS [*Aside to Brutus*] I know not what may fall, I like it not.
BRUTUS Mark Antony, here take you Caesar's body.
    You shall not in your funeral speech blame us,   245
    But speak all good you can devise of Caesar
    And say you do't by our permission,
    Else shall you not have any hand at all
    About his funeral. And you shall speak
    In the same pulpit whereto I am going,   250
    After my speech is ended.
ANTONY   Be it so,
    I do desire no more.
BRUTUS Prepare the body then and follow us.

                                    Exeunt [all but] Antony

ANTONY O, pardon me, thou bleeding piece of earth,
    That I am meek and gentle with these butchers!   255
    Thou art the ruins of the noblest man
    That ever livèd in the tide of times.
    Woe to the hand that shed this costly blood!
    Over thy wounds now do I prophesy –
    Which like dumb mouths do ope their ruby lips   260
    To beg the voice and utterance of my tongue –
    A curse shall light upon the limbs of men:
    Domestic fury and fierce civil strife
    Shall cumber all the parts of Italy;
    Blood and destruction shall be so in use   265
    And dreadful objects so familiar
    That mothers shall but smile when they behold
    Their infants quartered with the hands of war,
    All pity choked with custom of fell deeds;
    And Caesar's spirit, ranging for revenge,   270

---

243 SD] *Capell* 244 here] F; here, Q (1691) 251–2] *Steevens*³ *(Capell MS.)*; After … ended. / … so:/ … more.
F 254 SH ANTONY] Q (1691) 254 bleeding piece of] F; piece of bleeding *Reed* 258 hand] F; hands *White*
(conj. Thirlby) 262 limbs] F; kind *Hanmer*; line *Warburton*; lymms *conj. Johnson*; loines *Collier²* *(Collier MS.)*; lives
Dyce (conj. Johnson); tombs *conj. Staunton*; sonnes *conj. White*; heads *conj. John Hunter*; minds *Dyce²* *(conj. Jervis)*; times
conj. Walker

    243 **fall** befall, happen. See also 5.1.104.
    257 **times** history.
    258 **costly blood** blood whose shedding will
carry a great cost.
    260 **dumb** mute.

    264 **cumber** overwhelm.
    265 **so in use** so common.
    268 **quartered with** cut into pieces by.
    269 **custom … deeds** the regular occurrence of
cruel acts.

With Ate by his side come hot from hell,
Shall in these confines with a monarch's voice
Cry havoc and let slip the dogs of war,
That this foul deed shall smell above the earth
With carrion men groaning for burial.   275

Enter Octavio's SERVANT

You serve Octavius Caesar, do you not?
SERVANT I do, Mark Antony.
ANTONY Caesar did write for him to come to Rome.
SERVANT He did receive his letters, and is coming,
And bid me say to you by word of mouth–   280
[*Seeing the body*]
O Caesar!
ANTONY Thy heart is big, get thee apart and weep.
Passion, I see, is catching, for mine eyes,
Seeing those beads of sorrow stand in thine,
Began to water. Is thy master coming?   285
SERVANT He lies tonight within seven leagues of Rome.
ANTONY Post back with speed and tell him what hath chanced.
Here is a mourning Rome, a dangerous Rome,
No Rome of safety for Octavius yet:
Hie hence and tell him so. Yet stay awhile,   290
Thou shalt not back till I have borne this corse
Into the market-place. There shall I try
In my oration how the people take
The cruel issue of these bloody men,
According to the which thou shalt discourse   295
To young Octavius of the state of things.
Lend me your hand.

Exeunt [*with Caesar's body*]

---

275 SD Octavio's] F; Octavius's QU3   280 SD] *Rowe*   283 catching, for] F2; catching from F   285 Began] F; Begin QUI   287] *Rowe*; Post ... speede, / ... chanc'd: F   291 corse] Coarse F3; course F   297 SD *with Caesar's body*] *Rowe*

271 **Ate** in mythology, the daughter of Strife and sister of Lawlessness; a symbol of infatuation or moral blindness. Shakespeare equates her with discord, as in *John* 2.1.63.
272 **in these confines** within our borders. Antony is imagining civil war.
273 **havoc** destruction; originally, to give an army the order 'Havoc!' was the signal for soldiers to begin pillaging.
273 **let slip** unleash. A slip is a leash so

contrived that the dog can be readily released.
275 **carrion** dead and rotting.
286 **leagues** A league is a measurement of about 3 miles.
288 **Rome** For possible wordplay on 'room', see 1.2.156 n.
291 **corse** corpse.
292 **try** attempt to find out, test. See also 4.3.214, 5.3.110.
294 **cruel issue of** cruelty wrought by.

3.2 *Enter* BRUTUS *and Cassius with the* PLEBEIANS

ALL We will be satisfied! Let us be satisfied!
BRUTUS Then follow me and give me audience, friends.
          Cassius, go you into the other street
          And part the numbers.
          Those that will hear me speak, let 'em stay here;   5
          Those that will follow Cassius, go with him;
          And public reasons shall be renderèd
          Of Caesar's death.
1 PLEBEIAN   I will hear Brutus speak.
2 PLEBEIAN I will hear Cassius and compare their reasons
          When severally we hear them renderèd.   10
                    [*Exit Cassius with some of the Plebeians*]
                    [*Brutus goes into the pulpit*]
3 PLEBEIAN The noble Brutus is ascended, silence!
BRUTUS Be patient till the last.
          Romans, countrymen, and lovers, hear me for my cause, and be silent
          that you may hear. Believe me for mine honour, and have respect to
          mine honour that you may believe. Censure me in your wisdom, and   15
          awake your senses that you may the better judge. If there be any in this
          assembly, any dear friend of Caesar's, to him I say that Brutus' love to
          Caesar was no less than his. If then that friend demand why Brutus
          rose against Caesar, this is my answer: not that I loved Caesar less,
          but that I loved Rome more. Had you rather Caesar were living, and   20
          die all slaves, than that Caesar were dead, to live all freemen? As
          Caesar loved me, I weep for him; as he was fortunate, I rejoice at it; as
          he was valiant, I honour him; but, as he was ambitious, I slew him.
          There is tears for his love, joy for his fortune, honour for his valour,
          and death for his ambition. Who is here so base that would be a   25
          bondman? If any, speak, for him have I offended. Who is here so rude
          that would not be a Roman? If any, speak, for him have I offended.
          Who is here so vile that will not love his country? If any, speak, for him
          have I offended. I pause for a reply.

Act 3, Scene 2 3.2] *Rowe* Location] *Rowe* 10 SD.1 *Exit … Plebeians*] *Capell;* 10 SD.2 *Brutus … pulpit*] F (*at
0 SD*) 21 freemen] Q (1691); Free-men F; free men F2

Act 3, Scene 2
Location Rome. The Forum.
  4 part the numbers divide the crowd.
  10 severally separately, each in turn. See also
2.4.46 SD.

  13 lovers friends, well-wishers.
  14 have respect to consider, heed. See also
4.3.69.
  15 Censure judge (not necessarily negative in
connotation).
  26 rude ignorant.

ALL None, Brutus, none.   30

BRUTUS Then none have I offended. I have done no more to Caesar than
you shall do to Brutus. The question of his death is enrolled in the
Capitol, his glory not extenuated wherein he was worthy, nor his
offences enforced for which he suffered death.

Enter MARK ANTONY [*and others*] *with Caesar's body*

Here comes his body, mourned by Mark Antony, who, though he had   35
no hand in his death, shall receive the benefit of his dying, a place in
the commonwealth, as which of you shall not? With this I depart: that,
as I slew my best lover for the good of Rome, I have the same dagger
for myself when it shall please my country to need my death.

[*Comes down*]

ALL Live, Brutus, live, live!   40

1 PLEBEIAN Bring him with triumph home unto his house.

2 PLEBEIAN Give him a statue with his ancestors.

3 PLEBEIAN Let him be Caesar.

4 PLEBEIAN   Caesar's better parts
Shall be crowned in Brutus.

1 PLEBEIAN   We'll bring him to his house
With shouts and clamours.

BRUTUS   My countrymen –   45

2 PLEBEIAN Peace, silence, Brutus speaks!

1 PLEBEIAN   Peace ho!

BRUTUS Good countrymen, let me depart alone,
And, for my sake, stay here with Antony.
Do grace to Caesar's corpse, and grace his speech
Tending to Caesar's glories, which Mark Antony   50
(By our permission) is allowed to make.
I do entreat you, not a man depart,
Save I alone, till Antony have spoke.   *Exit*

---

34 SD *and others*] Malone (*after Capell*)   39 SD] Capell   42, 43 SH 2 PLEBEIAN . . . 4 PLEBEIAN] F; *on the assumption that the 'actual' Second Plebeian has left at* 10 *to hear Cassius, Humphreys substitutes* FOURTH *for* SECOND *and* FIFTH *for* FOURTH *throughout the rest of the scene. In 3.3, however, he reverts to* F's *four Plebeians. Bevington retains the 'arbitrary' numbering but notes, 'Not the same person who exited at l.10'*   42 ancestors] F; *ancestor's conj, Velz (privately)*   43–6] *Globe; 3. . . . Caesar. / . . . parts, / . . . Brutus. / . . . House, / . . . Clamors. / . . . Country-men. / . . . speakes. / . . . ho.* F; *3 Pleb. . . . Caesar. / . . . parts / . . . Brutus. / . . . clamours.* QU4; *3.* CIT. . . . *parts / . . . Brutus. / . . . clamours. / . . . speakes. / . . . ho!* Steevens[3]

---

32 The question … enrolled The reasons for
which we killed him have been recorded (i.e. written upon a roll of parchment).

34 enforced put forward (too) strongly,

emphasised.

38 best lover the man I loved best of all.

50 Tending giving attention to. See
1.2.307.

1 PLEBEIAN Stay ho, and let us hear Mark Antony.

3 PLEBEIAN Let him go up into the public chair,   55
       We'll hear him. Noble Antony, go up.

ANTONY For Brutus' sake, I am beholding to you.
                 [*Goes into the pulpit*]

4 PLEBEIAN What does he say of Brutus?

3 PLEBEIAN   He says for Brutus' sake
       He finds himself beholding to us all.

4 PLEBEIAN 'Twere best he speak no harm of Brutus here!   60

1 PLEBEIAN This Caesar was a tyrant.

3 PLEBEIAN   Nay, that's certain:
       We are blest that Rome is rid of him.

2 PLEBEIAN Peace, let us hear what Antony can say.

ANTONY You gentle Romans –

ALL   Peace ho, let us hear him.

ANTONY Friends, Romans, countrymen, lend me your ears!   65
       I come to bury Caesar, not to praise him.
       The evil that men do lives after them,
       The good is oft interrèd with their bones:
       So let it be with Caesar. The noble Brutus
       Hath told you Caesar was ambitious;   70
       If it were so, it was a grievous fault,
       And grievously hath Caesar answered it.
       Here, under leave of Brutus and the rest –
       For Brutus is an honourable man,
       So are they all, all honourable men –   75
       Come I to speak in Caesar's funeral.
       He was my friend, faithful and just to me,
       But Brutus says he was ambitious,
       And Brutus is an honourable man.
       He hath brought many captives home to Rome,   80
       Whose ransoms did the general coffers fill;
       Did this in Caesar seem ambitious?
       When that the poor have cried, Caesar hath wept:
       Ambition should be made of sterner stuff;
       Yet Brutus says he was ambitious,   85

---

57 SD] *Globe (after Capell/goes up)*   62 blest] F; *glad* F2   64 SH ALL] F; SECOND PLEBEIAN *Sanders*

55 **public chair** pulpit.   81 **general coffers** public treasury.
57, 59 **beholding** beholden, obligated.   83 **When that** When.
73 **under leave** by permission.

And Brutus is an honourable man.
You all did see that on the Lupercal
I thrice presented him a kingly crown,
Which he did thrice refuse. Was this ambition?
Yet Brutus says he was ambitious,   90
And sure he is an honourable man.
I speak not to disprove what Brutus spoke,
But here I am to speak what I do know.
You all did love him once, not without cause;
What cause withholds you then to mourn for him?   95
O judgement, thou art fled to brutish beasts,
And men have lost their reason! Bear with me,
My heart is in the coffin there with Caesar,
And I must pause till it come back to me.

1 PLEBEIAN Methinks there is much reason in his sayings.   100

2 PLEBEIAN If thou consider rightly of the matter,
    Caesar has had great wrong.

3 PLEBEIAN   Has he, masters!
    I fear there will a worse come in his place.

4 PLEBEIAN Marked ye his words? He would not take the crown,
    Therefore 'tis certain he was not ambitious.   105

1 PLEBEIAN If it be found so, some will dear abide it.

2 PLEBEIAN Poor soul, his eyes are red as fire with weeping.

3 PLEBEIAN There's not a nobler man in Rome than Antony.

4 PLEBEIAN Now mark him, he begins again to speak.

ANTONY But yesterday the word of Caesar might   110
    Have stood against the world; now lies he there,
    And none so poor to do him reverence.
    O masters, if I were disposed to stir
    Your hearts and minds to mutiny and rage,
    I should do Brutus wrong and Cassius wrong,   115
    Who (you all know) are honourable men.
    I will not do them wrong; I rather choose
    To wrong the dead, to wrong myself and you,

---

96 art] F2; are F   96 beasts] F; Breasts QU4   102 Has he] Ha's hee F; Has he my *Capell (conj. Thirlby);* Has he not
Craik; That has he *Mark Hunter (conj. Morley apud Mark Hunter);* Ha! has he *conj. Anon. (apud Cam.)*   102–3] *As verse,*
Steevens³ (Capell MS.); as prose (turnover), F

96 **brutish** possibly a pun on Latin 'brutus'   106 **abide** pay for. See also 3.1.94 n.
(= 'dull', 'without reason') and the name   112 **none so poor** 'The meanest man is now too
'Brutus'.   high' (Johnson).

Than I will wrong such honourable men.
But here's a parchment with the seal of Caesar,   120
I found it in his closet, 'tis his will.
Let but the commons hear this testament –
Which, pardon me, I do not mean to read –
And they would go and kiss dead Caesar's wounds
And dip their napkins in his sacred blood,   125
Yea, beg a hair of him for memory,
And, dying, mention it within their wills,
Bequeathing it as a rich legacy
Unto their issue.

4 PLEBEIAN We'll hear the will. Read it, Mark Antony.   130
ALL The will, the will, we will hear Caesar's will!
ANTONY Have patience, gentle friends, I must not read it.
It is not meet you know how Caesar loved you:
You are not wood, you are not stones, but men,
And, being men, hearing the will of Caesar,   135
It will inflame you, it will make you mad.
'Tis good you know not that you are his heirs,
For if you should, O, what would come of it?

4 PLEBEIAN Read the will, we'll hear it, Antony.
You shall read us the will, Caesar's will!   140
ANTONY Will you be patient? Will you stay awhile?
I have o'ershot myself to tell you of it.
I fear I wrong the honourable men
Whose daggers have stabbed Caesar, I do fear it.

4 PLEBEIAN They were traitors. Honourable men!   145
ALL The will! The testament!
2 PLEBEIAN They were villains, murderers! The will, read the will!
ANTONY You will compel me then to read the will?
Then make a ring about the corpse of Caesar
And let me show you him that made the will.   150
Shall I descend? And will you give me leave?

ALL Come down.

---

126 Yea] F; Nay *Capell*   145–6] F; *as one verse line, Keightley*   146–7] F; ALL … villains, / … Read the will! S. F.
Johnson²   147] *As prose,* F; *as verse, splitting after* murderers, *Irving; as one verse line, Craig*   148 will?] *Pope;* Will:
F   152–5] F; *Cit* … ring;/ … round. *Keightley (conj. Thirlby)*

121 **closet** private room, as at 2.1.35.   121 **issue** children.
122 **commons** people.   142 **o'ershot myself** gone too far.
125 **napkins** handkerchiefs.

2 PLEBEIAN Descend.

3 PLEBEIAN You shall have leave.

[*Antony comes down from the pulpit*]

4 PLEBEIAN A ring, stand round.   155

1 PLEBEIAN Stand from the hearse, stand from the body.

2 PLEBEIAN Room for Antony, most noble Antony.

ANTONY Nay, press not so upon me, stand far off.

ALL Stand back! Room, bear back!

ANTONY If you have tears, prepare to shed them now.   160
    You all do know this mantle. I remember
    The first time ever Caesar put it on,
    'Twas on a summer's evening, in his tent,
    That day he overcame the Nervii.
    Look, in this place ran Cassius' dagger through;   165
    See what a rent the envious Casca made;
    Through this the well-belovèd Brutus stabbed,
    And as he plucked his cursèd steel away,
    Mark how the blood of Caesar followed it,
    As rushing out of doors to be resolved   170
    If Brutus so unkindly knocked or no,
    For Brutus, as you know, was Caesar's angel.
    Judge, O you gods, how dearly Caesar loved him!
    This was the most unkindest cut of all.
    For when the noble Caesar saw him stab,   175
    Ingratitude, more strong than traitors' arms,
    Quite vanquished him. Then burst his mighty heart,
    And, in his mantle muffling up his face,
    Even at the base of Pompey's statue
    (Which all the while ran blood) great Caesar fell.   180
    O, what a fall was there, my countrymen!
    Then I, and you, and all of us fell down,
    Whilst bloody treason flourished over us.
    O, now you weep, and I perceive you feel

152–5] F; *Cit* ... ring;/ ... round. *Keightley (conj. Thirlby)*   154 SD] *Rowe (after 161)*   174 cut] F; act *Folger MS.*

156 **Stand from** stand back from.

156 **hearse** bier.

161 **mantle** cloak.

164 **Nervii** a mixed Celto-German tribe, occupying territory in what is now central Belgium. They were defeated by Caesar in

57 BC.

166 **rent** tear, gash.

170–1 **As rushing … If Brutus** as if it were rushing out of his body to see if it was really Brutus who.

170 **resolved** satisfied, convinced; as at 3.1.131.

The dint of pity. These are gracious drops.   185
Kind souls, what weep you when you but behold
Our Caesar's vesture wounded? Look you here,
Here is himself, marred as you see with traitors.

1 PLEBEIAN O piteous spectacle!

2 PLEBEIAN O noble Caesar!   190

3 PLEBEIAN O woeful day!

4 PLEBEIAN O traitors, villains!

1 PLEBEIAN O most bloody sight!

2 PLEBEIAN We will be revenged!

ALL Revenge! About! Seek! Burn! Fire! Kill!   195
Slay! Let not a traitor live!

ANTONY Stay, countrymen.

1 PLEBEIAN Peace there, hear the noble Antony.

2 PLEBEIAN We'll hear him, we'll follow him, we'll die with him.

ANTONY Good friends, sweet friends, let me not stir you up   200
To such a sudden flood of mutiny.
They that have done this deed are honourable.
What private griefs they have, alas, I know not,
That made them do it. They are wise and honourable,
And will no doubt with reasons answer you.   205
I come not, friends, to steal away your hearts.
I am no orator, as Brutus is,
But – as you know me all – a plain blunt man
That love my friend, and that they know full well
That gave me public leave to speak of him.   210
For I have neither wit, nor words, nor worth,
Action, nor utterance, nor the power of speech
To stir men's blood. I only speak right on.
I tell you that which you yourselves do know,
Show you sweet Caesar's wounds, poor, poor, dumb mouths,   215
And bid them speak for me. But were I Brutus,
And Brutus Antony, there were an Antony

186 what] F; what, *Pope*   189–98] F; 1 *Cit.* . . . Caesar! / . . . sight! / . . . burn,– / . . . live. / . . . Antony. *Keightley. There are numerous attempts to make verse of all or some of these lines*   194–6] *As prose, Pope; as verse,* We . . . Reuenge / . ., slay, / . . . liue. F   195 SHALL] *Collier²* (*Collier MS.*)   199] F; *as verse, Johnson²*   205 reasons] F; Reason QU4   210 gave] F; give F2   211 wit] F2; writ F

185 **dint** blow; especially one given with a weapon.
188 **with** by.

195 **About** Get to work, bestir yourself (Onions); an imperative use.
203 **griefs** grievances; as at 1.3.118.

Would ruffle up your spirits and put a tongue
In every wound of Caesar, that should move
The stones of Rome to rise and mutiny.   220
ALL We'll mutiny.
1 PLEBEIAN   We'll burn the house of Brutus.
3 PLEBEIAN Away then, come, seek the conspirators.
ANTONY Yet hear me, countrymen, yet hear me speak.
ALL Peace ho, hear Antony, most noble Antony!
ANTONY Why, friends, you go to do you know not what.   225
       Wherein hath Caesar thus deserved your loves?
       Alas, you know not! I must tell you then:
       You have forgot the will I told you of.
ALL Most true. The will, let's stay and hear the will!
ANTONY Here is the will, and under Caesar's seal: 230
       To every Roman citizen he gives,
       To every several man, seventy-five drachmaes.
2 PLEBEIAN Most noble Caesar, we'll revenge his death!
3 PLEBEIAN O royal Caesar!
ANTONY Hear me with patience.   235
ALL Peace ho!
ANTONY Moreover, he hath left you all his walks,
       His private arbours and new-planted orchards,
       On this side Tiber; he hath left them you,
       And to your heirs for ever – common pleasures,   240
       To walk abroad and recreate yourselves.
       Here was a Caesar! When comes such another?
1 PLEBEIAN Never, never! Come, away, away!
       We'll burn his body in the holy place
       And with the brands fire the traitors' houses.   245
       Take up the body.
2 PLEBEIAN Go fetch fire!
3 PLEBEIAN Pluck down benches!

234–6] F; *as one line, Keightley;* O . . . patience. / . . . ho! *Bevington*   **239** this] F; *that Theobald (after Plutarch)*   **245** fire]
F; *fire all* F2   **246–9**] F; *as* F, *adding* The *before* benches *as separate line, Capell;* Take . . . benches. / . . . thing.
Keightley

218 ruffle up stir up to indignation or rage.
230 under Caesar's seal authorised by Caesar
himself.
232 drachmaes silver coins.
234 royal noble, generous; as at 3.1.127.
239 this side Tiber this side of the Tiber.
240 common pleasures gardens (pleasure

grounds) for public enjoyment.
244 burn his body Burning on a pyre or *rogus*
was the general burial practice. Plutarch reports
that, after Caesar's funeral, the people 'plucked up
forms, tables, and stools, and laid them all about the
body [of Caesar], and setting them afire burnt the
corse' (Appendix, p. 155).

4 PLEBEIAN Pluck down forms, windows, anything!

                                    Exeunt Plebeians [with the body]

ANTONY Now let it work. Mischief, thou art afoot,   250
    Take thou what course thou wilt!

                        Enter SERVANT

                          How now, fellow?

SERVANT Sir, Octavius is already come to Rome.

ANTONY Where is he?

SERVANT He and Lepidus are at Caesar's house.

ANTONY And thither will I straight to visit him.   255
    He comes upon a wish. Fortune is merry,
    And in this mood will give us anything.

SERVANT I heard him say Brutus and Cassius
    Are rid like madmen through the gates of Rome.

ANTONY Belike they had some notice of the people,   260
    How I had moved them. Bring me to Octavius.

                                                Exeunt

3.3 *Enter* CINNA THE POET, *and after him the* PLEBEIANS

CINNA THE POET I dreamt tonight that I did feast with Caesar,
    And things unluckily charge my fantasy.
    I have no will to wander forth of doors,
    Yet something leads me forth.

1 PLEBEIAN What is your name?   5

2 PLEBEIAN Whither are you going?

3 PLEBEIAN Where do you dwell?

4 PLEBEIAN Are you a married man or a bachelor?

2 PLEBEIAN Answer every man directly.

1 PLEBEIAN Ay, and briefly.   10

4 PLEBEIAN Ay, and wisely.

---

249 SD *with the body*] *Rowe*   251 Take thou] F; Take now *conj. Craik;* Take then *conj. Anon. (apud Cam.)*   258 him] F; them *Capell*   Act 3, Scene 3   3.3] *Capell*   Location *Capell (Capell MS.)*   2 unluckily] F; unluckey *Warburton (Folger MS.);* unlikely *Collier*[2] *(Collier MS.)*   5–12] F; *1 Cit* ... dwell? / ... bachelor? / ... briefly. / ... best. *Keightley*

249 **forms** probably 'benches' (see *OED* 17), but possibly 'window frames' (*OED* 19a) as well.

256 **upon a wish** at just the moment I would wish.

Act 3, Scene 3
Location Rome. A street.

2 **unluckily ... fantasy** burden my imagination with ill omens.

3 **of** out of.

3 PLEBEIAN Ay, and truly, you were best.

CINNA THE POET What is my name? Whither am I going? Where do I
    dwell? Am I a married man or a bachelor? Then to answer every man
    directly and briefly, wisely and truly. Wisely I say I am a bachelor.   15

2 PLEBEIAN That's as much as to say they are fools that marry. You'll
    bear me a bang for that, I fear. Proceed directly.

CINNA THE POET Directly I am going to Caesar's funeral.

1 PLEBEIAN As a friend or an enemy?

CINNA THE POET As a friend.   20

2 PLEBEIAN That matter is answered directly.

4 PLEBEIAN For your dwelling – briefly.

CINNA THE POET Briefly, I dwell by the Capitol.

3 PLEBEIAN Your name, sir, truly.

CINNA THE POET Truly, my name is Cinna.   25

1 PLEBEIAN Tear him to pieces, he's a conspirator.

CINNA THE POET I am Cinna the poet, I am Cinna the poet.

4 PLEBEIAN Tear him for his bad verses, tear him for his bad verses.

CINNA THE POET I am not Cinna the conspirator.

4 PLEBEIAN It is no matter, his name's Cinna. Pluck but his name out of   30
    his heart and turn him going.

3 PLEBEIAN Tear him, tear him! Come, brands ho, firebrands! To
    Brutus', to Cassius', burn all! Some to Decius' house, and some to
    Casca's, some to Ligarius'! Away, go!

                    Exeunt all the Plebeians [forcing out Cinna]

4.1 *Enter* ANTONY, OCTAVIUS, *and* LEPIDUS

ANTONY These many then shall die, their names are pricked.

OCTAVIUS Your brother too must die; consent you, Lepidus?

LEPIDUS I do consent.

OCTAVIUS   Prick him down, Antony.

15 Wisely I say *Hudson;* wisely I say, F; Wisely, I say – *Rowe;* wisely, I say *Collier³*   28] F; *as one verse line, Staunton
(Capell MS.)*   33 Brutus' ... Cassius'] *Apostrophes, Capell*   33 Decius'] *Apostrophe,* F4   34 Ligarius'] *Apostrophe,*
Capell*   34 SD *forcing out Cinna*] *Collier²*   **Act 4, Scene 1**   4.1] *Actus Quartus.* F; ACT IV. SCENE I. *Rowe*   Location]
Rowe, Capell

    17 **bear me a bang** take a blow from me.
    31 **turn him going** drive him off.

Act 4, Scene 1
Shakespeare sets this scene in Rome, presumably at
Antony's house (see 10–11), but the triumvirs in

reality met on a small island in the river Lavinius
near Bononia.
    2 **brother** This is a detail mentioned in Plutarch
(*Antony,* Bullough, pp. 268–9). Lucius Aemilius
Paullus, elder brother of Lepidus, was named in
the proscriptions but allowed to escape.

LEPIDUS Upon condition Publius shall not live,
    Who is your sister's son, Mark Antony.   5
ANTONY He shall not live – look, with a spot I damn him.
    But, Lepidus, go you to Caesar's house,
    Fetch the will hither, and we shall determine
    How to cut off some charge in legacies.
LEPIDUS What, shall I find you here?   10
OCTAVIUS Or here or at the Capitol.

                                    Exit Lepidus

ANTONY This is a slight, unmeritable man,
    Meet to be sent on errands; is it fit,
    The threefold world divided, he should stand
    One of the three to share it?
OCTAVIUS   So you thought him   15
    And took his voice who should be pricked to die
    In our black sentence and proscription.
ANTONY Octavius, I have seen more days than you,
    And though we lay these honours on this man
    To ease ourselves of divers slanderous loads,   20
    He shall but bear them as the ass bears gold,
    To groan and sweat under the business,
    Either led or driven, as we point the way;
    And having brought our treasure where we will,
    Then take we down his load and turn him off   25

10–11] F; LEP. .... at / ... Capitol. *Steevens*³ *(Capell MS.)*   23 point] F; print F2

4–5 Publius … sister's son The historical Antony did not have a nephew named Publius. Plutarch (*Antony*, Bullough, p. 268) does mention that Antony offered his uncle, Lucius Julius Caesar, to be proscribed. Plutarch also tells a story, in his life of Brutus, about the proscription of a man named Publius Silicius (see *Brutus*, Bullough, p. 108). Possibly this is the 'Publius' Shakespeare had in mind for the character he put into 2.3 and 3.1. J. and S. Velz ('Publius, Mark Anthony's sister's son', *SQ* 26 (1975), 69–74) suggest that Shakespeare might have been misremembering Plutarch, and subsituting one historical person for another, when he gave Antony a nephew named Publius.

6 spot mark or stigma. See also 4.3.2 n.

6 damn condemn as guilty.

9 cut … charge avoid paying some of what has been promised.

11 Or here or Either here or.

14 threefold world For the Romans, the known world had a threefold structure: Europe, Asia, and Africa. The Roman empire, consisting of the East and West provinces and Africa, was divided among the triumvirate: Antony received Cisalpine and Transalpine Gaul (i.e. northern Italy on both sides of the Alps), Lepidus Old Gaul (i.e. the south of France) and all of Spain, and Octavius Africa, Sicily, and Sardinia.

16 took … who accepted his vote as to who.

17 black … proscription The *proscriptio* was a list of Roman citizens who were declared outlaws and whose goods were confiscated. This procedure was employed by Antony, Octavius, and Lepidus in 43–42 BC to get rid of personal and political opponents, and to obtain funds.

20 divers … loads various slanders that will be heaped upon us. That is, Lepidus can be used to take the blame for Antony and Octavius's unpopular acts.

24 where we will where we want him to.

25 turn him off send him away.

(Like to the empty ass) to shake his ears
And graze in commons.
OCTAVIUS   You may do your will,
But he's a tried and valiant soldier.
ANTONY So is my horse, Octavius, and for that
I do appoint him store of provender.   30
It is a creature that I teach to fight,
To wind, to stop, to run directly on,
His corporal motion governed by my spirit.
And, in some taste, is Lepidus but so:
He must be taught and trained and bid go forth,   35
A barren-spirited fellow, one that feeds
On objects, arts, and imitations,
Which, out of use and staled by other men,
Begin his fashion. Do not talk of him
But as a property. And now, Octavius,   40
Listen great things. Brutus and Cassius
Are levying powers; we must straight make head.
Therefore let our alliance be combined,
Our best friends made, our means stretched,
And let us presently go sit in counsel,   45
How covert matters may be best disclosed
And open perils surest answerèd.
OCTAVIUS Let us do so, for we are at the stake
And bayed about with many enemies,

---

37 objects, arts] F; abject Orts *Theobald*; abject arts *conj. Becket*; abjects, orts *Staunton*; objects, orts *White²*   38 staled] F; stall'd F4   44 our means stretched] F; and our best meanes stretcht out F2; our best means stretch'd out QU4; our best means stretcht *Johnson (Capell MS.)*; our meinies [*i.e.* followers] stretched *Wells and Taylor (conj. J.D.)*   45 counsel] *This edn;* Councell F; Council F3   47 surest] F; soonest *Folger MS.*

26 **shake his ears** a reference to the way an ass's ears move while it grazes. Used dismissively of a useless or idle person. See also *TN* 2.3.134.

27 **commons** public pastures.

30 **appoint ... provender** make sure he has enough food.

32 **wind** turn.

34 **in some taste** to some degree.

34 **but so** no more than this.

37 **objects, arts, and imitations** things, curiosities, and passing fashions.

38 **staled by** made stale by the attentions of. That is, people become tired of them and they go out of fashion.

39 **Begin his fashion** begin to capture his

attention. That is, Lepidus only takes an interest in something after everyone else is long-since bored by it.

40 **property** means to an end, instrument.

41 **Listen** Let me tell you of.

42 **make head** raise a force (see *OED* 54); or, press forward with our plans (see *OED* 55).

44 **Our ... made** our most loyal supporters selected.

45 **in counsel** in private.

46 How hidden dangers may be discovered.

49 **bayed about** brought to bay. See 3.1.204. The image here, however, is not of a deer cornered by hunting dogs but rather of the popular Elizabethan sport of bear-baiting, where a bear was tied to a stake and set upon by dogs.

And some that smile have in their hearts, I fear,   50
Millions of mischiefs.

Exeunt

4.2 *Drum. Enter* BRUTUS, LUCILIUS, [*Lucius,*] *and the army. Titinius and*
PINDARUS *meet them*

BRUTUS Stand ho!
LUCILIUS Give the word ho, and stand!
BRUTUS What now, Lucilius, is Cassius near?
LUCILIUS He is at hand, and Pindarus is come
        To do you salutation from his master.   5
BRUTUS He greets me well. Your master, Pindarus,
        In his own change or by ill officers,
        Hath given me some worthy cause to wish
        Things done undone, but if he be at hand
        I shall be satisfied.
PINDARUS   I do not doubt   10
        But that my noble master will appear
        Such as he is, full of regard and honour.
BRUTUS He is not doubted.
                [Brutus and Lucilius draw apart]
                        A word, Lucilius,
        How he received you; let me be resolved.
LUCILIUS With courtesy and with respect enough,   15
        But not with such familiar instances,
        Nor with such free and friendly conference,
        As he hath used of old.
BRUTUS   Thou hast described

Act 4, Scene 2 4.2] *Rowe* Location] *Rowe* 0 SD *Lucius*] *Capell* 1–2] F; *as one line, Keightley* 2 SH] *The speech
heading* / Luc. / *here and following, in all editions from* F2 *to Singer*², *may have contributed to the confusion of Lucilius and Lucius
in this scene* 7 change] F; *charge* QU3 13 SD] *Continues to 30, Sanders (after Capell)* 13–14 Lucilius, ... you;]
F *(subst.);* Lucilius, – / ... you, *Rowe (Folger MS.)*

51 **mischiefs** harms (stronger than in modern usage).

Act 4, Scene 2
Location Camp near Sardis. Before Brutus's tent.
0 SD.1 *Drum* The usual accompaniment for troops on the march. It is nearly interchangeable with *march* (24).
2 Send the word through the troops to halt.

5 **his master** i.e. Cassius.
6 **greets me well** greets me with a worthy ambassador.
8 **worthy** justifiable (Onions 3) or, perhaps, considerable.
14 **resolved** informed.
16 **familiar instances** gestures of friendship.
17 **free** frank.
17 **conference** conversation.

A hot friend cooling. Ever note, Lucilius,
When love begins to sicken and decay   20
It useth an enforcèd ceremony.
There are no tricks in plain and simple faith,
But hollow men, like horses hot at hand,
Make gallant show and promise of their mettle.
                    Low march within
But when they should endure the bloody spur   25
They fall their crests, and like deceitful jades
Sink in the trial. Comes his army on?
LUCILIUS They mean this night in Sardis to be quartered.
              The greater part, the horse in general,
              Are come with Cassius.

                    Enter CASSIUS *and his powers*

BRUTUS   Hark, he is arrived.   30
              March gently on to meet him.
CASSIUS Stand ho!
BRUTUS Stand ho, speak the word along!
1 SOLDIER Stand!
2 SOLDIER Stand!   35
3 SOLDIER Stand!
CASSIUS Most noble brother, you have done me wrong.
BRUTUS Judge me, you gods! Wrong I mine enemies?
              And if not so, how should I wrong a brother?
CASSIUS Brutus, this sober form of yours hides wrongs,   40
              And when you do them –
BRUTUS   Cassius, be content,
              Speak your griefs softly, I do know you well.
              Before the eyes of both our armies here –
              Which should perceive nothing but love from us –
              Let us not wrangle. Bid them move away.   45

---

24 SD] F; *placed after 30, Capell*   34, 35, 36 SH 1 SOLDIER, 2 SOLDIER, 3 SOLDIER] *Globe (after Capell,* 1. O[fficer],
etc.)

21 It depends upon forced gestures.
23 **hot at hand** lively at the start (i.e. in a race).
26 **fall their crests** become less proud. The *crest* is the ridge of a horse's neck.
26 **jades** 'A contemptuous name for a horse; a horse of inferior breed' (*OED* 1a).
27 **Sink in the trial** fail when put to the test.

28 **Sardis** the chief city of Lydia, made by the Romans the capital of a *conventus* (administrative division) of the province Asia. It was located in what is now western Turkey.
29 **the ... general** all the cavalry.
40 **this sober form** this solemn, grave demeanour.
42 **griefs** grievances; as at 1.3.118.

Then in my tent, Cassius, enlarge your griefs
And I will give you audience.
CASSIUS   Pindarus,
Bid our commanders lead their charges off
A little from this ground.
BRUTUS Lucius, do you the like, and let no man   50
Come to our tent till we have done our conference.
Let Lucilius and Titinius guard our door.

Exeunt [all but] Brutus and Cassius

4.3

CASSIUS That you have wronged me doth appear in this:
You have condemned and noted Lucius Pella
For taking bribes here of the Sardians,
Wherein my letters, praying on his side,
Because I knew the man, was slighted off.   5
BRUTUS You wronged yourself to write in such a case.
CASSIUS In such a time as this it is not meet
That every nice offence should bear his comment.
BRUTUS Let me tell you, Cassius, you yourself
Are much condemned to have an itching palm,   10
To sell and mart your offices for gold
To undeservers.
CASSIUS   I, an itching palm?
You know that you are Brutus that speaks this,
Or, by the gods, this speech were else your last.
BRUTUS The name of Cassius honours this corruption,   15

50, 52 Lucius ... Lucilius] *Craik (omitting* Let *at 52); Lucillius ... Lucius* F   **Act 4, Scene 3   4.3]** *Pope; although, as the / Mane[n]t / in* F *indicates, the scene obviously continues, the tradition since Pope (with very few exceptions) has been to observe the scene break*   Location] *Theobald*   **4** Wherein] F; Whereas *Hudson²*   **4–5** letters ... was] F; Letter ... was F2; letters ... were *Malone*   **5** man,] F2; man F   **5** off] F; of *Rowe³ (Folger MS.)*   **6** case] F; cause *conj. Thirlby*   **12** I] F; Ay *Rowe*   **13** speaks] F; speak *Pope*

46 enlarge give free vent to.
48 charges troops.

Act 4, Scene 3
Location Camp near Sardis. Brutus's tent.
2 noted stigmatised. See 4.1.6 n.
4–5 Cassius wrote letters on behalf of Lucius Pella, but Brutus ignored (*slighted off*) them. The use of the singular verb, 'was', with a plural subject, 'letters', may be attributed to confusion caused by the proximity of 'man'. See Abbott 412.

Or it may be that 'letters' is plural with a singular meaning like Latin *litterae* (*OED Letter* 4b).
8 nice slight, trivial.
8 his its. The phrase *bear his comment* means 'come under scrutiny' or 'be subjected to criticism'.
11 mart offer for sale.
11 offices important positions.
15 this corruption i.e. taking bribes. Brutus is saying, ironically, that Cassius's good name is almost sufficient to make corruption seem honourable.

And chastisement doth therefore hide his head.
CASSIUS Chastisement?
BRUTUS Remember March, the Ides of March remember:
Did not great Julius bleed for justice' sake?
What villain touched his body, that did stab   20
And not for justice? What, shall one of us,
That struck the foremost man of all this world,
But for supporting robbers, shall we now
Contaminate our fingers with base bribes
And sell the mighty space of our large honours   25
For so much trash as may be graspèd thus?
I had rather be a dog and bay the moon
Than such a Roman.
CASSIUS   Brutus, bait not me,
I'll not endure it. You forget yourself
To hedge me in. I am a soldier, I,   30
Older in practice, abler than yourself
To make conditions.
BRUTUS   Go to, you are not, Cassius!
CASSIUS I am.
BRUTUS I say you are not.
CASSIUS Urge me no more, I shall forget myself.   35
Have mind upon your health, tempt me no farther!
BRUTUS Away, slight man!
CASSIUS Is't possible?
BRUTUS   Hear me, for I will speak.
Must I give way and room to your rash choler?
Shall I be frighted when a madman stares?   40
CASSIUS O ye gods, ye gods, must I endure all this?
BRUTUS All this? Ay, more. Fret till your proud heart break.
Go show your slaves how choleric you are,
And make your bondmen tremble. Must I budge?
Must I observe you? Must I stand and crouch   45

27 bay] F; baite F2   28 bait] F; bay *Theobald*   30 soldier, I] F; soldier, ay *Steevens*   32 not,] QU4; not F   32–4]
*Steevens*³; To . . . Conditions. / . . . *Cassius*. / . . . am. / . . . not. F; To . . . Cassius. / . . . not. *Wordsworth (Capell MS.);*
To . . . conditions. / . . . am. / . . . not. *Humphreys*

23 But … robbers Plutarch (Appendix, p. 158)
writes of the conversation dramatised here, and has
Brutus tell Cassius that Caesar 'was a favourer and
suborner of all them that did rob and spoil'.
26 trash a contemptuous term for money (see
OED 3d).

28 bait harass, attack. See 4.1.49 n.
32 make conditions manage affairs.
36 tempt test.
44 budge wince, flinch.
45 observe show respectful or courteous attention to.

Under your testy humour? By the gods,
You shall digest the venom of your spleen
Though it do split you. For, from this day forth,
I'll use you for my mirth, yea, for my laughter,
When you are waspish.

CASSIUS   Is it come to this?   50

BRUTUS You say you are a better soldier:
Let it appear so, make your vaunting true
And it shall please me well. For mine own part
I shall be glad to learn of noble men.

CASSIUS You wrong me every way, you wrong me, Brutus.   55
I said an elder soldier, not a better.
Did I say 'better'?

BRUTUS   If you did, I care not.

CASSIUS When Caesar lived, he durst not thus have moved me.

BRUTUS Peace, peace, you durst not so have tempted him.

CASSIUS I durst not?   60

BRUTUS No.

CASSIUS What? Durst not tempt him?

BRUTUS   For your life you durst not.

CASSIUS Do not presume too much upon my love,
I may do that I shall be sorry for.

BRUTUS You have done that you should be sorry for.   65
There is no terror, Cassius, in your threats,
For I am armed so strong in honesty
That they pass by me as the idle wind,
Which I respect not. I did send to you
For certain sums of gold, which you denied me,   70
For I can raise no money by vile means.
By heaven, I had rather coin my heart
And drop my blood for drachmaes than to wring
From the hard hands of peasants their vile trash
By any indirection. I did send   75
To you for gold to pay my legions,
Which you denied me. Was that done like Cassius?

---

54 noble] F; abler *Collier²* (*Collier MS.*); able *conj. Singer* (*apud Cam.*); better *conj. Cartwright*; nobler *conj. Nicholson*   60 not?] Q (1684); not. F

47 **spleen** In early modern physiology and psychology, thought to be the source of sudden emotions and passions.
52 **vaunting** boasting.

69 **Which ... not** to which I pay no attention.
72 **coin** fashion into coins.
75 **indirection** deviousness. Brutus contrasts his means of raising money with that of Lucius Pella.

    Should I have answered Caius Cassius so?
    When Marcus Brutus grows so covetous
    To lock such rascal counters from his friends,   80
    Be ready, gods, with all your thunderbolts,
    Dash him to pieces!
CASSIUS   I denied you not.
BRUTUS You did.
CASSIUS I did not. He was but a fool that brought
    My answer back. Brutus hath rived my heart.   85
    A friend should bear his friend's infirmities,
    But Brutus makes mine greater than they are.
BRUTUS I do not, till you practise them on me.
CASSIUS You love me not.
BRUTUS   I do not like your faults.
CASSIUS A friendly eye could never see such faults.   90
BRUTUS A flatterer's would not, though they do appear
    As huge as high Olympus.
CASSIUS Come, Antony, and young Octavius, come,
    Revenge yourselves alone on Cassius,
    For Cassius is a-weary of the world: 95
    Hated by one he loves, braved by his brother,
    Checked like a bondman, all his faults observed,
    Set in a notebook, learned, and conned by rote,
    To cast into my teeth. O, I could weep
    My spirit from mine eyes! There is my dagger   100
    And here my naked breast: within, a heart
    Dearer than Pluto's mine, richer than gold.
    If that thou beest a Roman take it forth,
    I that denied thee gold will give my heart:
    Strike as thou didst at Caesar. For I know   105
    When thou didst hate him worst thou loved'st him better
    Than ever thou loved'st Cassius.

---

81 thunderbolts,] F; thunderbolts *Collier*   83–5] *Dyce; Bru.* ... did. / ... Foole / ... hart: F; BRU. ... fool. / ... heart:
Steevens[3] *(Capell MS.)*   88 not, till] F; not: will *Hanmer;* not. Still *Warburton (conj. Warburton apud Theobald)*
102 Pluto's] F; *Plutus' / Pope*

80 **rascal counters** worthless tokens, i.e. something as common as cash.
85 **rived** torn apart.
96 **braved** defied.
97 **Checked** rebuked.
98 **conned by rote** memorised.

99 **cast .. teeth** throw back in my face.
102 **Dearer** more precious.
102 **Pluto** Plutus, son of Demeter and Iasion,
who symbolises wealth. Shakespeare and his contemporaries connected this figure, and sometimes
confused him, with Pluto, god of the underworld.

BRUTUS   Sheathe your dagger.
         Be angry when you will, it shall have scope;
         Do what you will, dishonour shall be humour.
         O Cassius, you are yokèd with a lamb   110
         That carries anger as the flint bears fire,
         Who, much enforcèd, shows a hasty spark
         And straight is cold again.
CASSIUS   Hath Cassius lived
         To be but mirth and laughter to his Brutus
         When grief and blood ill-tempered vexeth him?   115
BRUTUS   When I spoke that, I was ill-tempered too.
CASSIUS Do you confess so much? Give me your hand.
BRUTUS   And my heart too.
CASSIUS   O Brutus!
BRUTUS   What's the matter?
CASSIUS Have not you love enough to bear with me
         When that rash humour which my mother gave me   120
         Makes me forgetful?
BRUTUS   Yes, Cassius, and from henceforth
         When you are over-earnest with your Brutus,
         He'll think your mother chides, and leave you so.

                Enter a POET, [LUCILIUS, *and Titinius*]

POET   Let me go in to see the generals.
         There is some grudge between 'em, 'tis not meet   125
         They be alone.
LUCILIUS You shall not come to them.
POET   Nothing but death shall stay me.
CASSIUS How now, what's the matter?
POET   For shame, you generals, what do you mean?   130
         Love and be friends, as two such men should be,
         For I have seen more years, I'm sure, than ye.

---

109 humour] F; honour *conj. Craik*   110 lamb] F; man *Pope*   123 SD LUCILIUS … *Titinius*] *Rowe; followed by Lucilius,
Titinius, and Lucius / Globe; entrance placed after 128, Theobald*   126–7] F; *as one line, Sisson (Capell MS.)*

108 **it … scope** you can let your anger go as far
as it likes.
109 **humour** your particular quirk.
110 **a lamb** i.e. Brutus.
112 **enforcèd** used with much force (i.e. a
flint must be struck to yield a spark). See also
1.2.177.

115, 116 **ill-tempered** wordplay on 'badly
mixed' (applied to the humours) and the modern
'bad-humoured'.
120 **rash humour** tendency to get irresponsibly
angry.
123 **leave you so** leave it at that.
128 **stay me** keep me back

CASSIUS Ha, ha, how vildly doth this cynic rhyme!
BRUTUS Get you hence, sirrah; saucy fellow, hence!
CASSIUS Bear with him, Brutus, 'tis his fashion.   135
BRUTUS I'll know his humour when he knows his time.
        What should the wars do with these jigging fools?
        Companion, hence!
CASSIUS   Away, away, be gone!

                                                    Exit Poet

BRUTUS Lucilius and Titinius, bid the commanders
        Prepare to lodge their companies tonight.   140
CASSIUS And come yourselves, and bring Messala with you
        Immediately to us.

                              [*Exeunt Lucilius and Titinius*]

BRUTUS [*To Lucius within*] Lucius, a bowl of wine!
CASSIUS I did not think you could have been so angry.
BRUTUS O Cassius, I am sick of many griefs.
CASSIUS Of your philosophy you make no use   145
        If you give place to accidental evils.
BRUTUS No man bears sorrow better. Portia is dead.
CASSIUS Ha? Portia?
BRUTUS She is dead.
CASSIUS How scaped I killing when I crossed you so?   150
        O insupportable and touching loss!
        Upon what sickness?
BRUTUS   Impatient of my absence,
        And grief that young Octavius with Mark Antony
        Have made themselves so strong – for with her death
        That tidings came. With this she fell distract   155

---

137 jigging] F; jingling *Pope*   142 SD.1 *Exeunt ... Titinius*] *Rowe*   142 SD.2 *To Lucius within*] *Evans*

---

133 vildly vilely.
133 cynic a rough, sneering railer. The word could also refer to a member of a school of philosophy 'marked by an ostentatious contempt for ease, wealth, and the enjoyments of life' (*OED* B.1).
134 sirrah See 3.1.10 n.
135 fashion usual habit.
136 'I will admit his right to be eccentric when he chooses a proper occasion to exhibit his eccentricity' (Kittredge). There is also a pun on 'time' in connection with poetic metre: that is, the Poet, with his doggerel rhymes, keeps bad time.
137 jigging Literally the word means 'dancing'; a jig is a 'lively, rapid, springy kind of dance' (*OED* 1a). Plays in Shakespeare's time often ended with a jig (see

Introduction, p. 2); the dance was a popular comic form, often performed by 'fools'. Brutus uses the word to refer to the sound and quality of the Poet's verse.
138 Companion a term of familiarity or contempt. Cf. *Cor.* 5.2.59: 'Now you companion, I'll say an errand for you'.
144 of as a result of.
145–6 Your philosophy [i.e. Stoicism] is of no use to you if you allow yourself to be shaken by bad things that happen by chance.
150 killing i.e. being killed.
152 Impatient of 'Unable or unwilling to endure' (*OED* A.1b).
155 fell distract became (esp. suddenly) anxious, perplexed.

And, her attendants absent, swallowed fire.

CASSIUS And died so?

BRUTUS   Even so.

CASSIUS   O ye immortal gods!

Enter BOY [LUCIUS] *with wine and tapers*

BRUTUS Speak no more of her. Give me a bowl of wine.
In this I bury all unkindness, Cassius.   *Drinks*

CASSIUS My heart is thirsty for that noble pledge.   160
Fill, Lucius, till the wine o'erswell the cup,
I cannot drink too much of Brutus' love.   [*Drinks*]

[*Exit Lucius*]

Enter TITINIUS *and* MESSALA

BRUTUS Come in, Titinius; welcome, good Messala.
Now sit we close about this taper here
And call in question our necessities.   165

CASSIUS Portia, art thou gone?

BRUTUS   No more, I pray you.
Messala, I have here receivèd letters
That young Octavius and Mark Antony
Come down upon us with a mighty power,
Bending their expedition toward Philippi.   170

MESSALA Myself have letters of the selfsame tenor.

BRUTUS With what addition?

MESSALA That by proscription and bills of outlawry
Octavius, Antony, and Lepidus
Have put to death an hundred senators.   175

BRUTUS Therein our letters do not well agree:
Mine speak of seventy senators that died
By their proscriptions, Cicero being one.

CASSIUS Cicero one?

MESSALA   Cicero is dead,

157] *Dyce (Capell MS.); Cas. . . . so? / . . . so. / . . . Gods!* F   157 SD LUCIUS] *Hanmer (omitting* BOY)   162 SD.1 *Drinks*]
Capell (Folger MS.)   162 SD.2 *Exit Lucius*] *Globe*   163] *Rowe;* Come . . . Titinius: / . . . Messala: F   179–80] *Thomas
Johnson²* (adding yes before Cicero is); *Cicero one? / . . . proscription* F

156 swallowed fire Plutarch (Appendix, p. 168)
says that Portia 'took hot burning coals and cast
them into her mouth, and kept her mouth so close
that she choked herself'.

165 call in question consider and discuss. This

is a legal phrase, meaning 'summon for trial or
examination' (*OED* Call *v* 18).

173 proscription . . . bills of outlawry See
4.1.17 n.

And by that order of proscription.   180
Had you your letters from your wife, my lord?
BRUTUS No, Messala.
MESSALA Nor nothing in your letters writ of her?
BRUTUS Nothing, Messala.
MESSALA   That, methinks, is strange.
BRUTUS Why ask you? Hear you aught of her in yours?   185
MESSALA No, my lord.
BRUTUS Now as you are a Roman tell me true.
MESSALA Then like a Roman bear the truth I tell,
For certain she is dead, and by strange manner.
BRUTUS Why, farewell, Portia. We must die, Messala.   190
With meditating that she must die once,
I have the patience to endure it now.
MESSALA Even so, great men great losses should endure.
CASSIUS I have as much of this in art as you,
But yet my nature could not bear it so.   195
BRUTUS Well, to our work alive. What do you think
Of marching to Philippi presently?
CASSIUS I do not think it good.
BRUTUS   Your reason?
CASSIUS   This it is:
'Tis better that the enemy seek us,
So shall he waste his means, weary his soldiers,   200
Doing himself offence, whilst we, lying still,
Are full of rest, defence, and nimbleness.
BRUTUS Good reasons must of force give place to better:
The people 'twixt Philippi and this ground
Do stand but in a forced affection,   205
For they have grudged us contribution.
The enemy, marching along by them,
By them shall make a fuller number up,
Come on refreshed, new added, and encouraged,

181–95] *First version of report of Portia's death; final version at 143–58, 166*   185] *Rowe;* Why ... you? / ... yours? F   193 so,]
This edn; so F   209 new added] F; *new-hearted Collier (Collier MS.);* new aided *Singer² (after Hall apud Thirlby)*

181–95 See Introduction, pp. 26–8.   197 **presently** immediately.
191 **once** in any case; at some time.   203 **of force** of necessity.
194 I have cultivated as much philosophical for-   205 Support us only under compulsion.
titude as you.   206 **contribution** 'An imposition levied upon
196 **to ... alive** either 'to the work that we, who a district for the support of an army in the field to
remain alive, must do', or 'to our work with full   secure immunity from plunder' (*OED* 2.b)
force and vigour'.   209 **new added** reinforced.

    From which advantage shall we cut him off   210
    If at Philippi we do face him there,
    These people at our back.
CASSIUS   Hear me, good brother.
BRUTUS Under your pardon. You must note beside
    That we have tried the utmost of our friends,
    Our legions are brimful, our cause is ripe;   215
    The enemy increaseth every day,
    We, at the height, are ready to decline.
    There is a tide in the affairs of men
    Which, taken at the flood, leads on to fortune;
    Omitted, all the voyage of their life   220
    Is bound in shallows and in miseries.
    On such a full sea are we now afloat,
    And we must take the current when it serves
    Or lose our ventures.
CASSIUS   Then with your will go on,
    We'll along ourselves and meet them at Philippi.   225
BRUTUS The deep of night is crept upon our talk,
    And nature must obey necessity,
    Which we will niggard with a little rest.
    There is no more to say?
CASSIUS   No more. Good night.
    Early tomorrow will we rise and hence.   230
BRUTUS Lucius!

Enter LUCIUS

    My gown.

                                 [Exit Lucius]

    Farewell, good Messala.
    Good night, Titinius. Noble, noble Cassius,
    Good night and good repose.
CASSIUS   O my dear brother!
    This was an ill beginning of the night.

224–5] *Capell;* Or ... Ventures. / ... along / ... *Philippi.* F   **229** say?] *Capell;* say. F   **231** SD.2 *Exit Lucius*]
Q (1691)

213 Under your pardon I beg your pardon.   **224 our ventures** all that we have risked.
214 tried the utmost demanded as much as we   **227 necessity** i.e. the necessity of sleep.
can.   **228 niggard ... rest** put off (the necessity of
219 at the flood when it is high.   sleep) with just a little rest.
220 Omitted neglected.

Never come such division 'tween our souls!   235
Let it not, Brutus.

Enter LUCIUS *with the gown*

BRUTUS   Everything is well.
CASSIUS Good night, my lord.
BRUTUS   Good night, good brother.
TITINIUS AND MESSALA Good night, Lord Brutus.
BRUTUS   Farewell every one.
              Exeunt [Cassius, Titinius, Messala]
Give me the gown. Where is thy instrument?
LUCIUS Here in the tent.
BRUTUS   What, thou speak'st drowsily.   240
Poor knave, I blame thee not, thou art o'erwatched.
Call Claudio and some other of my men,
I'll have them sleep on cushions in my tent.
LUCIUS Varrus and Claudio!

Enter VARRUS *and* CLAUDIO

VARRUS Calls my lord?   245
BRUTUS I pray you, sirs, lie in my tent and sleep,
It may be I shall raise you by and by
On business to my brother Cassius.
VARRUS So please you, we will stand and watch your pleasure.
BRUTUS I will not have it so. Lie down, good sirs,   250
It may be I shall otherwise bethink me.
        [Varrus and Claudio lie down]
Look, Lucius, here's the book I sought for so,
I put it in the pocket of my gown.
LUCIUS I was sure your lordship did not give it me.
BRUTUS Bear with me, good boy, I am much forgetful.   255
Canst thou hold up thy heavy eyes awhile
And touch thy instrument a strain or two?

---

236 SD] F; *placed after 239, Capell*   238 SD *Cassius . . . Messala*] Q (1691)   239 thy] F; my QU4   240 drowsily.] *This edn
(after Keightly)*; drowsily? F   242 Claudio] F; Claudius *Rowe*   244 Varrus and Claudio] F; *Varro* and *Claudius /
Rowe*   244–5] F; *as one line, Wells and Taylor*   244 SD] F; Varro *and* Claudius *Rowe*   249] *Rowe*; So . . . stand, / . . .
pleasure. F   250 will] F2; will it F   251 SD] *Capell (subst.)*

239 **instrument** most likely a lute.   249 **stand and watch** stand watch and wait
241 **thou art o'erwatched** you've been awake   for.
too long.   251 **otherwise bethink me** change my mind.
247 **raise** rouse.   257 **strain** melody, tune.

LUCIUS Ay, my lord, an't please you.
BRUTUS   It does, my boy.
        I trouble thee too much, but thou art willing.
LUCIUS It is my duty, sir.   260
BRUTUS I should not urge thy duty past thy might,
        I know young bloods look for a time of rest.
LUCIUS I have slept, my lord, already.
BRUTUS It was well done and thou shalt sleep again,
        I will not hold thee long. If I do live   265
        I will be good to thee.
                      Music, and a song
        This is a sleepy tune. O murd'rous slumber,
        Layest thou thy leaden mace upon my boy,
        That plays thee music? Gentle knave, good night,
        I will not do thee so much wrong to wake thee.   270
        If thou dost nod thou break'st thy instrument.
        I'll take it from thee and, good boy, good night.
        Let me see, let me see, is not the leaf turned down
        Where I left reading? Here it is, I think.

                  Enter the GHOST OF CAESAR

        How ill this taper burns! Ha, who comes here?   275
        I think it is the weakness of mine eyes
        That shapes this monstrous apparition.
        It comes upon me. Art thou any thing?
        Art thou some god, some angel, or some devil,
        That mak'st my blood cold and my hair to stare?   280
        Speak to me what thou art.
GHOST Thy evil spirit, Brutus.
BRUTUS   Why com'st thou?
GHOST To tell thee thou shalt see me at Philippi.
BRUTUS Well, then I shall see thee again?
GHOST Ay, at Philippi.   285
BRUTUS Why, I will see thee at Philippi then.

                                              [*Exit Ghost*]

284–5] F; Well; / ... Philippi. *Steevens*³   286 SD] *Rowe (after 285); placed as in Dyce*

258 an't if it.
261 should ought. See Abbott 323.
268 leaden mace Brutus imagines *slumber* as
a bailiff, who signals his intention to arrest a man
by laying a *mace*, i.e. a heavy metal staff or club,

upon the offender's shoulder (Mark Hunter).
273 leaf page.
277 shapes creates the shape of.
280 stare stand on end.

Now I have taken heart thou vanishest.
Ill spirit, I would hold more talk with thee.
Boy, Lucius! Varrus! Claudio! Sirs, awake!
Claudio!   290
LUCIUS The strings, my lord, are false.
BRUTUS He thinks he still is at his instrument.
Lucius, awake!
LUCIUS My lord?
BRUTUS Didst thou dream, Lucius, that thou so cried'st out?   295
LUCIUS My lord, I do not know that I did cry.
BRUTUS Yes, that thou didst. Didst thou see anything?
LUCIUS Nothing, my lord.
BRUTUS Sleep again, Lucius. Sirrah Claudio!
        [*To Varrus*] Fellow, thou, awake!   300
VARRUS My lord?
CLAUDIO My lord?
BRUTUS Why did you so cry out, sirs, in your sleep?
BOTH Did we, my lord?
BRUTUS   Ay. Saw you anything?
VARRUS No, my lord, I saw nothing.
CLAUDIO   Nor I, my lord.   305
BRUTUS Go and commend me to my brother Cassius.
        Bid him set on his powers betimes before,
        And we will follow.
BOTH   It shall be done, my lord.

                                            Exeunt

5.1 *Enter* OCTAVIUS, ANTONY, *and their army*

OCTAVIUS Now, Antony, our hopes are answerèd.
        You said the enemy would not come down

287–8 vanishest. Ill spirit,] F; vanishest, Ill Spirit; Rowe   289–90 Varrus! Claudio ... Claudio] F; *Varro! Claudius ...*
Claudius / Rowe   290–1] F; *as one line, Bevington*   295] *As verse, Theobald; as prose,* F   299 Claudio] F; *Claudius /*
Rowe   299–302] *Capell; Bru. ... Fellow, / ... Awake. / ... Lord. / ... Lord.* F; *Bru. ... Claudius! / ... lord ... lord?*
Dorsch (Capell MS.)   300 SD] *Globe (conj. Warburton)*   **Act 5, Scene 1 5.1]** *Actus Quintus.* F; ACT V. SCENE I.
Rowe   Location] *Capell (after Rowe)*

287 Now Now that.   **Act 5, Scene 1**
291 false out of tune.   Location The plains of Philippi.
306 commend me to greet.   1 our ... answerèd We have got what we hoped
307 betimes before early in the morning, and   for. Octavius is pleasantly surprised that Brutus's
before me.   troops have abandoned their strategically advanta-
                                           geous position in the hills.

But keep the hills and upper regions.
It proves not so: their battles are at hand,
They mean to warn us at Philippi here,   5
Answering before we do demand of them.
ANTONY Tut, I am in their bosoms, and I know
Wherefore they do it. They could be content
To visit other places and come down
With fearful bravery, thinking by this face   10
To fasten in our thoughts that they have courage.
But 'tis not so.

Enter a MESSENGER

MESSENGER   Prepare you, generals,
The enemy comes on in gallant show,
Their bloody sign of battle is hung out,
And something to be done immediately.   15
ANTONY Octavius, lead your battle softly on
Upon the left hand of the even field.
OCTAVIUS Upon the right hand I, keep thou the left.
ANTONY Why do you cross me in this exigent?
OCTAVIUS I do not cross you, but I will do so.   20
March

Drum. Enter BRUTUS, CASSIUS, *and their army;* [LUCILIUS, *Titinius,*
MESSALA, *and others*]

BRUTUS They stand and would have parley.
CASSIUS Stand fast, Titinius, we must out and talk.

---

5 warn] F; wage *Hanmer;* wait *conj. Mason*   12 Prepare you,] Q (1691); Prepare you F; Prepare, you *Jennens*   20 SD.2
LUCILIUS ... others] *Capell*

4 **battles** troops in battle array, usually the main force.

5 **warn** summon to battle.

9 **come down** attack (by surprise). See also 5.2.6.

8–9 **They ... places** They would rather be elsewhere, i.e. maintaining their places in the hills.

9–11 **and come ... courage** and they come down on the plains with a show of bravery, hoping to make us think they are courageous.

10 **fearful bravery** that induces fear; or, possibly, bravery that conceals their own fear. The word *bravery* refers both to the apparent courage of the soldiers and to the splendour of their armour and weaponry. See also *gallant*

show (13).

10 **face** appearance.

14 **bloody sign of battle** Plutarch (Appendix, p. 161) says that the 'signal of battle was set out' in Brutus's camp on the morning of the battle. This signal was an 'arming scarlet coat', i.e. a 'vest of rich material embroidered with heraldic devices' (*OED* coat-armour 1), suspended above the soldiers' tents.

16 **softly** slowly.

19 **cross** oppose.

19 **exigent** moment of crisis.

21 **parley** 'A meeting between opposing sides in a dispute', especially a 'conference with an enemy, under truce' during wartime (*OED* 2.a).

OCTAVIUS Mark Antony, shall we give sign of battle?
ANTONY No, Caesar, we will answer on their charge.
         Make forth, the generals would have some words.   25
OCTAVIUS Stir not until the signal.
BRUTUS Words before blows; is it so, countrymen?
OCTAVIUS Not that we love words better, as you do.
BRUTUS Good words are better than bad strokes, Octavius.
ANTONY In your bad strokes, Brutus, you give good words.   30
         Witness the hole you made in Caesar's heart,
         Crying, 'Long live, hail, Caesar!'
CASSIUS   Antony,
         The posture of your blows are yet unknown;
         But for your words, they rob the Hybla bees
         And leave them honeyless.
ANTONY   Not stingless too?   35
BRUTUS O yes, and soundless too,
         For you have stolen their buzzing, Antony,
         And very wisely threat before you sting.
ANTONY Villains! You did not so when your vile daggers
         Hacked one another in the sides of Caesar.   40
         You showed your teeth like apes and fawned like hounds,
         And bowed like bondmen, kissing Caesar's feet,
         Whilst damnèd Casca, like a cur, behind
         Struck Caesar on the neck. O you flatterers!
CASSIUS Flatterers? Now, Brutus, thank yourself.   45
         This tongue had not offended so today
         If Cassius might have ruled.
OCTAVIUS Come, come, the cause. If arguing make us sweat,
         The proof of it will turn to redder drops.

---

33 posture] F; puncture *conj. Singer 1858;* portents *conj. Bulloch*   35 too?] *Macmillan (conj. Thirlby);* too. F   35–6]
Steevens³; And ... Hony-lesse. / ... too. / ... soundlesse too: F; And ... honeyless. / ... soundless too. *Bevington (Capell MS.)*   41] *Rowe;* You ... Apes, / ... Hounds, F   41 teeth] F3; teethes F

24 **answer on their charge** respond when they attack.

33 **posture ... blows** the manner in which you will strike.

34 **Hybla** town in Sicily famous for honey.
38 **threat** threaten.
39 **did not so** i.e. did not first threaten or give warning.

46 **this tongue** i.e. Antony's tongue.

47 **ruled** had his way. See 2.1.155–61, where Cassius advised that Antony should be killed along with Caesar.

48 **Come ... cause** Let's get to the matter at hand.

49 **The proof of it** settling it in battle.

Look,   50
I draw a sword against conspirators;
When think you that the sword goes up again?
Never, till Caesar's three and thirty wounds
Be well avenged, or till another Caesar
Have added slaughter to the sword of traitors.   55

BRUTUS Caesar, thou canst not die by traitors' hands
Unless thou bring'st them with thee.

OCTAVIUS   So I hope.
I was not born to die on Brutus' sword.

BRUTUS O, if thou wert the noblest of thy strain,
Young man, thou couldst not die more honourable.   60

CASSIUS A peevish schoolboy, worthless of such honour,
Joined with a masker and a reveller!

ANTONY Old Cassius still!

OCTAVIUS   Come, Antony, away!
Defiance, traitors, hurl we in your teeth.
If you dare fight today, come to the field;   65
If not, when you have stomachs.

                    Exeunt Octavius, Antony, and army

CASSIUS Why now blow wind, swell billow, and swim bark!
The storm is up, and all is on the hazard.

BRUTUS Ho, Lucilius, hark, a word with you.

                    Lucilius and Messala stand forth

LUCILIUS   My lord.

            [Brutus speaks apart to Lucilius]

CASSIUS Messala!

50–1] *Steevens³*; Looke . . . Conspirators, F   53 thirty] F; twenty *Theobald (after Plutarch)*   55 sword] F; word *Collier²*
(Collier MS.)   57 So I hope.] So I hope: F; So I hope QUI; So; I hope *Collier⁴*   67] *Rowe*; Why . . . Billow, / . . .
Barke: F   69 SD.2 *Brutus . . . Lucilius*] *Rowe*

52 goes up will be sheathed.

53 three and thirty In Plutarch and other classical sources the number is twenty-three.

54–5 till . . . traitors i.e. until you traitors have
killed me (*another Caesar*) as well.

56–8 Brutus suggests that the only traitors are
the soldiers who support Octavius. Octavius replies
that he would rather be killed by his own soldiers
than by Brutus.

59 strain lineage.

61 peevish silly, foolish.

61 worthless unworthy.

62 masker one who takes part in a masque or
masquerade – i.e. someone involved in trivial and
light-hearted matters. Earlier, Caesar had praised
Antony for loving plays (1.2.203–4).

63 Old Cassius still the same old Cassius.

66 have stomachs have the inclination, or
appetite; see 1.2.290. *Stomach* could also mean
'Spirit, courage, valour, bravery' (*OED* 8.a).

67 bark small ship.

68 all . . . hazard everything is at stake.

MESSALA   What says my general?
CASSIUS   Messala,   70
          This is my birthday, as this very day
          Was Cassius born. Give me thy hand, Messala.
          Be thou my witness that against my will
          (As Pompey was) am I compelled to set
          Upon one battle all our liberties.   75
          You know that I held Epicurus strong
          And his opinion. Now I change my mind
          And partly credit things that do presage.
          Coming from Sardis, on our former ensign
          Two mighty eagles fell, and there they perched,   80
          Gorging and feeding from our soldiers' hands,
          Who to Philippi here consorted us.
          This morning are they fled away and gone,
          And in their steads do ravens, crows, and kites
          Fly o'er our heads and downward look on us   85
          As we were sickly prey. Their shadows seem
          A canopy most fatal under which
          Our army lies, ready to give up the ghost.
MESSALA Believe not so.
CASSIUS   I but believe it partly,
          For I am fresh of spirit and resolved   90
          To meet all perils very constantly.
BRUTUS Even so, Lucilius. [*Advancing*]
CASSIUS   Now, most noble Brutus,
          The gods today stand friendly that we may,
          Lovers in peace, lead on our days to age!
          But since the affairs of men rests still incertain,   95

70–1] *Pope; Cassi Messala. / . . . Generall? / . . . day* F   79 former] F; foremost *Rowe;* forward *Collier² (Collier MS.)*
79 ensign] F; ensigns *Humphreys (conj. Lettsom)*   92 SD] *Staunton*   94 Lovers in peace,] F; Lovers, in peace, *Capell;*
Lovers, in peace *conj. Furness*

76 **Epicurus** moral and natural philosopher
(341–270 BC), whose main doctrine, that 'pleasure
is the beginning and end of living happily', entailed
a distrust of the supernatural. Plutarch twice mentions Cassius's aberration: before the murder of
Caesar and before the battle at Philippi (see
Appendix, p. 143 and pp. 159–60).
    78 **things … presage** omens.
    79 **former** foremost.

79 **ensign** banner, standard.
80 **fell** swooped.
82 **Who** i.e. the eagles.
82 **consorted** accompanied.
87 **fatal** foreboding, ominous.
88 **give … ghost** breathe its last.
91 **constantly** resolutely.
93 **The gods … stand** May the gods stand.

Let's reason with the worst that may befall.
If we do lose this battle, then is this
The very last time we shall speak together.
What are you then determined to do?
BRUTUS Even by the rule of that philosophy   100
By which I did blame Cato for the death
Which he did give himself – I know not how,
But I do find it cowardly and vile,
For fear of what might fall, so to prevent
The time of life – arming myself with patience   105
To stay the providence of some high powers
That govern us below.
CASSIUS   Then if we lose this battle,
You are contented to be led in triumph
Through the streets of Rome?
BRUTUS No, Cassius, no. Think not, thou noble Roman,   110
That ever Brutus will go bound to Rome:
He bears too great a mind. But this same day
Must end that work the Ides of March begun.
And whether we shall meet again I know not,
Therefore our everlasting farewell take: 115
For ever and for ever, farewell, Cassius!
If we do meet again, why, we shall smile;
If not, why then this parting was well made.
CASSIUS For ever and for ever, farewell, Brutus!
If we do meet again, we'll smile indeed;   120
If not, 'tis true this parting was well made.
BRUTUS Why then, lead on. O, that a man might know
The end of this day's business ere it come!
But it sufficeth that the day will end,
And then the end is known. Come ho, away!   125

Exeunt

---

105 time] F; turn [of death] *conj. Thirlby;* term *Capell*   106 some] F; those *Collier²*   109 Rome?] Q (1691); Rome.
F   110] *Rowe;* No ... no: / ... Romane, F

96 **reason with** consider.
100 **that philosophy** Stoicism, which held that
committing suicide in order to avoid further pain was
'cowardly and vile' (103); the Stoic ought to face pain
'with patience' (105) and an acknowledgement that

one's fate is in the hands of 'some high powers' (106).
101 **Cato** See 2.1.295 n.
104 **fall** befall, i.e. happen, as at 3.1.243.
104 **prevent** forestall.
106 **stay** await, stay for.

5.2 *Alarum. Enter* BRUTUS *and Messala*

BRUTUS Ride, ride, Messala, ride, and give these bills
Unto the legions on the other side.
Loud alarum
Let them set on at once, for I perceive
But cold demeanour in Octavio's wing,
And sudden push gives them the overthrow.   5
Ride, ride, Messala, let them all come down.

Exeunt

5.3 *Alarums. Enter* CASSIUS *and* TITINIUS

CASSIUS O, look, Titinius, look, the villains fly!
Myself have to mine own turned enemy.
This ensign here of mine was turning back;
I slew the coward and did take it from him.
TITINIUS O Cassius, Brutus gave the word too early,   5
Who, having some advantage on Octavius,
Took it too eagerly. His soldiers fell to spoil
Whilst we by Antony are all enclosed.

Enter PINDARUS

PINDARUS Fly further off, my lord, fly further off!
Mark Antony is in your tents, my lord,   10
Fly therefore, noble Cassius, fly far off.
CASSIUS This hill is far enough. Look, look, Titinius,
Are those my tents where I perceive the fire?
TITINIUS They are, my lord.

Act 5, Scene 2   5.2] *Capell*   Location] *Capell*   4 Octavio's] f; *Octavius' / Thomas Johnson²*   5 And] f; One *Hanmer*
(Folger MS.); A *Warburton*   Act 5, Scene 3   5.3] *Capell* Location] *Capell*

Act 5, Scene 2
Location The field of battle.

   0 SD **Alarum** the sound of a drum, and possibly
a trumpet as well, signalling the beginning of military action, and used to 'create an atmosphere of
conflict and confusion during battle scenes' (Dessen
and Thomson).
   1 **bills** written orders.
   4 **cold** fearful.
   4 **wing** side of the army.

6 **come down** come down from the hills and
join the attack.

Act 5, Scene 3
Location Another part of the field.
   1 **the villains** Cassius refers to his own men.
   3 **ensign** standard-bearer.
   4 **it** the standard, or banner, held by the ensign.
   7 **fell to spoil** began plundering.
   8 **enclosed** surrounded.

CASSIUS   Titinius, if thou lovest me,
      Mount thou my horse and hide thy spurs in him   15
      Till he have brought thee up to yonder troops
      And here again that I may rest assured
      Whether yond troops are friend or enemy.
TITINIUS I will be here again even with a thought.   *Exit*
CASSIUS Go, Pindarus, get higher on that hill,   20
      My sight was ever thick: regard Titinius
      And tell me what thou not'st about the field.
                [Pindarus goes up]
      This day I breathèd first, time is come round
      And where I did begin there shall I end:
      My life is run his compass. Sirrah, what news?   25
PINDARUS *[Above]* O my lord!
CASSIUS What news?
PINDARUS Titinius is enclosèd round about
      With horsemen that make to him on the spur,
      Yet he spurs on. Now they are almost on him.   30
      Now Titinius – Now some light; O, he lights too.
      He's ta'en.
                   [Shout]
      And hark, they shout for joy.
CASSIUS Come down, behold no more.
      O, coward that I am to live so long
      To see my best friend ta'en before my face.   35
            Pindarus [descends]
      Come hither, sirrah.
      In Parthia did I take thee prisoner,
      And then I swore thee, saving of thy life,
      That whatsoever I did bid thee do
      Thou shouldst attempt it. Come now, keep thine oath.   40

---

20 higher] F; thither F2 **22** SD] *Dyce (after Hanmer / Exit Pin.)* **28–33**] *As Pope (not omitting* Now *before* Titinius *at 31);* Pind. . . . about / . . . Spurre, / . . . him: / . . . too. / . . . Showt. / . . . ioy. / . . . more: F; Pin. . . . is / . . . that / . . . on.– / . . . Titinius! – / . . . hark! / . . . joy. / . . . more. –*Malone; as Malone, except 32–3:* They . . . more. – *Steevens³; as Pope, except 31–3:* Now . . . ta'en; – / And . . . more. – *Boswell; as Pope, except 32–3:* He's . .–. more. – *Singer²; as Pope, except 31–3:* Now, Titinius! – / . . . too: – / . . . hark! / . . . joy. / . . . more. *Craik; as Pope, except 31–3:* Now . . . Now, / . . . hark! / . . . more. – *Wordsworth; as Pope, except 31–3:* Now, Titinius! – / . . . hark! / . . . more. *Dyce²; as Pope, except 31–2:* Now . . . he / . . . joy. *Bevington (conj. Nicholson, who adds* now *after* Now) **31** Titinius –] *Jennens;* Titinius. F **35** SD] *Dyce (Douai MS.);* Enter Pindarus F **36–7**] *Pope;* Come . . . Prisoner, F

  19 even … thought as swift as thought, in an instant.
  21 thick misty, dim.
  31 light alight (i.e. from their horses).

  37 In Parthia Cassius refers to the disastrous Roman military expedition in Parthia (modern northern Iran) in 53 BC.

Now be a freeman, and with this good sword,
That ran through Caesar's bowels, search this bosom.
Stand not to answer; here, take thou the hilts
And when my face is covered, as 'tis now,
Guide thou the sword.
             [Pindarus stabs him]
                Caesar, thou art revenged   45
Even with the sword that killed thee.   *[Dies]*

PINDARUS So I am free, yet would not so have been
    Durst I have done my will. O Cassius,
    Far from this country Pindarus shall run,
    Where never Roman shall take note of him.   *[Exit]*   50

          Enter TITINIUS *and* MESSALA

MESSALA It is but change, Titinius, for Octavius
    Is overthrown by noble Brutus' power,
    As Cassius' legions are by Antony.
TITINIUS These tidings will well comfort Cassius.
MESSALA Where did you leave him?
TITINIUS   All disconsolate,   55
    With Pindarus his bondman, on this hill.
MESSALA Is not that he that lies upon the ground?
TITINIUS He lies not like the living. O my heart!
MESSALA Is not that he?
TITINIUS   No, this was he, Messala,
    But Cassius is no more. O setting sun,   60
    As in thy red rays thou dost sink to night,
    So in his red blood Cassius' day is set.
    The sun of Rome is set. Our day is gone,
    Clouds, dews, and dangers come. Our deeds are done.
    Mistrust of my success hath done this deed.   65
MESSALA Mistrust of good success hath done this deed.
    O hateful error, melancholy's child,
    Why dost thou show to the apt thoughts of men
    The things that are not? O error, soon conceived,

---

41 freeman] F3; Free-man F; free man *Humphreys*   45 SD] *Globe (Douai MS.)*   46 SD] *Capell (Folger MS.); Kills him*
F2; *Kills himself / Rowe²*   47] *Rowe;* So ... free,/ ... beene F   50 SD. 1 *Exit*] *Rowe (Folger MS.)*   61 to night] F;
to-night *Thomas Johnson*   62 is] F; it F2   63 sun] F; Sonne F2; Son F3

51 It is but change It is merely the alternating   **65 my success** the result of my errand; as at 2.2.6.
fortunes of war.   **68 apt** susceptible to impressions.

Thou never com'st unto a happy birth 70
But kill'st the mother that engendered thee.
TITINIUS What, Pindarus? Where art thou, Pindarus?
MESSALA Seek him, Titinius, whilst I go to meet
The noble Brutus, thrusting this report
Into his ears. I may say 'thrusting' it, 75
For piercing steel and darts envenomèd
Shall be as welcome to the ears of Brutus
As tidings of this sight.
TITINIUS   Hie you, Messala,
And I will seek for Pindarus the while.

                                           [*Exit Messala*]

Why didst thou send me forth, brave Cassius? 80
Did I not meet thy friends? And did not they
Put on my brows this wreath of victory
And bid me give it thee? Didst thou not hear their shouts?
Alas, thou hast misconstrued everything.
But hold thee, take this garland on thy brow; 85
Thy Brutus bid me give it thee, and I
Will do his bidding. Brutus, come apace,
And see how I regarded Caius Cassius.
By your leave, gods! – This is a Roman's part.
Come, Cassius' sword, and find Titinius' heart.   *Dies* 90

Alarum. Enter BRUTUS, MESSALA, YOUNG CATO, *Strato,*
Volumnius, and Lucilius, [Labeo, and Flavius]

BRUTUS Where, where, Messala, doth his body lie?
MESSALA Lo yonder, and Titinius mourning it.
BRUTUS Titinius' face is upward.
CATO   He is slain.
BRUTUS O Julius Caesar, thou art mighty yet,
Thy spirit walks abroad and turns our swords 95
In our own proper entrails.
                              Low alarums
CATO   Brave Titinius!
Look whe'er he have not crowned dead Cassius.
BRUTUS Are yet two Romans living such as these?

79 SD] Q (1691)   90 SD.2 *Labeo,* and *Flavius*] *Wilson*   95 walks] F; wa'kes F2; wakes *Folger MS.*   97 whe'er] whe'r
Capell; where F   97 not] F; *omitted in* F *(uncorrected)*

76 darts arrows.   **96 own proper** our very own.

The last of all the Romans, fare thee well!
It is impossible that ever Rome   100
Should breed thy fellow. Friends, I owe mo tears
To this dead man than you shall see me pay.
I shall find time, Cassius, I shall find time.
Come therefore and to Thasos send his body;
His funerals shall not be in our camp   105
Lest it discomfort us. Lucilius, come,
And come, young Cato, let us to the field.
Labeo and Flavio, set our battles on.
'Tis three o'clock, and, Romans, yet ere night
We shall try fortune in a second fight.   110

                                                Exeunt

5.4 *Alarum. Enter* BRUTUS, *Messala,* [YOUNG] CATO, LUCILIUS, *and Flavius,*
[*Labeo*]

BRUTUS Yet, countrymen, O, yet hold up your heads!
                    [*Exit with Messala, Flavius, and Labeo*]
CATO What bastard doth not? Who will go with me?
I will proclaim my name about the field.
I am the son of Marcus Cato, ho!
A foe to tyrants, and my country's friend.   5
I am the son of Marcus Cato, ho!

                    Enter SOLDIERS *and fight*

99 The] F; Thou *Rowe*   101 owe mo] F; owe no F *(uncorrected)*; own mo Q (1684); own my QU3; own more Q (1691);
owe more *Rowe (Folger MS.)*   104 Thasos] Thassos *Theobald (after Plutarch): Tharsus* F   108 Flavio] F; *Flavius* F2
(after Plutarch)   108 Flavio,] F4, *Flavio* F   109 and, Romans, yet] *Rowe*; and Romans yet F; and, Romans yet, *conj. this*
edn   **Act 5, Scene 4   5.4**] *Capell*   Location] *Capell*   **o** SD YOUNG] *Dyce*   **o** SD *Labeo*] *This edn*   **1** SD] *Wilson*
(subst.)

101 mo more; see 2.1.72 n.
104 **Thasos** an island in the north Aegean Sea,
not far from Philippi.
105 **funerals** i.e. funeral. Until the end of the
seventeenth century the plural and singular forms
of this word were interchangeable. North's translation of Plutarch uses the plural in connection with
Caesar's burial (see Appendix, p. 155). See also *Tit.*
1.1.381, *MND* 1.1.14.
106 **discomfort** dishearten.
108 **battles** See 5.1.4 n.
109–10 **yet   …   second   fight** Shakespeare

makes the two battles occur in a single afternoon; in reality, they took place some twenty
days apart.

Act 5, Scene 4
Location Another part of the field.
   o SD It is likely that Labeo, who is coupled with
Flavius at 5.3.108, also enters here and exits after
line 1. Plutarch mentions Brutus's grieving over his
friends slain in battle, 'specially when he came to
name Labio and Flavius' (Appendix, p. 167).
   4 **Marcus Cato** See 2.1.295 n.

LUCILIUS And I am Brutus, Marcus Brutus, I,
      Brutus, my country's friend. Know me for Brutus!
                [*Young Cato is slain*]
      O young and noble Cato, art thou down?
      Why, now thou diest as bravely as Titinius   10
      And mayst be honoured, being Cato's son.
I SOLDIER Yield, or thou diest.
LUCILIUS   Only I yield to die.
      There is so much that thou wilt kill me straight.
      Kill Brutus and be honoured in his death.
I SOLDIER We must not. A noble prisoner!   15

Enter ANTONY

2 SOLDIER Room ho! Tell Antony, Brutus is ta'en.
I SOLDIER I'll tell the news. Here comes the general.
      Brutus is ta'en, Brutus is ta'en, my lord!
ANTONY Where is he?
LUCILIUS Safe, Antony, Brutus is safe enough.   20
      I dare assure thee that no enemy
      Shall ever take alive the noble Brutus.
      The gods defend him from so great a shame!
      When you do find him, or alive or dead,
      He will be found like Brutus, like himself.   25
ANTONY This is not Brutus, friend, but, I assure you,
      A prize no less in worth. Keep this man safe,
      Give him all kindness. I had rather have
      Such men my friends than enemies. Go on,
      And see whe'er Brutus be alive or dead,   30
      And bring us word unto Octavius' tent
      How everything is chanced.
                                Exeunt

---

7 SH LUCILIUS] *Macmillan; Bru./Rowe*   8 SD] Cato *falls/Capell*   9 O young] *Macmillan; Luc.* O yong F   **12, 15** SH I]
Capell   **17** the news] Q (1684) *(Folger MS.)*; thee newes F   **30** whe'er] whe'r *Capell* (whether *Folger MS.*); where
F

7 SH Most editors assign to Lucilius, who imper-
sonates Brutus to protect him from harm. The ruse
is referred to by Antony at 26. For this action, see
Plutarch (Appendix, p. 167).
  12 **Only I yield** i.e. I yield only.

13 **so much** so many strong reasons (i.e. honour
and fame).
  13 **straight** straight away, immediately.
  24 **or ... or** either ... or.

5.5 *Enter* BRUTUS, DARDANIUS, CLITUS, STRATO, *and* VOLUMNIUS

BRUTUS Come, poor remains of friends, rest on this rock.
CLITUS Statilius showed the torchlight but, my lord,
    He came not back. He is or ta'en or slain.
BRUTUS Sit thee down, Clitus. Slaying is the word,
    It is a deed in fashion. Hark thee, Clitus. [*Whispering*]   5
CLITUS What, I, my lord? No, not for all the world.
BRUTUS Peace then, no words.
CLITUS   I'll rather kill myself.
BRUTUS Hark thee, Dardanius. [*Whispers*]
DARDANIUS   Shall I do such a deed?
CLITUS O Dardanius!
DARDANIUS O Clitus!   10
CLITUS What ill request did Brutus make to thee?
DARDANIUS To kill him, Clitus. Look, he meditates.
CLITUS Now is that noble vessel full of grief,
    That it runs over even at his eyes.
BRUTUS Come hither, good Volumnius, list a word.   15
VOLUMNIUS What says my lord?
BRUTUS   Why, this, Volumnius:
    The ghost of Caesar hath appeared to me
    Two several times by night, at Sardis once
    And this last night here in Philippi fields.
    I know my hour is come.
VOLUMNIUS   Not so, my lord.   20
BRUTUS Nay, I am sure it is, Volumnius.
    Thou seest the world, Volumnius, how it goes:
    Our enemies have beat us to the pit.
        Low alarums
    It is more worthy to leap in ourselves
    Than tarry till they push us. Good Volumnius,   25
    Thou know'st that we two went to school together;

Act 5, Scene 5   5.5] *Capell*   Location] *Pope*   1] *As verse, Pope²; as prose,* F   5 SD] *Rowe (Douai MS.)*   8 SD] *Capell (Douai MS.)*   23 SD *Low*] F; *Loud* F *(uncorrected)*

Act 5, Scene 5
Location Another part of the field.
  2 **showed the torchlight** For this episode in Plutarch, see Appendix, p. 167.

3 **or … or** either … or.
18 **several** separate.
23 **beat … pit** i.e. driven us into a hole (like hunted animals), or into the grave.

Even for that our love of old, I prithee
Hold thou my sword-hilts whilst I run on it.
VOLUMNIUS That's not an office for a friend, my lord.
                    Alarum still
CLITUS Fly, fly, my lord, there is no tarrying here.   30
BRUTUS Farewell to you, and you, and you, Volumnius.
        Strato, thou hast been all this while asleep:
        Farewell to thee too, Strato. Countrymen,
        My heart doth joy that yet in all my life
        I found no man but he was true to me.   35
        I shall have glory by this losing day
        More than Octavius and Mark Antony
        My this vile conquest shall attain unto.
        So fare you well at once, for Brutus' tongue
        Hath almost ended his life's history.   40
        Night hangs upon mine eyes, my bones would rest,
        That have but laboured to attain this hour.
                Alarum. Cry within, 'Fly, fly, fly!'
CLITUS Fly, my lord, fly!
BRUTUS   Hence! I will follow.
                [Exeunt Clitus, Dardanius, and Volumnius]
        I prithee, Strato, stay thou by thy lord.
        Thou art a fellow of a good respect,   45
        Thy life hath had some smatch of honour in it.
        Hold then my sword and turn away thy face,
        While I do run upon it. Wilt thou, Strato?
STRATO Give me your hand first. Fare you well, my lord.
BRUTUS Farewell, good Strato.
                [Runs on his sword]
                        Caesar, now be still,   50
        I killed not thee with half so good a will.   *Dies*

        Alarum. Retreat. Enter ANTONY, OCTAVIUS, MESSALA,
                LUCILIUS, *and the army*

OCTAVIUS What man is that?
MESSALA My master's man. Strato, where is thy master?

28 sword-hilts] *Malone;* Sword Hilts F; Swords Hilt QU3; Sword's hilt *Rowe*   33 thee too] *Thomas Johnson;* thee, to
F   43 SD] *Capell*   50 SD] *Rowe (after 51)*

45 **respect** reputation.
46 **smatch** taste, i.e. your life has generally been
an honourable one.

51 SD *Retreat* The sound of a trumpet or drum
signalling the retreat of one or both sides in battle
(Dessen and Thomson).

STRATO Free from the bondage you are in, Messala.
　　　　The conquerors can but make a fire of him: 55
　　　　For Brutus only overcame himself,
　　　　And no man else hath honour by his death.
LUCILIUS So Brutus should be found. I thank thee, Brutus,
　　　　That thou hast proved Lucilius' saying true.
OCTAVIUS All that served Brutus I will entertain them.   60
　　　　Fellow, wilt thou bestow thy time with me?
STRATO Ay, if Messala will prefer me to you.
OCTAVIUS Do so, good Messala.
MESSALA How died my master, Strato?
STRATO I held the sword, and he did run on it.   65
MESSALA Octavius, then take him to follow thee,
　　　　That did the latest service to my master.
ANTONY This was the noblest Roman of them all:
　　　　All the conspirators, save only he,
　　　　Did that they did in envy of great Caesar.   70
　　　　He only, in a general honest thought
　　　　And common good to all, made one of them.
　　　　His life was gentle, and the elements
　　　　So mixed in him that Nature might stand up
　　　　And say to all the world, 'This was a man!'   75
OCTAVIUS According to his virtue let us use him,
　　　　With all respect and rites of burial.
　　　　Within my tent his bones tonight shall lie,
　　　　Most like a soldier, ordered honourably.
　　　　So call the field to rest, and let's away   80
　　　　To part the glories of this happy day.

Exeunt

63–4] F; *as one line, omitting* good, Steevens³ *(Capell MS.); as one line, Singer*　71 He only,] Q (1691); He, onely
F　71–2 general … And] F; *generous … Of Collier²* *(Collier MS.)*

55 make a fire See 3.2.244 n.	humours (blood, phlegm, choler, melancholy),
56 only alone.	thought in ancient and medieval medicine to regulate
60 entertain them take them into my service.	the health and temperament of a person; the ideal
62 prefer recommend.	mixture of humours was a balanced one. Since
67 latest last.	Antony calls Brutus a paragon of Nature in this
69 save only excepting only.	passage, he might also be referring to the four funda-
70 that what.	mental natural elements: earth, air, water, and fire.
72 made one of them joined their conspiracy.	**79 ordered** dealt with, treated.
73 gentle noble.	**80 field** army.
73 elements Probably a reference to the four	**81 part** share.

APPENDIX: EXCERPTS FROM PLUTARCH

The following excerpts are from Sir Thomas North's translation (1579) of Plutarch's lives of Julius Caesar and Marcus Brutus, the two major sources of Shakespeare's play. Longer, continuous sections are given for a better understanding not merely of the characters and events but also of the distinctive art of both Plutarch and Shakespeare. Although the life of Caesar is used mainly for the first half of the play, and of Brutus for the second, there is some overlapping. The spelling has been modernised and, occasionally, very slightly altered to accord with recognised usage. The punctuation reflects North's, though somewhat modified.

The Life of Julius Caesar

After all these things were ended, he was chosen Consul the fourth time, and went into Spain to make war with the sons of Pompey; who were yet but very young, but had notwithstanding raised a marvellous great army together, and showed to have had manhood and courage worthy to command such an army, insomuch as they put Caesar himself in great danger of his life. The greatest battle that was fought between them in all this war was by the city of Munda. For then Caesar seeing his men sorely distressed, and having their hands full of their enemies, he ran into the press among his men that fought, and cried out unto them: 'What, are ye not ashamed to be beaten and taken prisoners, yielding yourselves with your own hands to these young boys?' And so, with all the force he could make, having with much ado put his enemies to flight, he slew above thirty thousand of them in the field, and lost of his own men a thousand of the best he had. After this battle he went into his tent, and told his friends that he had often before fought for victory, but, this last time now, that he had fought for the safety of his own life. He won this battle on the very feast day of the Bacchanalians, in the which men say that Pompey the Great went out of Rome, about four years before, to begin this civil war. For his sons, the younger scaped from the battle; but, within few days after, Didius brought the head of the elder.

This was the last war that Caesar made. But the Triumph he made into Rome for the same did as much offend the Romans, and more, than anything that ever he had done before; because he had not overcome captains that were strangers, nor barbarous kings, but had destroyed the sons of the noblest man in Rome, whom fortune had overthrown. And, because he had plucked up his race by the roots, men did not think it meet for him to triumph so for the calamities of his country, rejoicing at a thing for the which he had but one excuse to allege in his defence unto the gods and men – that he was compelled to do that he did. And the rather they thought it not meet, because he had never before sent letters nor messengers unto the commonwealth at Rome, for any victory that he had ever won in all the civil wars, but did always for shame refuse the glory of it.

This notwithstanding, the Romans inclining to Caesar's prosperity, and taking the bit in the mouth, supposing that, to be ruled by one man alone, it would be a good mean for them to take breath a little after so many troubles and miseries as they had abidden in these civil wars, they chose him perpetual Dictator. This was a plain tyranny. For to this absolute power of Dictator they added this, never to be afraid to be deposed. Cicero propounded before the Senate that they should give him such honours as were meet for a man. Howbeit others afterwards added to honours beyond all reason. For, men striving who should most honour him, they made him hateful and troublesome to themselves that most favoured him, by reason of the unmeasurable greatness and honours which they gave him. Thereupon, it is reported that even they that most hated him were no less favourers and furtherers of his honours than they that most flattered him, because they might have greater occasions to rise, and that it might appear they had just cause and colour to attempt that they did against him.

And now for himself, after he had ended his civil wars, he did so honourably behave himself that there was no fault to be found in him; and therefore, methinks, amongst other honours they gave him, he rightly deserved this – that they should build him a Temple of Clemency, to thank him for his courtesy he had used unto them in his victory. For he pardoned many of them that had borne arms against him, and, furthermore, did prefer some of them to honour and office in the commonwealth: as, amongst others, Cassius and Brutus, both the which were made Praetors. And, where Pompey's images had been thrown down, he caused them to be set up again. Whereupon Cicero said then that Caesar setting up Pompey's images again he made his own to stand the surer. And when some of his friends did counsel him to have a guard for the safety of his person, and some also did offer themselves to serve him, he would never consent to it, but said it was better to die once than always to be afraid of death.

But to win himself the love and good will of the people, as the honourablest guard and best safety he could have, he made common feasts again and general distribution of corn. Furthermore, to gratify the soldiers also, he replenished many cities again with inhabitants, which before had been destroyed, and placed them there that had no place to repair unto; of the which the noblest and chiefest cities were these two, Carthage and Corinth; and it chanced so that, like as aforetime they had been both taken and destroyed together, even so were they both set afoot again, and replenished with people, at one self time.

And, as for great personages, he won them also, promising some of them to make them Praetors and Consuls in time to come, and unto others honours and preferments, but to all men generally good hope, seeking all the ways he could to make every man contented with his reign ... Furthermore, Caesar being born to attempt all great enterprises and having an ambitious desire besides to covet great honours, the prosperous good success he had of his former conquests bred no desire in him quietly to enjoy the fruits of his labours, but rather gave him hope of things to come, still kindling more and more in him thoughts of greater enterprises and desire of new glory, as if that which he had present were stale and nothing worth. This humour of his was no other but an emulation with himself as with another man, and a certain contention to overcome the things he prepared to attempt . . .

But the chiefest cause that made him mortally hated was the covetous desire he had to be called king, which first gave the people just cause, and next his secret enemies honest colour, to bear him ill will. This notwithstanding, they that procured him this honour and dignity gave it out among the people that it was written in the Sibylline prophecies how the Romans might overcome the Parthians, if they made war with them and were led by a king, but otherwise that they were unconquerable. And furthermore they were so bold besides that, Caesar returning to Rome from the city of Alba, when they came to salute him, they called him king. But the people being offended, and Caesar also angry, he said he was not called king, but Caesar. Then, every man keeping silence, he went his way heavy and sorrowful.

When they had decreed divers honours for him in the Senate, the Consuls and Praetors accompanied with the whole assembly of the Senate went unto him in the market-place, where he was set by the pulpit for orations, to tell him what honours they had decreed for him in his absence. But he, sitting still in his majesty, disdaining to rise up unto them when they came in, as if they had been private men, answered them that his honours had more need to be cut off than enlarged. This did not only offend the Senate, but the common people also, to see that he should so lightly esteem of the magistrates of the commonwealth; insomuch as every man that might lawfully go his way departed thence very sorrowfully. Thereupon also Caesar rising departed home to his house, and tearing open his doublet collar, making his neck bare, he cried out aloud to his friends that his throat was ready to offer to any man that would come and cut it. Notwithstanding, it is reported that afterwards, to excuse this folly, he imputed it to his disease, saying that their wits are not perfect which have his disease of the falling evil, when standing of their feet they speak to the common people, but are soon troubled with a trembling of their body and a sudden dimness and giddiness. But that was not true. For he would have risen up to the Senate, but Cornelius Balbus one of his friends (but rather a flatterer) would not let him, saying: 'What, do you not remember that you are Caesar, and will you not let them reverence you and do their duties?'

Besides these occasions and offences, there followed also his shame and reproach, abusing the Tribunes of the People in this sort. At that time the feast Lupercalia was celebrated, the which in old time men say was the feast of shepherds or herdmen and is much like unto the feast of the Lycians in Arcadia. But, howsoever it is, that day there are divers noblemen's sons, young men – and some of them magistrates themselves that govern then – which run naked through the city, striking in sport them they meet in their way with leather thongs, hair and all on, to make them give place. And many noblewomen and gentlewomen also go of purpose to stand in their way, and do put forth their hands to be stricken, as scholars hold them out to their schoolmaster to be stricken with the ferula; persuading themselves that, being with child, they shall have good delivery, and also, being barren, that it will make them to conceive with child. Caesar sat to behold that sport upon the pulpit for orations, in a chair of gold, apparelled in triumphing manner. Antonius, who was Consul at that time, was one of them that ran this holy course. So, when he came into the market-place, the people made a lane for him to run at liberty; and he came to Caesar and presented him a diadem wreathed about with laurel. Whereupon there rose a certain cry of rejoicing, not very great, done only by a few appointed for the purpose. But when Caesar refused the diadem, then all the people together made an outcry of joy. Then, Antonius offering it him again, there was a second shout of joy, but yet of a few. But when Caesar refused it again the second time, then all the whole people shouted. Caesar, having made this proof, found that the people did not like of it, and thereupon rose out of his chair, and commanded the crown to be carried unto Jupiter in the Capitol.

After that, there were set up images of Caesar in the city with diadems upon their heads, like kings. Those the two Tribunes, Flavius and Marullus, went and pulled down; and furthermore, meeting with them that first saluted Caesar as king, they committed them to prison. The people followed them rejoicing at it, and called them 'Brutes', because of Brutus, who had in old time driven the kings out of Rome and that brought the kingdom of one person unto the government of the Senate and people. Caesar was so offended withal that he deprived Marullus and Flavius of their Tribuneships, and, accusing them, he spake also against the people, and called them *Bruti* and *Cumani* (to wit, 'beasts' and 'fools').

Hereupon the people went straight unto Marcus Brutus, who from his father came of the first Brutus and by his mother of the house of the Servilians, a noble house as any was in Rome, and was also nephew and son-in-law of Marcus Cato. Notwithstanding, the great honours and favour Caesar showed unto him kept him back, that of himself alone he did not conspire nor consent to depose him of his kingdom. For Caesar did not only save his life after the battle of Pharsalia when Pompey fled, and did at his request also save many more of his friends besides. But, furthermore, he put a marvellous confidence in him. For he had already preferred him to the Praetorship for that year, and furthermore was appointed to be Consul the fourth year after that, having through Caesar's friendship obtained it before Cassius, who likewise made suit for the same. And Caesar also, as it is reported, said in this contention: 'Indeed Cassius hath alleged best reason, but yet shall he not be chosen before Brutus.' Some one day accusing Brutus while he practised this conspiracy, Caesar would not hear of it, but, clapping his hand on his body, told them: 'Brutus will look for this skin' – meaning thereby that Brutus for his virtue deserved to rule after him, but yet that for ambition's sake he would not show himself unthankful nor dishonourable.

Now they that desired change and wished Brutus only their prince and governor above all other, they durst not come to him themselves to tell him what they would have him to do, but in the night did cast sundry papers into the Praetor's seat where he gave audience and the most of them to this effect: 'Thou sleepest, Brutus, and art not Brutus indeed.' Cassius, finding Brutus' ambition stirred up the more by these seditious bills, did prick him forward and egg him on the more for a private quarrel he had conceived against Caesar – the circumstance whereof we have set down more at large in Brutus' *Life*.

Caesar also had Cassius in great jealousy and suspected him much. Whereupon he said on a time to his friends: 'What will Cassius do, think ye? I like not his pale looks.' Another time, when Caesar's friends complained unto him of Antonius and Dolabella, that they pretended some mischief towards him, he answered them again: 'As for those fat men and smooth-combed heads', quoth he, 'I never reckon of them. But these pale-visaged and carrion lean people, I fear them most' – meaning Brutus and Cassius.

Certainly destiny may easier be foreseen than avoided, considering the strange and wonderful signs that were said to be seen before Caesar's death. For, touching the fires in the element and spirits running up and down in the night, and also these solitary birds to be seen at noondays sitting in the great market-place – are not all these signs perhaps worth the noting, in such a wonderful chance as happened? But Strabo the Philosopher writeth that divers men were seen going up and down in fire; and, furthermore, that there was a slave of the soldiers that did cast a marvellous burning flame out of his hand, insomuch as they that saw it thought he had been burnt, but, when the fire was out, it was found he had no hurt. Caesar self also, doing sacrifice unto the gods, found that one of the beasts which was sacrificed had no heart; and that was a strange thing in nature, how a beast could live without a heart.

Furthermore, there was a certain soothsayer that had given Caesar warning long time afore to take heed of the day of the Ides of March (which is the fifteenth of the month), for on that day he should be in great danger. That day being come, Caesar, going unto the Senate-house and speaking merrily unto the soothsayer, told him: 'The Ides of March be come.' 'So be they', softly answered the soothsayer, 'but yet they are not past.' And the very day before, Caesar, supping with Marcus Lepidus, sealed certain letters as he was wont to do at the board; so, talk falling out amongst them, reasoning what death was best, he preventing their opinions cried out aloud: 'Death unlooked for.'

Then going to bed the same night as his manner was and lying with his wife Calpurnia, all the windows and doors of his chamber flying open, the noise awoke him and made him afraid when he saw such light; but more, when he heard his wife Calpurnia, being fast asleep, weep and sigh and put forth many fumbling lamentable speeches. For she dreamed that Caesar was slain, and that she had him in her arms. Others also do deny that she had any such dream; as, amongst other, Titus Livius writeth that it was in this sort: the Senate having set upon the top of Caesar's house, for an ornament and setting forth of the same, a certain pinnacle, Calpurnia dreamed that she saw it broken down and that she thought she lamented and wept for it. Insomuch that, Caesar rising in the morning, she prayed him if it were possible not to go out of the doors that day, but to adjourn the session of the Senate until another day. And if that he made no reckoning of her dream, yet that he would search further of the soothsayers by their sacrifices, to know what should happen him that day. Thereby it seemed that Caesar likewise did fear and suspect somewhat, because his wife Calpurnia until that time was never given to any fear or superstition, and then, for that he saw her so troubled in mind with this dream she had. But much more afterwards, when the soothsayers, having sacrificed many beasts one after another, told him that none did like them; then he determined to send Antonius to adjourn the session of the Senate.

But in the meantime came Decius Brutus, surnamed Albinus, in whom Caesar put such confidence that in his last will and testament he had appointed him to be his next heir, and yet was of the conspiracy with Cassius and Brutus. He, fearing that if Caesar did adjourn the session that day the conspiracy would out, laughed the soothsayers to scorn, and reproved Caesar, saying that he gave the Senate occasion to mislike with him, and that they might think he mocked them, considering that by his commandment they were assembled, and that they were ready willingly to grant him all things, and to proclaim him king of all the provinces of the Empire of Rome out of Italy, and that he should wear his diadem in all other places both by sea and land; and furthermore, that if any man should tell them from him they should depart for that present time, and return again when Calpurnia should have better dreams – what would his enemies and ill-willers say, and how could they like of his friends' words? And who could persuade them otherwise, but that they would think his dominion a slavery unto them, and tyrannical in himself? 'And yet, if it be so', said he, 'that you utterly mislike of this day, it is better that you go yourself in person, and saluting the Senate to dismiss them till another time.'

Therewithal he took Caesar by the hand and brought him out of his house. Caesar was not gone far from his house but a bondman, a stranger, did what he could to speak with him; and, when he saw he was put back by the great press and multitude of people that followed him, he went straight unto his house, and put himself into Calpurnia's hands to be kept till Caesar came back again, telling her that he had great matters to impart unto him. And one Artemidorus also, born in the isle of Cnidos, a doctor of rhetoric in the Greek tongue, who by means of his profession was very familiar with certain of Brutus' confederates and therefore knew the most part of all their practices against Caesar, came and brought him a little bill written with his own hand, of all that he meant to tell him. He, marking how Caesar received all the supplications that were offered him, and that he gave them straight to his men that were about him, pressed nearer to him and said: 'Caesar, read this memorial to yourself, and that quickly, for they be matters of great weight and touch you nearly.' Caesar took it of him, but could never read it, though he many times attempted it, for the number of people that did salute him; but holding it still in his hand, keeping it to himself, went on withal into the Senate-house. Howbeit other are of opinion that it was some man else that gave him that memorial, and not Artemidorus, who did what he could all the way as he went to give it Caesar, but he was always repulsed by the people.

For these things, they may seem to come by chance. But the place where the murder was prepared, and where the Senate were assembled, and where also there stood up an image of Pompey dedicated by himself amongst other ornaments which he gave unto the Theatre – all these were manifest proofs that it was the ordinance of some god that made this treason to be executed specially in that very place. It is also reported that Cassius – though otherwise he did favour the doctrine of Epicurus – beholding the image of Pompey before they entered into the action of their traitorous enterprise, he did softly call upon it to aid him. But the instant danger of the present time, taking away his former reason, did suddenly put him into a furious passion and made him like a man half besides himself. Now Antonius, that was a faithful friend to Caesar and a valiant man besides of his hands, him Decius Brutus Albinus entertained out of the Senate-house, having begun a long tale of set purpose.

So, Caesar coming into the house, all the Senate stood up on their feet to do him honour. Then part of Brutus' company and confederates stood round about Caesar's chair, and part of them also came towards him, as though they made suit with Metellus Cimber, to call home his brother again from banishment; and thus, prosecuting still their suit, they followed Caesar till he was set in his chair; who denying their petitions and being offended with them one after another, because the more they were denied, the more they pressed upon him and were the earnester with him. Metellus at length, taking his gown with both his hands, pulled it over his neck, which was the sign given the confederates to set upon him. Then Casca behind him strake him in the neck with his sword. Howbeit the wound was not great nor mortal, because, it seemed, the fear of such a devilish attempt did amaze him and take his strength from him, that he killed him not at the first blow. But Caesar, turning straight unto him, caught hold of his sword and held it hard; and they both cried out, Caesar in Latin: 'O vile traitor Casca, what doest thou?' And Casca in Greek to his brother: 'Brother, help me.' At the beginning of this stir, they that were present, not knowing of the conspiracy, were so amazed with the horrible sight they saw that they had no power to fly, neither to help him, not so much as once to make any outcry. They on the other side that had conspired his death compassed him in on every side with their swords drawn in their hands, that Caesar turned him nowhere but he was stricken at by some, and still had naked swords in his face, and was hacked and mangled among them, as a wild beast taken of hunters. For it was agreed among them that every man should give him a wound, because all their parts should be in this murder. And then Brutus himself gave him one wound about his privities. Men report also that Caesar did still defend himself against the rest, running every way with his body. But when he saw Brutus with his sword drawn in his hand, then he pulled his gown over his head and made no more resistance, and was driven, either casually or purposedly by the counsel of the conspirators, against the base whereupon Pompey's image stood, which ran all of a gore-blood till he was slain. Thus it seemed that the image took just revenge of Pompey's enemy, being thrown down on the ground at his feet and yielding up his ghost there for the number of wounds he had upon him. For it is reported that he had three-and-twenty wounds upon his body; and divers of the conspirators did hurt themselves, striking one body with so many blows.

When Caesar was slain, the Senate, though Brutus stood in the midst amongst them as though he would have said somewhat touching this fact, presently ran out of the house, and flying filled all the city with marvellous fear and tumult; insomuch as some did shut-to their doors, others forsook their shops and warehouses, and others ran to the place to see what the matter was; and others also that had seen it ran home to their houses again. But Antonius and Lepidus, which were two of Caesar's chiefest friends, secretly conveying themselves away, fled into other men's houses and forsook their own.

Brutus and his confederates on the other side, being yet hot with this murder they had committed, having their swords drawn in their hands, came all in a troop together out of the Senate, and went into the market-place, not as men that made countenance to fly, but otherwise boldly holding up their heads like men of courage, and called to the people to defend their liberty, and stayed to speak with every great personage whom they met in their way. Of them, some followed this troop and went amongst them as if they had been of the conspiracy, and falsely challenged part of the honour with them. Among them was Caius Octavius and Lentulus Spinther. But both of them were afterwards put to death, for their vain covetousness of honour, by Antonius and Octavius Caesar the younger; and yet had no part of that honour for the which they were put to death, neither did any man believe that they were any of the confederates or of counsel with them. For they that did put them to death took revenge rather of the will they had to offend than of any fact they had committed.

The next morning Brutus and his confederates came into the market-place to speak unto the people, who gave them such audience that it seemed they neither greatly reproved nor allowed the fact. For by their great silence they showed that they were sorry for Caesar's death, and also that they did reverence Brutus. Now the Senate granted general pardon for all that was past and, to pacify every man, ordained besides that Caesar's funerals should be honoured as a god, and established all things that he had done, and gave certain provinces also and convenient honours unto Brutus and his confederates, whereby every man thought all things were brought to good peace and quietness again. But when they had opened Caesar's testament and found a liberal legacy of money bequeathed unto every citizen of Rome, and that they saw his body (which was brought into the market-place) all bemangled with gashes of swords, then there was no order to keep the multitude and common people quiet. But they plucked up forms, tables, and stools, and laid them all about the body, and setting them afire burnt the corse. Then, when the fire was well kindled, they took the firebrands and went unto their houses that had slain Caesar, to set them afire. Other also ran up and down the city to see if they could meet with any of them to cut them in pieces; howbeit they could meet with never a man of them, because they had locked themselves up safely in their houses.

There was one of Caesar's friends called Cinna, that had a marvellous strange and terrible dream the night before. He dreamed that Caesar bade him to supper, and that he refused, and would not go; then that Caesar took him by the hand, and led him against his will. Now Cinna hearing at that time that they burnt Caesar's body in the market-place, notwithstanding that he feared his dream and had an ague on him besides, he went into the market-place to honour his funerals. When he came thither, one of the mean sort asked what his name was. He was straight called by his name. The first man told it to another, and that other unto another, so that it ran straight through them all that he was one of them that murdered Caesar; for indeed one of the traitors to Caesar was also called Cinna as himself. Wherefore, taking him for Cinna the murderer, they fell upon him with such fury that they presently dispatched him in the market-place.

This stir and fury made Brutus and Cassius more afraid than of all that was past; and therefore, within few days after, they departed out of Rome. And touching their doings afterwards, and what calamity they suffered till their deaths, we have written it at large in the *Life of Brutus*.

Caesar died at six-and-fifty years of age; and Pompey also lived not passing four years more than he. So he reaped no other fruit of all his reign and dominion, which he had so vehemently desired all his life and pursued with such extreme danger, but a vain name only and a superficial glory that procured him the envy and hatred of his country. But his great prosperity and good fortune, that favoured him all his lifetime, did continue afterwards in the revenge of his death, pursuing the murderers both by sea and land, till they had not left a man more to be executed, of all them that were actors or counsellors in the conspiracy of his death. Furthermore, of all the chances that happen unto men upon the earth, that which came to Cassius above all other is most to be wondered at. For he, being overcome in battle at the journey of Philippes, slew himself with the same sword with the which he strake Caesar. Again, of signs in the element, the great comet, which seven nights together was seen very bright after Caesar's death, the eighth night after was never seen more. Also the brightness of the sun was darkened, the which all that year through rose very pale and shined not out, whereby it gave but small heat; therefore the air being very cloudy and dark, by the weakness of the heat that could not come forth, did cause the earth to bring forth but raw and unripe fruit, which rotted before it could ripe.

But, above all, the ghost that appeared unto Brutus showed plainly that the gods were offended with the murder of Caesar. The vision was thus. Brutus, being ready to pass over his army from the city of Abydos to the other coast lying directly against it, slept every night, as his manner was, in his tent; and being yet awake thinking of his affairs – for by report he was as careful a captain and lived with as little sleep as ever man did – he thought he heard a noise at his tent door; and, looking towards the light of the lamp that waxed very dim, he saw a horrible vision of a man, of a wonderful greatness and dreadful look, which at the first made him marvellously afraid. But when he saw that it did him no hurt, but stood by his bedside and said nothing, at length he asked him what he was. The image answered him: 'I am thy ill angel, Brutus, and thou shalt see me by the city of Philippes.' Then Brutus replied again, and said: 'Well, I shall see thee then.' Therewithal the spirit presently vanished from him.

After that time Brutus being in battle near unto the city of Philippes against Antonius and Octavius Caesar, at the first battle he won the victory, and, overthrowing all them that withstood him, he drave them into young Caesar's camp, which he took. The second battle being at hand, this spirit appeared again unto him, but spake never a word. Thereupon Brutus, knowing he should die, did put himself to all hazard in battle, but yet fighting could not be slain. So, seeing his men put to flight and overthrown, he ran unto a little rock not far off; and there setting his sword's point to his breast fell upon it and slew himself, but yet, as it is reported, with the help of his friend that dispatched him.

The Life of Marcus Brutus

Now there were divers sorts of Praetorships at Rome, and it was looked for that Brutus or Cassius would make suit for the chiefest Praetorship, which they called the

Praetorship of the City, because he that had that office was as a judge to minister justice unto the citizens. Therefore they strove one against the other, though some say that there was some little grudge betwixt them for other matters before, and that this contention did set them further out, though they were allied together. For Cassius had married Junia, Brutus' sister. Others say, that this contention betwixt them came by Caesar himself, who secretly gave either of them both hope of his favour. So their suit for the Praetorship was so followed and laboured of either party that one of them put another in suit of law. Brutus with his virtue and good name contended against many noble exploits in arms which Cassius had done against the Parthians. So Caesar, after he had heard both their objections, he told his friends with whom he consulted about this matter: 'Cassius' cause is the juster', said he, 'but Brutus must be first preferred.' Thus Brutus had the first Praetorship, and Cassius the second; who thanked not Caesar so much for the Praetorship he had, as he was angry with him for that he had lost. But Brutus in many other things tasted of the benefit of Caesar's favour in anything he requested. For, if he had listed, he might have been one of Caesar's chiefest friends and of greatest authority and credit about him. Howbeit Cassius' friends did dissuade him from it (for Cassius and he were not yet reconciled together sithence their first contention and strife for the Praetorship) and prayed him to beware of Caesar's sweet enticements and to fly his tyrannical favours; the which they said Caesar gave him, not to honour his virtue but to weaken his constant mind, framing it to the bent of his bow.

Now Caesar on the other side did not trust him overmuch, nor was not without tales brought unto him against him; howbeit he feared his great mind, authority, and friends. Yet, on the other side also, he trusted his good nature and fair conditions. For, intelligence being brought him one day that Antonius and Dolabella did conspire against him, he answered that these fat long-haired men made him not afraid, but the lean and whitely-faced fellows, meaning that by Brutus and Cassius. At another time also when one accused Brutus unto him and bade him beware of him: 'What', said he again, clapping his hand on his breast, 'think ye that Brutus will not tarry till this body die?'– meaning that none but Brutus after him was meet to have such power as he had. And surely, in my opinion, I am persuaded that Brutus might indeed have come to have been the chiefest man of Rome, if he could have contented himself for a time to have been next unto Caesar and to have suffered his glory and authority which he had gotten by his great victories to consume with time.

But Cassius being a choleric man and hating Caesar privately, more than he did the tyranny openly, he incensed Brutus against him. It is also reported that Brutus could evil away with the tyranny, and that Cassius hated the tyrant, making many complaints for the injuries he had done him, and, amongst others, for that he had taken away his lions from him. Cassius had provided them for his sports, when he should be Aedilis, and they were found in the city of Megara when it was won by Calenus, and Caesar kept them. The rumour went that these lions did marvellous great hurt to the Megarians. For, when the city was taken, they brake their cages where they were tied up, and turned them loose, thinking they would have done great mischief to the enemies, and have kept them from setting upon them. But the lions, contrary to expectation, turned upon themselves that fled unarmed, and did so cruelly tear some in pieces that it pitied their enemies to see them. And this was the cause, as some do report, that made Cassius conspire against Caesar. But this holdeth no water. For Cassius even from his cradle could not abide any manner of tyrants, as it appeared when he was but a boy, and went unto the same school that Faustus the son of Sylla did. And Faustus, bragging among other boys, highly boasted of his father's kingdom. Cassius rose up on his feet, and gave him two good wirts on the ear. Faustus' governors would have put this matter in suit against Cassius. But Pompey would not suffer them, but caused the two boys to be brought before him, and asked them how the matter came to pass. Then Cassius, as it is written of him, said unto the other: 'Go to, Faustus, speak again, and thou darest, before this nobleman here, the same words that made me angry with thee, that my fists may walk once again about thine ears.' Such was Cassius' hot stirring nature.

But for Brutus, his friends and countrymen, both by divers procurements and sundry rumours of the city and by many bills also, did openly call and procure him to do that he did. For, under the image of his ancestor Junius Brutus, that drave the kings out of Rome, they wrote: 'O, that it pleased the gods thou wert now alive, Brutus.' And again: 'That thou wert here among us now.' His tribunal, or chair, where he gave audience during the time he was Praetor, was full of such bills: 'Brutus, thou art asleep, and art not Brutus indeed.' And of all this, Caesar's flatterers were the cause; who beside many other exceeding and unspeakable honours they daily devised for him, in the night-time they did put diadems upon the heads of his images, supposing thereby to allure the common people to call him King, instead of Dictator. Howbeit it turned to the contrary, as we have written more at large in Julius Caesar's *Life*.

Now when Cassius felt his friends and did stir them up against Caesar, they all agreed and promised to take part with him, so Brutus were the chief of their conspiracy. For they told him that so high an enterprise and attempt as that did not so much require men of manhood and courage to draw their swords, as it stood them upon to have a man of such estimation as Brutus, to make every man boldly think that by his only presence the fact were holy and just. If he took not this course, then that they should go to it with fainter hearts; and when they had done it they should be more fearful, because every man would think that Brutus would not have refused to have made one with them, if the cause had been good and honest. Therefore Cassius, considering this matter with himself, did first of all speak to Brutus since they grew strange together for the suit they had for the Praetorship. So when he was reconciled to him again, and that they had embraced one another, Cassius asked him if he were determined to be in the Senate-house the first day of the month of March, because he heard say that Caesar's friends should move the council that day that Caesar should be called King by the Senate. Brutus answered him, he would not be there. 'But if we be sent for', said Cassius, 'how then?' 'For myself then', said Brutus, 'I mean not to hold my peace, but to withstand it, and rather die than lose my liberty.' Cassius, being bold and taking hold of this word, 'Why', quoth he, 'what Roman is he alive that will suffer thee to die for thy liberty? What, knowest thou not that thou art Brutus? Thinkest thou that they be cobblers, tapsters, or suchlike base mechanical people, that write these bills and scrolls which are found daily in thy Praetor's chair, and not the noblest men and best citizens that do it? No, be thou well assured that of other Praetors they look for gifts, common distributions amongst the people, and for common plays, and to see fencers fight at the sharp, to show the people pastime. But at thy hands they specially require, as a due debt unto them, the taking away of the tyranny, being fully bent to suffer any extremity for thy sake, so that thou wilt show thyself to be the man thou art taken for, and that they hope thou art.' Thereupon he kissed Brutus, and embraced him; and so, each taking leave of other, they went both to speak with their friends about it.

Now amongst Pompey's friends there was one called Caius Ligarius, who had been accused unto Caesar for taking part with Pompey, and Caesar discharged him. But Ligarius thanked not Caesar so much for his discharge, as he was offended with him for that he was brought in danger by his tyrannical power. And therefore in his heart he was alway his mortal enemy, and was besides very familiar with Brutus, who went to see him being sick in his bed, and said unto him: 'O Ligarius, in what a time art thou sick!' Ligarius, rising up in his bed and taking him by the right hand, said unto him: 'Brutus', said he, 'if thou hast any great enterprise in hand worthy of thyself, I am whole.'

After that time they began to feel all their acquaintance whom they trusted, and laid their heads together consulting upon it, and did not only pick out their friends, but all those also whom they thought stout enough to attempt any desperate matter, and that were not afraid to lose their lives. For this cause they durst not acquaint Cicero with their conspiracy, although he was a man whom they loved dearly and trusted best. For they were afraid that he being a coward by nature, and age also having increased his fear, he would quite turn and alter all their purpose, and quench the heat of their enterprise (the which specially required hot and earnest execution), seeking by persuasion to bring all things to such safety as there should be no peril.

Brutus also did let other of his friends alone, as Statilius Epicurean and Fa[v]onius, that made profession to follow Marcus Cato: because that having cast out words afar off, disputing together in philosophy to feel their minds, Fa[v]onius answered that civil war was worse than tyrannical government usurped against the law. And Statilius told him also that it were an unwise part of him to put his life in danger for a sight of ignorant fools and asses. Labeo was present at this talk, and maintained the contrary against them both. But Brutus held his peace, as though it had been a doubtful matter and a hard thing to have decided. But afterwards, being out of their company, he made Labeo privy to his intent, who very readily offered himself to make one. And they thought good also to bring in another Brutus to join with him, surnamed Albinus, who was no man of his hands himself, but because he was able to bring good force of a great number of slaves and fencers at the sharp, whom he kept to show the people pastime with their fighting; besides also that Caesar had some trust in him. Cassius and Labeo told Brutus Albinus of it at the first, but he made them no answer. But when he had spoken with Brutus himself alone, and that Brutus had told him he was the chief ringleader of all this conspiracy, then he willingly promised him the best aid he could. Furthermore the only name and great calling of Brutus did bring on the most of them to give consent to this conspiracy; who having never taken oaths together nor taken or given any caution or assurance, nor binding themselves one to another by any religious oaths, they all kept the matter so secret to themselves and could so cunningly handle it that, notwithstanding the gods did reveal it by manifest signs and tokens from above and by predictions of sacrifices, yet all this would not be believed.

Now Brutus (who knew very well that for his sake all the noblest, valiantest, and most courageous men of Rome did venture their lives) weighing with himself the greatness of the danger, when he was out of his house he did so frame and fashion his countenance and looks that no man could discern he had anything to trouble his mind. But when night came that he was in his own house, then he was clean changed. For, either care did wake him against his will when he would have slept, or else oftentimes of himself he fell into such deep thoughts of this enterprise, casting in his mind all the dangers that might happen, that his wife, lying by him, found that there was some marvellous great matter that troubled his mind, not being wont to be in that taking, and that he could not well determine with himself. His wife Porcia (as we have told you before) was the daughter of Cato, whom Brutus married being his cousin, not a maiden, but a young widow after the death of her first husband Bibulus, by whom she had also a young son called Bibulus, who afterwards wrote a book *Of the Acts and Gests of Brutus*, extant at this present day.

This young lady being excellently well seen in philosophy, loving her husband well, and being of a noble courage, as she was also wise – because she would not ask her husband what he ailed before she had made some proof by her self – she took a little razor such as barbers occupy to pare men's nails, and, causing all her maids and women to go out of her chamber, gave her self a great gash withal in her thigh, that she was straight all of a gore-blood; and, incontinently after, a vehement fever took her, by reason of the pain of her wound. Then, perceiving her husband was marvellously out of quiet and that he could take no rest, even in her greatest pain of all, she spake in this sort unto him: 'I being, O Brutus', said she, 'the daughter of Cato, was married unto thee, not to be thy bedfellow and companion in bed and at board only, like a harlot, but to be partaker also with thee of thy good and evil fortune. Now for thyself, I can find no cause of fault in thee touching our match. But for my part, how may I show my duty towards thee and how much I would do for thy sake, if I cannot constantly bear a secret mischance or grief with thee, which requireth secrecy and fidelity? I confess that a woman's wit commonly is too weak to keep a secret safely. But yet, Brutus, good education and the company of virtuous men have some power to reform the defect of nature. And for myself, I have this benefit moreover: that I am the daughter of Cato and wife of Brutus. This notwithstanding, I did not trust to any of these things before, until that now I have found by experience that no pain nor grief whatsoever can overcome me.' With those words she showed him her wound on her thigh and told him what she had done to prove herself. Brutus was amazed to hear what she said unto him, and, lifting up his hands to heaven, he besought the gods to give him the grace he might bring his enterprise to so good pass, that he might be found a husband worthy of so noble a wife as Porcia. So he then did comfort her the best he could.

Now a day being appointed for the meeting of the Senate, at what time they hoped Caesar would not fail to come, the conspirators determined then to put their enterprise in execution, because they might meet safely at that time without suspicion, and the rather, for that all the noblest and chiefest men of the city would be there; who when they should see such a great matter executed, would every man then set-to their hands, for the defence of their liberty. Furthermore, they thought also that the appointment of the place where the council should be kept was chosen of purpose by divine providence and made all for them. For it was one of the porches about the Theatre, in the which there was a certain place full of seats for men to sit in, where also was set up the image of Pompey which the city had made and consecrated in honour of him, when he did beautify that part of the city with the Theatre he built, with divers porches about it. In this place was the assembly of the Senate appointed to be, just on the fifteenth day of the month of March, which the Romans call *Idus Martias*. So that it seemed some god of purpose had brought Caesar thither to be slain, for revenge of Pompey's death.

So, when the day was come, Brutus went out of his house with a dagger by his side under his long gown, that nobody saw nor knew, but his wife only. The other conspirators were all assembled at Cassius' house, to bring his son into the market-place, who on that day did put on the man's gown, called *toga virilis*; and from thence they came all in a troop together unto Pompey's porch, looking that Caesar would straight come thither. But here is to be noted the wonderful assured constancy of these conspirators in so dangerous and weighty an enterprise as they had undertaken. For many of them being Praetors, by reason of their office, whose duty is to minister justice to everybody, they did not only with great quietness and courtesy hear them that spake unto them or that pleaded matters before them, and gave them attentive ear as if they had had no other matter in their heads; but moreover they gave just sentence and carefully dispatched the causes before them. So there was one among them who, being condemned in a certain sum of money, refused to pay it and cried out that he did appeal unto Caesar. Then Brutus, casting his eyes upon the conspirators, said: 'Caesar shall not let me to see the law executed.'

Notwithstanding this, by chance there fell out many misfortunes unto them which was enough to have marred the enterprise. The first and chiefest was Caesar's long tarrying, who came very late to the Senate. For, because the signs of the sacrifices appeared unlucky, his wife Calpurnia kept him at home, and the soothsayers bade him beware he went not abroad. The second cause was when one came unto Casca being a conspirator, and, taking him by the hand, said unto him:'O Casca, thou keptest it close from me, but Brutus hath told me all.' Casca being amazed at it, the other went on with his tale and said: 'Why, how now, how cometh it to pass thou art thus rich, that thou dost sue to be Aedilis?' Thus Casca being deceived by the other's doubtful words, he told them it was a thousand to one he blabbed not out all the conspiracy. Another Senator, called Popilius Laena, after he had saluted Brutus and Cassius more friendly than he was wont to do, he rounded softly in their ears and told them: 'I pray the gods you may go through with that you have taken in hand. But withal, dispatch I rede you, for your enterprise is bewrayed.' When he had said, he presently departed from them, and left them both afraid that their conspiracy would out.

Now in the meantime there came one of Brutus' men post-haste unto him and told him his wife was a-dying. For Porcia being very careful and pensive for that which was to come and being too weak to away with so great and inward grief of mind, she could hardly keep within, but was frighted with every little noise and cry she heard, as those that are taken and possessed with the fury of the Bacchants, asking every man that came from the market-place what Brutus did, and still sent messenger after messenger to know what news. At length, Caesar's coming being prolonged as you have heard, Porcia's weakness was not able to hold out any lenger, and thereupon she suddenly swounded, that she had no leisure to go to her chamber, but was taken in the midst of her house, where her speech and senses failed her. Howbeit she soon came to herself again, and so was laid in her bed and tended by her women. When Brutus heard these news, it grieved him, as it is to be presupposed. Yet he left not off the care of his country and commonwealth, neither went home to his house for any news he heard.

Now it was reported that Caesar was coming in his litter; for he determined not to stay in the Senate all that day, because he was afraid of the unlucky signs of the sacrifices, but to adjourn matters of importance unto the next session and council holden, feigning himself not to be well at ease. When Caesar came out of his litter, Popilius Laena, that had talked before with Brutus and Cassius and had prayed the gods they might bring this enterprise to pass, went unto Caesar and kept him a long time with a talk. Caesar gave good ear unto him. Wherefore the conspirators (if so they should be called), not hearing what he said to Caesar, but conjecturing, by that he had told them a little before, that his talk was none other but the very discovery of their conspiracy, they were afraid every man of them; and, one looking in another's face, it was easy to see that they all were of a mind that it was no tarrying for them till they were apprehended, but rather that they should kill themselves with their own hands. And when Cassius and certain other clapped their hands on their swords under their gowns to draw them, Brutus marking the countenance and gesture of Laena, and considering that he did use himself rather like an humble and earnest suitor than like an accuser, he said nothing to his companion (because there were many amongst them that were not of the conspiracy), but with a pleasant countenance encouraged Cassius. And immediately after, Laena went from Caesar and kissed his hand; which showed plainly that it was for some matter concerning himself that he had held him so long in talk.

Now all the Senators being entered first into this place or chapter house where the council should be kept, all the other conspirators straight stood about Caesar's chair, as if they had had something to have said unto him. And some say that Cassius, casting his eyes upon Pompey's image, made his prayer unto it, as if it had been alive. Trebonius, on the other side, drew Antonius at one side as he came into the house where the Senate sat, and held him with a long talk without.

When Caesar was come into the house, all the Senate rose to honour him at his coming in. So, when he was set, the conspirators flocked about him, and amongst them they presented one Tullius Cimber, who made humble suit for the calling home again of his brother that was banished. They all made as though they were intercessors for him, and took him by the hands and kissed his head and breast. Caesar at the first simply refused their kindness and entreaties. But afterwards, perceiving they still pressed on him, he violently thrust them from him. Then Cimber with both his hands plucked Caesar's gown over his shoulders; and Casca that stood behind him drew his dagger first, and strake Caesar upon the shoulder, but gave him no great wound. Caesar, feeling himself hurt, took him straight by the hand he held his dagger in, and cried out in Latin: 'O traitor, Casca, what doest thou?' Casca on the other side cried in Greek and called his brother to help him. So divers running on a heap together to fly upon Caesar, he looking about him to have fled, saw Brutus with a sword drawn in his hand ready to strike at him. Then he let Casca's hand go, and, casting his gown over his face, suffered every man to strike at him that would. Then the conspirators thronging one upon another because every man was desirous to have a cut at him, so many swords and daggers lighting upon one body, one of them hurt another; and among them Brutus caught a blow on his hand, because he would make one in murdering of him, and all the rest also were every man of them bloodied.

Caesar being slain in this manner, Brutus, standing in the midst of the house, would have spoken, and stayed the other Senators that were not of the conspiracy, to have told them the reason why they had done this fact. But they, as men both afraid and amazed, fled one upon another's neck in haste to get out at the door; and no man followed them. For it was set down and agreed between them that they should kill no man but Caesar only, and should entreat all the rest to look to defend their liberty. All the conspirators but Brutus, determining upon this matter, thought it good also to kill Antonius, because he was a wicked man and that in nature favoured tyranny; besides also, for that he was in great estimation with soldiers, having been conversant of long time amongst them; and specially, having a mind bent to great enterprises, he was also of great authority at that time, being Consul with Caesar. But Brutus would not agree to it. First, for that he said it was not honest; secondly, because he told them there was hope of change in him. For he did not mistrust but that Antonius, being a noble-minded and courageous man, when he should know that Caesar was dead, would willingly help his country to recover her liberty, having them an example unto him, to follow their courage and virtue. So Brutus by this means saved Antonius' life, who at that present time disguised himself and stale away.

But Brutus and his consorts, having their swords bloody in their hands, went straight to the Capitol, persuading the Romans, as they went, to take their liberty again. Now at the first time, when the murder was newly done, there were sudden outcries of people that ran up and down the city, the which indeed did the more increase the fear and tumult. But when they saw they slew no man, neither did spoil or make havoc of anything, then certain of the Senators and many of the people, emboldening themselves, went to the Capitol unto them. There a great number of men being assembled together one after another, Brutus made an oration unto them to win the favour of the people and to justify that they had done. All those that were by said they had done well, and cried unto them that they should boldly come down from the Capitol. Whereupon Brutus and his companions came boldly down into the market-place. The rest followed in troop; but Brutus went foremost, very honourably compassed in round about with the noblest men of the city, which brought him from the Capitol, through the market-place, to the pulpit for orations.

When the people saw him in the pulpit, although they were a multitude of rakehells of all sorts and had a good will to make some stir, yet, being ashamed to do it for the reverence they bare unto Brutus, they kept silence, to hear what he would say. When Brutus began to speak, they gave him quiet audience. Howbeit, immediately after, they showed that they were not all contented with the murder. For when another called Cinna would have spoken and began to accuse Caesar, they fell into a great uproar among them and marvellously reviled him. Insomuch that the conspirators returned again into the Capitol. There Brutus, being afraid to be besieged, sent back again the noblemen that came thither with him, thinking it no reason that they, which were no partakers of the murder, should be partakers of the danger.

Then the next morning the Senate being assembled and holden within the Temple of the goddess Tellus (to wit, 'the Earth'), and Antonius, Plancus, and Cicero having made a motion to the Senate in that assembly that they should take an order to pardon and forget all that was past and to stablish friendship and peace again, it was decreed that they should not only be pardoned, but also that the Consuls should refer it to the Senate what honours should be appointed unto them. This being agreed upon, the Senate brake up, and Antonius the Consul, to put them in heart that were in the Capitol, sent them his son for a pledge. Upon this assurance, Brutus and his companions came down from the Capitol, where every man saluted and embraced each other; among the which Antonius himself did bid Cassius to supper to him, and Lepidus also bade Brutus, and so one bade another, as they had friendship and acquaintance together.

The next day following, the Senate being called again to council did first of all commend Antonius, for that he had wisely stayed and quenched the beginning of a civil war. Then they also gave Brutus and his consorts great praises; and lastly they appointed them several governments of provinces. For unto Brutus they appointed Creta, Afric unto Cassius, Asia unto Trebonius, Bithynia unto Cimber, and unto the other Decius Brutus Albinus, Gaul on this side the Alps. When this was done, they came to talk of Caesar's will and testament, and of his funerals and tomb. Then Antonius thinking good his testament should be read openly, and also that his body should be honourably buried and not in hugger-mugger, lest the people might thereby take occasion to be worse offended if they did otherwise, Cassius stoutly spake against it. But Brutus went with the motion, and agreed unto it; wherein it seemeth he committed a second fault. For the first fault he did was when he would not consent to his fellow conspirators that Antonius should be slain; and therefore he was justly accused that thereby he had saved and strengthened a strong and grievous enemy of their conspiracy. The second fault was when he agreed that Caesar's funerals should be as Antonius would have them, the which indeed marred all. For first of all, when Caesar's testament was openly read among them, whereby it appeared that he bequeathed unto every citizen of Rome seventy-five drachmas a man, and that he left his gardens and arbours unto the people, which he had on this side of the river of Tiber (in the place where now the Temple of Fortune is built), the people then loved him and were marvellous sorry for him.

Afterwards, when Caesar's body was brought into the market-place, Antonius making his funeral oration in praise of the dead, according to the ancient custom of Rome, and perceiving that his words moved the common people to compassion, he framed his eloquence to make their hearts yearn the more; and, taking Caesar's gown all bloody in his hand, he laid it open to the sight of them all, showing what a number of cuts and holes it had upon it. Therewithal the people fell presently into such a rage and mutiny that there was no more order kept amongst the common people. For some of them cried out: 'Kill the murderers.' Others plucked up forms, tables, and stalls about the market-place, as they had done before at the funerals of Clodius; and, having laid them all on a heap together, they set them on fire, and thereupon did put the body of Caesar, and burnt it in the middest of the most holy places. And furthermore, when the fire was thoroughly kindled, some here, some there, took burning fire-brands, and ran with them to the murderers' houses that had killed him, to set them a-fire. Howbeit the conspirators, foreseeing the danger before, had wisely provided for themselves, and fled.

But there was a poet called Cinna, who had been no partaker of the conspiracy but was alway one of Caesar's chiefest friends. He dreamed, the night before, that Caesar bade him to supper with him and that, he refusing to go, Caesar was very importunate with him and compelled him, so that at length he led him by the hand into a great dark place, where, being marvellously afraid, he was driven to follow him in spite of his heart. This dream put him all night into a fever. And yet, notwithstanding, the next morning when he heard that they carried Caesar's body to burial, being ashamed not to accompany his funerals, he went out of his house, and thrust himself into the press of the common people that were in a great uproar. And because some one called him by his name, Cinna, the people thinking he had been that Cinna who in an oration he made had spoken very evil of Caesar, they falling upon him in their rage slew him outright in the market-place.

This made Brutus and his companions more afraid than any other thing, next unto the change of Antonius. Wherefore they got them out of Rome, and kept at the first in the city of Antium, hoping to return again to Rome when the fury of the people were a little assuaged; the which they hoped would be quickly, considering that they had to deal with a fickle and unconstant multitude, easy to be carried, and that the Senate stood for them; who notwithstanding made no inquiry of them that had torn poor Cinna the poet in pieces, but caused them to be sought for and apprehended that went with fire-brands to set fire of the conspirators' houses . . .

After that, these three, Octavius Caesar, Antonius, and Lepidus, made an agreement between themselves, and by those articles divided the provinces belonging to the Empire of Rome among themselves, and did set up bills of proscription and outlawry, condemning two hundred of the noblest men of Rome to suffer death; and among that number Cicero was one. News being brought thereof into Macedon, Brutus, being then enforced to it, wrote unto Hortensius that he should put Caius Antonius to death, to be revenged of the death of Cicero and of the other Brutus, of the which the one was his friend and the other his kinsman. For this cause therefore, Antonius afterwards taking Hortensius at the battle of Philippes, he made him to be slain upon his brother's tomb. But then Brutus said that he was more ashamed of the cause for the which Cicero was slain than he was otherwise sorry for his death; and that he could not but greatly reprove his friends he had at Rome who were slaves more through their own fault than through their valiantness or manhood which usurped the tyranny, considering that they were so cowardly and faint-hearted as to suffer the sight of those things before their eyes, the report whereof should only have grieved them to the heart.

Now when Brutus had passed over his army (that was very great) into Asia, he gave order for the gathering of a great number of ships together, as well in the coast of Bithynia, as also in the city of Cyzicum, because he would have an army by sea; and himself in the meantime went unto the cities, taking order for all things and giving audience unto princes and noblemen of the country that had to do with him. Afterwards he sent unto Cassius in Syria, to turn him from his journey into Egypt, telling him that it was not for the conquest of any kingdom for themselves that they wandered up and down in that sort, but, contrarily, that it was to restore their country again to their liberty; and that the multitude of soldiers they gathered together was to subdue the tyrants that would keep them in slavery and subjection. Wherefore, regarding their chief purpose and intent, they should not be far from Italy, as near as they could possible, but should rather make all the haste they could to help their countrymen. Cassius believed him and returned. Brutus went to meet him; and they both met at the city of Smyrna, which was the first time that they saw together since they took leave of each other at the haven of Piraea in Athens, the one going into Syria and the other into Macedon. So they were marvellous joyful, and no less courageous when they saw the great armies together which they had both levied; considering that they departing out of Italy like naked and poor banished men, without armour and money, nor having any ship ready, nor soldier about them, nor any one town at their commandment; yet, notwithstanding, in a short time after they were now met together, having ships, money, and soldiers enow, both footmen and horsemen, to fight for the Empire of Rome.

Now Cassius would have done Brutus as much honour as Brutus did unto him. But Brutus most commonly prevented him and went first unto him, both because he was the elder man, as also for that he was sickly of body. And men reputed him commonly to be very skilful in wars, but otherwise marvellous choleric and cruel, who sought to rule men by fear rather than with lenity; and on the other side he was too familiar with his friends and would jest too broadly with them. But Brutus in contrary manner, for his virtue and valiantness was well-beloved of the people and his own, esteemed of noblemen, and hated of no man, not so much as of his enemies; because he was a marvellous lowly and gentle person, noble minded, and would never be in any rage, nor carried away with pleasure and covetousness, but had ever an upright mind with him, and would never yield to any wrong or injustice, the which was the chiefest cause of his fame, of his rising, and of the good will that every man bare him; for they were all persuaded that his intent was good. For they did not certainly believe that if Pompey himself had overcome Caesar he would have resigned his authority to the law; but rather they were of opinion that he would still keep the sovereignty and absolute government in his hands, taking only, to please the people, the title of Consul or Dictator, or of some other more civil office. And as for Cassius, a hot, choleric, and cruel man, that would oftentimes be carried away from justice for gain, it was certainly thought that he made war, and put himself into sundry dangers, more to have absolute power and authority than to defend the liberty of his country. For they that will also consider others that were elder men than they – as Cinna, Marius, and Carbo: it is out of doubt that the end and hope of their victory was to be lords of their country; and in manner they did all confess that they fought for the tyranny and to be lords of the Empire of Rome. And in contrary manner, his enemies themselves did never reprove Brutus for any such change or desire. For it was said that Antonius spake it openly divers times that he thought that of all them that had slain Caesar there was none but Brutus only that was moved to do it as thinking the act commendable of itself; but that all the other conspirators did conspire his death for some private malice or envy that they otherwise did bear unto him.

Hereby it appeareth that Brutus did not trust so much to the power of his army as he did to his own virtue, as is to be seen by his writings. For, approaching near to the instant danger, he wrote unto Pomponius Atticus that his affairs had the best hap that could be. 'For', said he, 'either I will set my country at liberty by battle, or by honourable death rid me of this bondage.' And furthermore, that, they being certain and assured of all things else, this one thing only was doubtful to them: whether they should live or die with liberty. He wrote also that Antonius had his due payment for his folly. For, where he might have been a partner equally of the glory of Brutus, Cassius, and Cato, and have made one with them, he liked better to choose to be joined with Octavius Caesar alone, 'with whom, though now he be not overcome by us, yet shall he shortly after also have war with him'. And truly he proved a true prophet, for so came it indeed to pass.

Now, whilst Brutus and Cassius were together in the city of Smyrna, Brutus prayed Cassius to let him have some part of his money, whereof he had great store, because all that he could rap and rend of his side he had bestowed it in making so great a number of ships, that by means of them they should keep all the sea at their commandment. Cassius' friends hindered this request and earnestly dissuaded him from it, persuading him that it was no reason that Brutus should have the money which Cassius hath gotten together by sparing and levied with great evil will of the people their subjects, for him to bestow liberally upon his soldiers and by this means to win their good wills by Cassius' charge. This notwithstanding, Cassius gave him the third part of his total sum . . .

About that time Brutus sent to pray Cassius to come to the city of Sardis; and so he did. Brutus, understanding of his coming, went to meet him with all his friends. There, both their armies being armed, they called them both emperors. Now, as it commonly happeneth in great affairs between two persons, both of them having many friends and so many captains under them, there ran tales and complaints betwixt them. Therefore before they fell in hand with any other matter, they went into a little chamber together, and bade every man avoid, and did shut the doors to them. Then they began to pour out their complaints one to the other, and grew hot and loud, earnestly accusing one another, and at length fell both a-weeping. Their friends that were without the chamber hearing them loud within and angry between themselves, they were both amazed and afraid also lest it would grow to further matter. But yet they were commanded that no man should come to them. Notwithstanding, one Marcus Fa[v]onius, that had been a friend and follower of Cato while he lived, and took upon him to counterfeit a philosopher, not with wisdom and discretion but with a certain bedlam and frantic motion, he would needs come into the chamber, though the men offered to keep him out. But it was no boot to let Fa[v]onius, when a mad mood or toy took him in the head, for he was a hot hasty man and sudden in all his doings, and cared for never a senator of them all. Now though he used this bold manner of speech after the profession of the Cynic philosophers (as who would say, 'dogs'), yet this boldness did no hurt many times, because they did but laugh at him to see him so mad. This Fa[v]onius at that time, in despite of the doorkeepers, came into the chamber, and, with a certain scoffing and mocking gesture which he counterfeited of purpose, he rehearsed the verses which old Nestor said in Homer:

> *My lords, I pray you hearken both to me,*
> *For I have seen mo years than suchye three.*

Cassius fell a-laughing at him. But Brutus thrust him out of the chamber, and called him dog and counterfeit Cynic. Howbeit his coming in brake their strife at that time, and so they left each other.

The self-same night Cassius prepared his supper in his chamber, and Brutus brought his friends with him. So when they were set at supper, Fa[v]onius came to sit down after he had washed. Brutus told him aloud, no man sent for him; and bade them set him at the upper end, meaning indeed at the lower end of the bed. Fa[v]onius made no ceremony, but thrust in amongst the midst of them, and made all the company laugh at him. So they were merry all supper-time and full of their philosophy. The next day after, Brutus, upon complaint of the Sardians, did condemn and noted Lucius Pella for a defamed person, that had been a Praetor of the Romans and whom Brutus had given charge unto; for that he was accused and convicted of robbery and pilfery in his office. This judgement much misliked Cassius, because he himself had secretly, not many days before, warned two of his friends, attainted and convicted of the like offences, and openly had cleared them; but yet he did not therefore leave to employ them in any manner of service as he did before. And therefore he greatly reproved Brutus for that he would show himself so strait and severe in such a time as was meeter to bear a little than to take things at the worst. Brutus in contrary manner answered that he should remember the Ides of March, at which time they slew Julius Caesar; who neither pilled nor polled the country, but only was a favourer and suborner of all them that did rob and spoil by his countenance and authority. And, if there were any occasion whereby they might honestly set aside justice and equity, they should have had more reason to have suffered Caesar's friends to have robbed and done what wrong and injury they had would, than to bear with their own men. For then, said he, they could but have said they had been cowards, 'And now they may accuse us of injustice, beside the pains we take, and the danger we put ourselves into.' And thus may we see what Brutus' intent and purpose was.

But, as they both prepared to pass over again out of Asia into Europe, there went a rumour that there appeared a wonderful sign unto him. Brutus was a careful man and slept very little, both for that his diet was moderate, as also because he was continually occupied. He never slept in the day time, and in the night no lenger than the time he was driven to be alone, and when everybody else took their rest. But now whilst he was in war and his head ever busily occupied to think of his affairs, and what would happen, after he had slumbered a little after supper, he spent all the rest of the night in dispatching of his weightiest causes; and after he had taken order for them, if he had any leisure left him, he would read some book till the third watch of the night, at what time the captains, petty-captains, and colonels did use to come unto him.

So, being ready to go into Europe, one night very late, when all the camp took quiet rest, as he was in his tent with a little light, thinking of weighty matters, he thought he heard one come in to him and, casting his eye towards the door of his tent, that he saw a wonderful strange and monstruous shape of a body coming towards him, and said never a word. So Brutus boldly asked what he was, a god or a man, and what cause brought him thither. The spirit answered him: 'I am thy evil spirit, Brutus; and thou shalt see me by the city of Philippes.' Brutus, being no otherwise afraid, replied again unto it: 'Well, then I shall see thee again.' The spirit presently vanished away; and Brutus called his men unto him, who told him that they heard no noise, nor saw anything at all. Thereupon Brutus returned again to think on his matters as he did before. And when the day brake he went unto Cassius to tell him what vision had appeared unto him in the night. Cassius being in opinion an Epicurean, and reasoning thereon with Brutus, spake to him touching the vision thus: 'In our sect, Brutus, we have an opinion that we do not always feel or see that which we suppose we do both see and feel; but that our senses being credulous, and therefore easily abused, when they are idle and unoccupied in their own objects, are induced to imagine they see and conjecture that which they in truth do not. For our mind is quick and cunning to work, without either cause or matter, anything in the imagination whatsoever. And therefore the imagination is resembled to clay, and the mind to the potter, who, without any other cause than his fancy and pleasure, changeth it into what fashion and form he will. And this doth the diversity of our dreams show unto us. For our imagination doth upon a small fancy grow from conceit to conceit, altering both in passions and forms of things imagined. For the mind of man is ever occupied, and that continual moving is nothing but an imagination. But yet there is a further cause of this in you. For, you being by nature given to melancholic discoursing, and of late continually occupied, your wits and senses having been overlaboured do easilier yield to such imaginations. For, to say that there are spirits or angels, and, if there were, that they had the shape of men, or such voices, or any power at all to come unto us, it is a mockery. And for mine own part I would there were such, because that we should not only have soldiers, horses, and ships, but also the aid of the gods, to guide and further our honest and honourable attempts.' With these words Cassius did somewhat comfort and quiet Brutus.

When they raised their camp, there came two eagles that, flying with a marvellous force, lighted upon two of the foremost ensigns, and always followed the soldiers, which gave them meat, and fed them, until they came near to the city of Philippes; and there, one day only before the battle, they both flew away.

Now Brutus had conquered the most part of all the people and nations of that country. But if there were any other city or captain to overcome, then they made all clear before them, and so drew towards the coasts of Thasos. There Norbanus lying in camp in a certain place called the Straits, by another place called Symbolon (which is a port of the sea), Cassius and Brutus compassed him in in such sort that he was driven to forsake the place, which was of great strength for him, and he was also in danger beside to have lost all his army. For Octavius Caesar could not follow him because of his sickness, and therefore stayed behind. Whereupon they had taken his army, had not Antonius' aid been, which made such wonderful speed that Brutus could scant believe it. So Caesar came not thither of ten days after; and Antonius camped against Cassius, and Brutus on the other side against Caesar.

The Romans called the valley between both camps, the Philippian fields; and there were never seen two so great armies of the Romans, one before the other, ready to fight. In truth, Brutus' army was inferior to Octavius Caesar's in number of men. But, for bravery and rich furniture, Brutus' army far excelled Caesar's. For the most part of their armours were silver and gilt, which Brutus had bountifully given them, although in all other things he taught his captains to live in order without excess. But, for the bravery of armour and weapon which soldiers should carry in their hands or otherwise wear upon their backs, he thought that it was an encouragement unto them that by nature are greedy of honour, and that it maketh them also fight like devils, that love to get and be afraid to lose; because they fight to keep their armour and weapon, as also their goods and lands.

Now when they came to muster their armies, Octavius Caesar took the muster of his army within the trenches of his camp, and gave his men only a little corn, and five silver drachmas to every man to sacrifice to the gods and to pray for victory. But Brutus, scorning this misery and niggardliness, first of all mustered his army and did purify it in the fields, according to the manner of the Romans. And then he gave unto every band a number of wethers to sacrifice, and fifty silver drachmas to every soldier. So that Brutus' and Cassius' soldiers were better pleased, and more courageously bent to fight at the day of battle, than their enemies' soldiers were.

Notwithstanding, being busily occupied about the ceremonies of this purification, it is reported that there chanced certain unlucky signs unto Cassius. For one of his sergeants that carried the rods before him brought him the garland of flowers turned backwards, the which he should have worn on his head in the time of sacrificing. Moreover it is reported also that at another time before, in certain sports and triumph where they carried an image of Cassius' victory of clean gold, it fell by chance, the man stumbling that carried it. And yet further, there were seen a marvellous number of fowls of prey, that feed upon dead carcases. And beehives also were found, where bees were gathered together in a certain place within the trenches of the camp; the which place the soothsayers thought good to shut out of the precinct of the camp, for to take away the superstitious fear and mistrust men would have of it. The which began somewhat to alter Cassius' mind from Epicurus' opinions, and had put the soldiers also in a marvellous fear. Thereupon Cassius was of opinion not to try this war at one battle, but rather to delay time and to draw it out in length, considering that they were the stronger in money and the weaker in men and armours. But Brutus in contrary manner did alway before, and at that time also, desire nothing more than to put all to the hazard of battle, as soon as might be possible, to the end he might either quickly restore his country to her former liberty, or rid him forthwith of this miserable world, being still troubled in following and maintaining of such great armies together. But perceiving that in the daily skirmishes and bickerings they made his men were alway the stronger and ever had the better, that yet quickened his spirits again, and did put him in better heart. And furthermore, because that some of their own men had already yielded themselves to their enemies, and that it was suspected moreover divers others would do the like, that made many of Cassius' friends which were of his mind before (when it came to be debated in council whether the battle should be fought or not) that they were then of Brutus' mind. But yet was there one of Brutus' friends called Atilius, that was against it, and was of opinion that they should tarry the next winter. Brutus asked him what he should get by tarrying a year lenger? 'If I get nought else', quoth Atilius again, 'yet have I lived so much lenger.' Cassius was very angry with this answer; and Atilius was maliced and esteemed the worse for it of all men. Thereupon it was presently determined they should fight battle the next day.

So Brutus all supper time looked with a cheerful countenance, like a man that had good hope, and talked very wisely of philosophy, and after supper went to bed. But touching Cassius, Messala reporteth that he supped by himself in his tent with a few of his friends, and that all supper time he looked very sadly, and was full of thoughts, although it was against his nature; and that after supper he took him by the hand, and holding him fast, in token of kindness as his manner was, told him in Greek: 'Messala, I protest unto thee, and make thee my witness, that I am compelled against my mind and will, as Pompey the Great was, to jeopard the liberty of our country to the hazard of a battle. And yet we must be lively and of good courage, considering our good fortune, whom we should wrong too much to mistrust her, although we follow evil counsel.' Messala writeth that Cassius having spoken these last words unto him, he bade him farewell and willed him to come to supper to him the next night following, because it was his birthday.

The next morning, by break of day, the signal of battle was set out in Brutus' and Cassius' camp, which was an arming scarlet coat; and both the chieftains spake together in the midst of their armies. There Cassius began to speak first, and said: 'The gods grant us, O Brutus, that this day we may win the field and ever after to live all the rest of our life quietly one with another. But sith the gods have so ordained it that the greatest and chiefest things amongst men are most uncertain, and that, if the battle fall out otherwise today than we wish or look for, we shall hardly meet again, what art thou then determined to do – to fly, or die? Brutus answered him: 'Being yet but a young man and not over greatly experienced in the world, I trust (I know not how) a certain rule of philosophy by the which I did greatly blame and reprove Cato for killing of himself, as being no lawful nor godly act, touching the gods, nor, concerning men, valiant; not to give place and yield to divine providence, and not constantly and patiently to take whatsoever it pleaseth him to send us, but to draw back and fly. But being now in the midst of the danger, I am of a contrary mind. For, if it be not the will of God that this battle fall out fortunate for us, I will look no more for hope, neither seek to make any new supply for war again, but will rid me of this miserable world, and content me with my fortune. For I gave up my life for my country in the Ides of March, for the which I shall live in another more glorious world.' Cassius fell a-laughing to hear what he said, and embracing him, 'Come on then', said he, 'let us go and charge our enemies with this mind. For either we shall conquer, or we shall not need to fear the conquerors.'

After this talk, they fell to consultation among their friends for the ordering of the battle. Then Brutus prayed Cassius he might have the leading of the right wing, the which men thought was far meeter for Cassius, both because he was the elder man, and also for that he had the better experience. But yet Cassius gave it him, and willed that Messala, who had charge of one of the warlikest legions they had, should be also in that wing with Brutus. So Brutus presently sent out his horsemen, who were excellently well appointed; and his footmen also were as willing and ready to give charge.

Now Antonius' men did cast a trench from the marsh by the which they lay, to cut off Cassius' way to come to the sea; and Caesar, at the least, his army stirred not. As for Octavius Caesar himself, he was not in his camp, because he was sick. And for his people, they little thought the enemies would have given them battle, but only have made some light skirmishes to hinder them that wrought in the trench, and with their darts and slings to have kept them from finishing of their work. But they, taking no heed to them that came full upon them to give them battle, marvelled much at the great noise they heard, that came from the place where they were casting their trench. In the meantime Brutus, that led the right wing, sent little bills to the colonels and captains of private bands, in the which he wrote the word of the battle; and he himself, riding a-horseback by all the troops, did speak to them and encouraged them to stick to it like men. So by this means very few of them understood what was the word of the battle, and, besides, the, most part of them never tarried to have it told them, but ran with great fury to assail the enemies; whereby, through this disorder, the legions were marvellously scattered and dispersed one from the other.

For first of all, Messala's legion, and then the next unto them, went beyond the left wing of the enemies, and did nothing, but glancing by them overthrew some as they went; and so going on further fell right upon Caesar's camp, out of the which (as himself writeth in his *Commentaries*) he had been conveyed away a little before, through the counsel and advice of one of his friends called Marcus Artorius; who, dreaming in the night, had a vision appeared unto him, that commanded Octavius Caesar should be carried out of his camp, insomuch as it was thought he was slain, because his litter, which had nothing in it, was thrust through and through with pikes and darts. There was great slaughter in this camp. For amongst others there were slain two thousand Lacedaemonians, who were arrived but even a little before, coming to aid Caesar. The other also that had not glanced by, but had given a charge full upon Caesar's battle; they easily made them fly, because they were greatly troubled for the loss of their camp, and of them there were slain by hand three legions. Then, being very earnest to follow the chase of them that fled, they ran in amongst them hand over head into their camp, and Brutus among them.

But that which the conquerors thought not of, occasion showed it unto them that were overcome; and that was the left wing of their enemies left naked and unguarded of them of the right wing, who were strayed too far off, in following of them that were overthrown. So they gave a hot charge upon them. But notwithstanding all the force they made, they could not break into the midst of their battle, where they found men that received them and valiantly made head against them. Howbeit they brake and overthrew the left wing where Cassius was, by reason of the great disorder among them, and also because they had no intelligence how the right wing had sped. So they chased them, beating them into their camp, the which they spoiled, none of both the chieftains being present there. For Antonius, as it is reported, to fly the fury of the first charge, was gotten into the next marsh; and no man could tell what became of Octavius Caesar after he was carried out of his camp; insomuch that there were certain soldiers that showed their swords bloodied, and said that they had slain him, and did describe his face and showed what age he was of. Furthermore, the vaward and the midst of Brutus' battle had already put all their enemies to flight that withstood them, with great slaughter; so that Brutus had conquered all of his side, and Cassius had lost all on the other side. For nothing undid them but that Brutus went not to help Cassius, thinking he had overcome them, as himself had done; and Cassius on the other side tarried not for Brutus, thinking he had been overthrown, as himself was. And, to prove that the victory fell on Brutus' side, Messala confirmeth it, that they won three eagles and divers other ensigns of their enemies, and their enemies won never a one of theirs.

Now Brutus returning from the chase after he had slain and sacked Caesar's men, he wondered much that he could not see Cassius' tent standing up high as it was wont, neither the other tents of his camp standing as they were before, because all the whole camp had been spoiled and the tents thrown down, at the first coming in of the enemies. But they that were about Brutus, whose sight served them better, told him that they saw a great glistering of harness and a number of silvered targets, that went and came into Cassius' camp and were not, as they took it, the armours nor the number of men that they had left there to guard the camp; and yet that they saw not such a number of dead bodies, and great overthrow, as there should have been if so many legions had been slain.

This made Brutus at the first mistrust that which had happened. So he appointed a number of men to keep the camp of his enemy which he had taken, and caused his men to be sent for that yet followed the chase, and gathered them together, thinking to lead them to aid Cassius, who was in this state as you shall hear. First of all he was marvellous angry to see how Brutus' men ran to give charge upon their enemies and tarried not for the word of the battle nor commandment to give charge; and it grieved him beside that, after he had overcome them, his men fell straight to spoil and were not careful to compass in the rest of the enemies behind. But with tarrying too long also, more than through the valiantness or foresight of the captains his enemies, Cassius found himself compassed in with the right wing of his enemies' army. Whereupon his horsemen brake immediately, and fled for life towards the sea. Furthermore, perceiving his footmen to give ground, he did what he could to keep them from flying, and took an ensign from one of the ensign-bearers that fled, and stuck it fast at his feet, although with much ado he could scant keep his own guard together. So Cassius himself was at length compelled to fly, with a few about him, unto a little hill from whence they might easily see what was done in all the plain; howbeit Cassius himself saw nothing, for his sight was very bad, saving that he saw, and yet with much ado, how the enemies spoiled his camp before his eyes. He saw also a great troop of horsemen whom Brutus sent to aid him, and thought that they were his enemies that followed him. But yet he sent Titinius, one of them that was with him, to go and know what they were. Brutus' horsemen saw him coming afar off, whom when they knew that he was one of Cassius' chiefest friends, they shouted out for joy; and they that were familiarly acquainted with him lighted from their horses, and went and embraced him. The rest compassed him in round about a-horseback, with songs of victory and great rushing of their harness, so that they made all the field ring again for joy.

But this marred all. For Cassius thinking indeed that Titinius was taken of the enemies, he then spake these words: 'Desiring too much to live, I have lived to see one of my best friends taken, for my sake, before my face.' After that, he got into a tent where nobody was, and took Pindarus with him, one of his freed bondmen, whom he reserved ever for such a pinch, since the cursed battle of the Parthians where Crassus was slain, though he notwithstanding scaped from that overthrow. But then casting his cloak over his head and holding out his bare neck unto Pindarus, he gave him his head to be stricken off. So the head was found severed from the body. But after that time Pindarus was never seen more. Whereupon some took occasion to say that he had slain his master without his commandment.

By and by they knew the horsemen that came towards them, and might see Titinius crowned with a garland of triumph, who came before with great speed unto Cassius. But when he perceived, by the cries and tears of his friends which tormented themselves, the misfortune that had chanced to his captain Cassius by mistaking, he drew out his sword, cursing himself a thousand times that he had tarried so long, and so slew himself presently in the field. Brutus in the meantime came forward still, and understood also that Cassius had been overthrown. But he knew nothing of his death, till he came very near to his camp. So when he was come thither, after he had lamented the death of Cassius, calling him the last of all the Romans, being unpossible that Rome should ever breed again so noble and valiant a man as he, he caused his body to be buried and sent it to the city of Thasos, fearing lest his funerals within the camp should cause great disorder.

Then he called his soldiers together and did encourage them again. And when he saw that they had lost all their carriage, which they could not brook well, he promised every man of them two thousand drachmas in recompense. After his soldiers had heard his oration, they were all of them prettily cheered again, wondering much at his great liberality, and waited upon him with great cries when he went his way, praising him for that he only of the four chieftains was not overcome in battle. And, to speak the truth, his deeds showed that he hoped not in vain to be conqueror. For with few legions he had slain and driven all them away that made head against him. And yet if all his people had fought, and that the most of them had not out-gone their enemies to run to spoil their goods, surely it was like enough he had slain them all and had left never a man of them alive . . .

The self-same night, it is reported that the monstrous spirit, which had appeared before unto Brutus in the city of Sardis, did now appear again unto him in the self-same shape and form, and so vanished away, and said never a word. Now Publius Volumnius, a grave and wise philosopher, that had been with Brutus from the beginning of this war, he doth make [no] mention of this spirit; but saith that the greatest eagle and ensign was covered over with a swarm of bees, and that there was one of the captains whose arm suddenly fell a-sweating, that it dropped oil of roses from him, and that they oftentimes went about to dry him, but all would do no good. And that, before the battle was fought, there were two eagles fought between both armies, and all the time they fought there was a marvellous great silence all the valley over, both the armies, being one before the other, marking this fight between them; and that in the end the eagle towards Brutus gave over and flew away. But this is certain, and a true tale: that, when the gate of the camp was open, the first man the standard-bearer met that carried the eagle was an Ethiopian, whom the soldiers for ill-luck mangled with their swords.

Now after that Brutus had brought his army into the field and had set them in battle ray, directly against the vaward of his enemy, he paused a long time before he gave the signal of battle. For Brutus riding up and down to view the bands and companies, it came in his head to mistrust some of them, besides that some came to tell him so much as he thought. Moreover, he saw his horsemen set forward but faintly, and did not go lustily to give charge, but still stayed to see what the footmen would do. Then suddenly one of the chiefest knights he had in all his army, called Camulatius [the Celt Camulatus], and that was alway marvellously esteemed of for his valiantness until that time, he came hard by Brutus a-horseback and rode before his face to yield himself unto his enemies. Brutus was marvellous sorry for it, wherefore, partly for anger and partly for fear of greater treason and rebellion, he suddenly caused his army to march, being past three of the clock in the afternoon. So, in that place where he himself fought in person he had the better and brake into the left wing of his enemies, which gave him way, through the help of his horsemen that gave charge with his footmen, when they saw the enemies in a maze and afraid. Howbeit the other also on the right wing, when the captains would have had them to have marched, they were afraid to have been compassed in behind, because they were fewer in number than their enemies; and therefore did spread themselves and leave the midst of their battle. Whereby they having weakened themselves, they could not withstand the force of their enemies, but turned tail straight and fled. And those that had put them to flight came in straight upon it to compass Brutus behind, who in the midst of the conflict did all that was possible for a skilful captain and valiant soldier, both for his wisdom as also for his hardiness, for the obtaining of victory. But that which won him the victory at the first battle did now lose it him at the second. For at the first time the enemies that were broken and fled were straight cut in pieces; but at the second battle, of Cassius' men that were put to flight, there were few slain; and they that saved themselves by speed, being afraid because they had been overcome, did discourage the rest of the army when they came to join with them and filled all the army with fear and disorder.

There was the son of M. Cato slain, valiantly fighting amongst the lusty youths. For, notwithstanding that he was very weary and overharried, yet would he not therefore fly but manfully fighting and laying about him, telling aloud his name and also his father's name, at length he was beaten down amongst many other dead bodies of his enemies which he had slain round about him. So there were slain in the field all the chiefest gentlemen and nobility that were in his army, who valiantly ran into any danger to save Brutus' life.

Amongst them there was one of Brutus' friends called Lucilius, who seeing a troop of barbarous men making no reckoning of all men else they met in their way, but going all together right against Brutus, he determined to stay them with the hazard of his life, and, being left behind, told them that he was Brutus; and, because they should believe him, he prayed them to bring him to Antonius, for he said he was afraid of Caesar, and that he did trust Antonius better. These barbarous men being very glad of this good hap, and thinking themselves happy men, they carried him in the night, and sent some before unto Antonius to tell him of their coming. He was marvellous glad of it, and went out to meet them that brought him. Others also understanding of it that they had brought Brutus prisoner, they came out of all parts of the camp to see him, some pitying his hard fortune and others saying that it was not done like himself, so cowardly to be taken alive of the barbarous people for fear of death. When they came near together, Antonius stayed awhile bethinking himself how he should use Brutus. In the meantime Lucilius was brought to him, who stoutly with a bold countenance said: 'Antonius, I dare assure thee that no enemy hath taken nor shall take Marcus Brutus alive; and I beseech God keep him from that fortune. For wheresoever he be found, alive or dead, he will be found like himself. And now for myself, I am come unto thee, having deceived these men of arms here, bearing them down that I was Brutus; and do not refuse to suffer any torment thou wilt put me to.' Lucilius' words made them all amazed that heard him. Antonius on the other side, looking upon all them that had brought him, said unto them: 'My companions, I think ye are sorry you have failed of your purpose, and that you think this man hath done you great wrong. But, I do assure you, you have taken a better booty than that you followed. For, instead of an enemy, you have brought me a friend; and for my part, if you had brought me Brutus alive, truly I cannot tell what I should have done to him. For I had rather have such men my friends as this man here, than enemies.' Then he embraced Lucilius and at that time delivered him to one of his friends in custody; and Lucilius ever after served him faithfully, even to his death.

Now Brutus having passed a little river walled in on either side with high rocks and shadowed with great trees, being then dark night he went no further, but stayed at the foot of a rock with certain of his captains and friends that followed him. And looking up to the firmament that was full of stars, sighing, he rehearsed two verses, of the which Volumnius wrote the one, to this effect:

Let not the wight from whom this mischief went,
O Jove, escape without due punishment.

And saith that he had forgotten the other. Within a little while after, naming his friends that he had seen slain in battle before his eyes, he fetched a greater sigh than before; specially when he came to name Labio and Flavius, of the which the one was his lieutenant and the other captain of the pioneers of his camp.

In the meantime, one of the company being a-thirst and seeing Brutus a-thirst also, he ran to the river for water and brought it in his sallet. At the self-same time they heard a noise on the other side of the river. Whereupon Volumnius took Dardanus, Brutus' servant, with him to see what it was; and, returning straight again, asked if there were any water left. Brutus, smiling, gently told them all was drunk; 'but they shall bring you some more'. Thereupon he sent him again that went for water before, who was in great danger of being taken by the enemies, and hardly scaped, being sore hurt. Furthermore, Brutus thought that there was no great number of men slain in battle; and, to know the truth of it, there was one called Statilius that promised to go through his enemies, for otherwise it was impossible to go see their camp, and from thence, if all were well, that he would lift up a torch-light in the air, and then return again with speed to him. The torch-light was lift up as he had promised, for Statilius went thither. Now Brutus seeing Statilius tarry long after that, and that he came not again, he said: 'If Statilius be alive, he will come again.' But his evil fortune was such that as he came back he lighted in his enemies' hands and was slain.

Now, the night being far spent, Brutus as he sat bowed towards Clitus, one of his men, and told him somewhat in his ear, the other answered him not, but fell a-weeping. Thereupon he proved Dardanus, and said somewhat also to him. At length he came to Volumnius himself, and, speaking to him in Greek, prayed him, for the study's sake which brought them acquainted together, that he would help him to put his hand to his sword, to thrust it in him to kill him. Volumnius denied his request, and so did many others. And, amongst the rest, one of them said, there was no tarrying for them there, but that they must needs fly. Then Brutus rising up: 'We must fly indeed', said he, 'but it must be with our hands not with our feet.' Then, taking every man by the hand, he said these words unto them with a cheerful countenance: 'It rejoiceth my heart that not one of my friends hath failed me at my need, and I do not complain of my fortune, but only for my country's sake. For, as for me, I think myself happier than they that have overcome, considering that I leave a perpetual fame of our courage and manhood, the which our enemies the conquerors shall never attain unto by force nor money, neither can let their posterity to say that they, being naughty and unjust men, have slain good men, to usurp tyrannical power not pertaining to them.'

Having said so, he prayed every man to shift for themselves. And then he went a little aside with two or three only, among the which Strato was one, with whom he came first acquainted by the study of rhetoric. He came as near to him as he could, and, taking his sword by the hilts with both his hands and falling down upon the point of it, ran himself through. Others say that not he, but Strato, at his request, held the sword in his hand, and turned his head aside, and that Brutus fell down upon it; and so ran himself through, and died presently.

Messala, that had been Brutus' great friend, became afterwards Octavius Caesar's friend. So, shortly after, Caesar being at good leisure, he brought Strato, Brutus' friend, unto him and weeping said: 'Caesar, behold, here is he that did the last service to my Brutus.' Caesar welcomed him at that time, and afterwards he did him as faithful service in all his affairs as any Grecian else he had about him, until the battle of Actium. It is reported also that this Messala himself answered Caesar one day, when he gave him great praise before his face that he had fought valiantly and with great affection for him at the battle of Actium (notwithstanding that he had been his cruel enemy before, at the battle of Philippes, for Brutus' sake): 'I ever loved', said he, 'to take the best and justest part.'

Now, Antonius having found Brutus' body, he caused it to be wrapped up in one of the richest coat-armours he had. Afterwards also, Antonius understanding that this coat-armour was stolen, he put the thief to death that had stolen it, and sent the ashes of his body unto Servilia his mother. And for Porcia, Brutus' wife, Nicolaus the philosopher and Valerius Maximus do write that she, determining to kill herself (her parents and friends carefully looking to her to keep her from it), took hot burning coals and cast them into her mouth, and kept her mouth so close that she choked herself. There was a letter of Brutus found written to his friends, complaining of their negligence, that, his wife being sick, they would not help her but suffered her to kill herself, choosing to die rather than to languish in pain. Thus it appeareth that Nicolaus knew not well that time, sith the letter (at the least if it were Brutus' letter) doth plainly declare the disease and love of this lady and also the manner of her death.

READING LIST

Blits, Jan H. *The End of the Ancient Republic: Essays on 'Julius Caesar'*, 1982
Bonjour, Adrien. *The Structure of 'Julius Caesar'*, 1958
Bono, Barbara. 'The birth of tragedy: action in *Julius Caesar*', *English Literary Renaissance* 24 (1994), 449–70
Cantor, Paul A. *Shakespeare's Rome: Republic and Empire*, 1976
Carnegie, David. *Shakespeare Handbooks: 'Julius Caesar'*, 2009
Charney, Maurice. *Shakespeare's Roman Plays: The Function of Imagery in the Drama*, 1961
Clayton, Thomas. '"Should Brutus never taste of Portia's death but once?": text and performance in *Julius Caesar*', *Studies in English Literature* 23 (1983), 237–55
Drakakis, John. '"Fashion it thus": Julius Caesar and the politics of theatrical representation', in *Shakespeare's Tragedies: Contemporary Critical Essays*, ed. Susan Zimmerman, 1998
Granville-Barker, Harley. 'Julius Caesar', in his *Prefaces to Shakespeare*, 1928
Hadfield, Andrew. *Shakespeare and Republicanism*, 2004
Hartley, Andrew James. *Shakespeare in Performance: 'Julius Caesar'*, 2014
Kahn, Coppélia. *Roman Shakespeare: Warriors, Wounds, and Women*, 1997
Kewes, Paulina. '*Julius Caesar* in Jacobean England', *Seventeenth Century* 17 (2002), 155–86
Knight, G. Wilson. *The Imperial Theme: Further Interpretations of Shakespeare's Tragedies Including the Roman Plays*, 1931
Leggatt, Alexander. 'Julius Caesar', in *Shakespeare's Political Drama: The History Plays and the Roman Plays*, 1988
MacCallum, M. W. *Shakespeare's Roman Plays and their Background*, 1910
Marshall, Cynthia. 'Portia's wound, Calphurnia's dream: reading character in *Julius Caesar*', *English Literary Renaissance* 24 (1994), 471–88
Maxwell, J. C. 'Shakespeare's Roman plays: 1900–1956', *Shakespeare Survey* 10 (1957), 1–11
Miles, Geoffrey. *Shakespeare and the Constant Romans*, 1996
Miola, Robert S. *Shakespeare's Rome*, 1983
Paster, Gail Kern. '"In the spirit of men there is no blood": blood as trope of gender in *Julius Caesar*', *Shakespeare Quarterly* 40 (1989), 284–98
Phillips Jr, James Emerson. *The State in Shakespeare's Greek and Roman Plays*, 1940
Ripley, John. *'Julius Caesar' on Stage in England and America, 1599–1973*, 1980
Ronan, Clifford J. *'Antike Roman': Power Symbology and the Roman Play in Early Modern England, 1585–1635*, 1995
Rutter, Carol Chillington. 'Facing history, facing now: Deborah Warner's *Julius Caesar* at the Barbican Theatre', *Shakespeare Quarterly* 57 (2006), 71–85

Schanzer, Ernest, ed. *Shakespeare's Appian*, 1956

Shackford, Martha Hale. *Plutarch in Renaissance England*, 1929

Simmons, J. L. *Shakespeare's Pagan World: The Roman Tragedies*, 1974

Smith, Warren D. 'The duplicate revelation of Portia's death', *Shakespeare Quarterly* 4 (1953), 1–11

Spencer, T. J. B. 'Shakespeare and the Elizabethan Romans', *Shakespeare Survey* 10 (1957), 27–38

Stirling, Brents. '*Julius Caesar* in revision', *Shakespeare Quarterly* 13 (1962), 187–205

Suetonius. *Lives of the Caesars*, trans. C. Rolfe, The Loeb Classical Library, 2 vols., revised 1951

Traversi, Derek. *Shakespeare: The Roman Plays*, 1963

Velz, John W. *Shakespeare and the Classical Tradition*, 1968

    '*Julius Caesar* 1937–1997: where we are; how we got there', *The Shakespearean International Yearbook* 1 (1999), 257–65

Walker, Roy. 'The northern star: an essay on the Roman plays', *Shakespeare Quarterly* 2 (1951), 287–93

Wills, Gary. *Rome and Rhetoric: Shakespeare's 'Julius Caesar'*, 2011

Wilson, Richard, ed. *'Julius Caesar': A Casebook*, 2001

Zander, Horst, ed. *'Julius Caesar': New Critical Essays*, 2004